# Waltzing

## A Manual for Dancing and Living

Richard Powers and Nick Enge

Redowa Press

ISBN-10: 0982799543
ISBN-13: 978-0-9827995-4-3

First Edition

Original Illustrations
by Tamarind King

Cover Illustration by
Manuel Avendano

Additional Illustrations
from the collection of
Richard Powers

www.waltzingbook.com

Redowa Press
Stanford, CA

# Table of Contents

"Let us read, and let us dance.
These two amusements will never
do any harm to the world."
— Voltaire

# Dear Reader

*Welcome to the wonderful world of waltzing!*

In this guidebook, *Waltzing: A Manual for Dancing and Living,* you will find many ideas about waltzing, dancing, and living, including descriptions of how to waltz, along with advice on how to find greater fulfillment in your dancing (and *through* your dancing), and general advice on how to find greater fulfillment in your life.

## Our Focus: *Social* Waltzing

As explained in "The Three Worlds of Ballroom Dance" (p. 29), there are three different kinds of ballroom dancing: *social, competitive,* and *exhibition.* All three of these worlds are wonderful. For the purpose of this book, **our focus will be on *social* waltzing, where the purpose of waltzing is having fun with your partners**. Many of our ideas about *social* waltzing can also be applied to the other two worlds of ballroom dance, but some can't be. If you're a competitive or exhibition dancer, we encourage you to take what's of value to you, leaving what isn't.

## Our Focus: Social *Waltzing*

Likewise, we realize that there are many genres of dance, both in the ballroom and beyond— from swing to salsa, bhangra to belly dancing. Each of these genres has something to offer. Many of our ideas about waltzing will also be relevant to these other genres, but some won't be. Again, we'll leave that judgment to you.

## For Dancers and Yet-to-Be Dancers Alike

**Even if you don't see yourself as a dancer yet, we strongly encourage you to read this book**. Whether explicitly laid out in our essays on waltzing through life, or hidden in our tips for better waltzing, this book is overflowing with ideas that you can use to improve your life and relationships, regardless of whether you currently dance or not.

Of course, we also strongly encourage you to dance, as dancing itself does have unique benefits, and we hope that this book will inspire you to start dancing, if you don't already. If you happen to be someone who believes that you "can't dance," you may want to begin your journey through this book by reading our essay about *fixed* vs. *growth mindsets* on p. 73.

## *Suggestions* for Social Waltzing

In the spirit of social waltzing, which is flexible, accepting, and in which we *value others' truths,* we want to note explicitly upfront that **everything in this book is merely a suggestion**, an idea which we have found useful in improving our dancing and our lives. In offering these ideas to you, we trust that you won't use them as new ways to disapprove of a future partner (or yourself), i.e. *"Richard and Nick said that you must _____."* We feel that we can trust this because a flexible and accepting attitude is embodied on nearly every page.

## Who Wrote What?

The authorship of the first drafts of these chapters was evenly divided.

At first, we were going to note the primary author of each chapter, but then we realized that we both agree on everything, we have similar writing styles, and we each made significant improvements in each other's chapters.

So we agreed that the author of each chapter is "us." If we don't care who wrote what, we think we can safely assume that you don't either.

## Our Writing Style

Each chapter of this book is carefully and thoroughly researched (see "References" on p. 237), but we want to avoid the dense writing style and jargon of academic papers. We chose an **informal conversational style** for two reasons.

1) Our primary goal is communicating our ideas clearly and directly. We also aim for quick comprehension by our readers. Therefore, straightforward descriptions and explanations are preferable to esoteric jargon, dense blocks of text, and sentences that must be re-read several times to be understood.

2) The non-verbal communication of social dance partnering is informal and friendly, with the wish to communicate clearly and quickly. So it makes sense that our writing style matches our topic.

Specifically, we found that breaking up long paragraphs into easily identifiable points facilitates quick comprehension. We know that you're busy and may be skimming some of our chapters. The line breaks assist your navigation through our thoughts.

Likewise, our use of **bold** type is to help you quickly identify **key points**. It isn't shouting.

We edited each topic down to its most concise essence, so that most fit into a two-page spread. This way, you can pick up our book, open randomly to any chapter, and gain a complete insight about dancing (and living) in just a few minutes. People usually learn their life lessons in random, serendipitous order, not as a linear progression, so you can read our book in the same way.

We hope you enjoy the book!

*Richard & Nick*

# What Is Waltz?

The word "waltz" has several definitions, each of which we will honor in this book.

> Waltz is:
> a kind of dance,
> a kind of music, and
> a way of approaching life.

## A Kind of Dance

Etymologically speaking, the word "waltz" comes from the German *walzen* "to roll, dance," from the Proto-Indo-European root *wel-* "to turn, revolve."

It is little surprise then, that historically, the term "waltz" has been applied to a variety of dance forms which **turn**, **revolve**, and **roll**.

In the early days of dancing these "waltzes," the meter of each "waltz" had to be specified. While many "waltzes," such as the original rotary waltz, were in 3/4 time, dances in other meters, like the polka and schottische (in 2/4 time), and the five-step waltz (in 5/4 time), were also commonly referred to as "waltzes" in the 19th century dance manuals which described them.

## A Kind of Music

Over the years, however, people came to associate the word "waltz" not only with the idea of turning dances in general, but also with the music for those particular turning dances which happened to be performed in **3/4 time**, now commonly known as "waltz time."

In this book, we will respect both of these historical usages.

We will focus on "waltzes" that are danced in 3/4 "waltz time" (cross-step waltz, box step waltz, rotary waltz, reverse waltz, redowa, mazurka, and hambo), but we will also look at "waltzes" that are danced in other meters (2/4 time: polka and schottische, 5/4 time: five-step waltz, 7/4 time: seven-step waltz), as well as dance forms that do not revolve but which are danced in "waltz time" (swing waltz, Latin waltz, tango vals, and others).

## A Way of Approaching Life

Finally, there is a third common usage of the word "waltz," this time as a metaphorical verb, where it is variously defined by Merriam-Webster as **"to move in a lively manner,"** **"to advance easily and successfully,"** and **"to approach boldly."**

With respect to this third meaning of the word, in addition to the physical descriptions of the various waltz steps, this book contains a diverse selection of essays on dancing and living. Our hope is that these essays will help you "waltz" through your entire life as skillfully as you "waltz" across the dance floor.

# Waltz Essentials

## Waltz Position

All of the dances we describe in this book will be danced primarily in waltz position, or some variation thereof.

The name "waltz position" is appropriate, as it is the waltz that introduced it to the world, creating quite a scandal by doing so. Prior to the introduction of the waltz in the early 19th century, public social dancing in such a close embrace would have been unthinkable. Indeed, for many it remained unthinkable, at least until polkamania swept the world in the 1840s and finally made waltz position seem innocent enough.

The basic waltz position is illustrated at left.

- The Lead's right arm and the Follow's left arm are somewhat raised. His* arm is below hers, with their elbows lightly touching. Both partners are individually responsible for keeping these arms floating together, like a raft on the water. He doesn't push her arm up, nor does she push his arm down.

- The Lead's right hand is up between the Follow's shoulder blades, not low on her back. If he holds her too low, her back may cantilever painfully backward. His fingertips just about reach her vertebrae, depending on the relative sizes of the dancers.

- The Lead's left and Follow's right hands are held about halfway between him and her, neither pulled back toward him nor pushed back toward her. Their arms are comfortably extended beside them, not too close, but not too far. Holding the hands straight out to the side can be dangerous for other dancers.

- In waltzing, these free hands tend to be held palm to palm, with her fingers more vertical and his more horizontal. Her fingers are pointing up between his thumb and forefinger, and his are pointed off toward the side of her palm. Other similar handholds are also possible. In any case, there is usually push-back pressure in the arms by both partners, so that any movement in the arms is immediately translated to the body.

- In social dancing, the Follow's left hand is *wherever she wants to place it*. The five most common placements found in ballroom dance are:

    1) She places her left hand palm down on the top of his shoulder.

    2) She holds her left hand flat, palm down, behind his back so that the knuckle of her thumb is the only part of her hand touching his back ("Knife Edge" hold).

---

\* In this book, we use gendered terms—his, her, he, she—only as a convenience, based on the observation that the vast majority of men choose to lead most of the time, and the vast majority of women choose to follow most of the time, though many enjoy occasional role reversal too (p. 161). In light of our use of gendered terms for the sake of convenience, we wish to make perfectly clear that we wholeheartedly support all dancers in their choice of role(s), and equally appreciate male Leads and male Follows, female Follows and female Leads, and all possible partnerships thereof.

3) She lightly pinches his upper arm, near his bicep, between her left thumb and forefinger.

4) She braces away from him with her left palm pressed against his upper arm, near his bicep.

5) She reaches around and holds onto his right shoulder blade with the palm of her left hand.

Dance teachers usually give a plausible reason why their preferred version is "better," so all five of these handholds are defended by someone. For instance, those who prefer version 5 report that many men love it when their partner helps hold on to them during a fast turning waltz, so that his right arm isn't doing all of the work. Some cite aesthetic reasons for their preference, and some say, "This is the only correct way because that's the way I learned it." As a result, different ballroom dance studies argue with each other over the one-and-only "correct" placement of the woman's left hand.

As we mention in "Sketchy Guys" (p. 137), some men try to correct their partner's choice of where to place their left hand, making her conform to the only way they know. In social dancing, however, the Lead respects his partner's choice of where to place her left hand.

Then, regardless of minor personal preferences, there are a few suggestions about the frame that are held in general agreement:

- Leads: Don't poke the fingertips of your right hand inward, into her back.

- Leads and Follows: Face your partner squarely, aiming your heart toward your partner's heart. Some stylings prefer a slight offset to the left, which is fine, but you don't want to twist out of the frame so that the Lead is facing toward his left hand. When that happens, his partner starts slipping off his right hand, resulting in him poking his fingertips into her back to catch her.

- Leads: Keep the frame comfortable for her, i.e., don't hold your arms up too high, and don't hold your partner closer than is comfortable for her. Give her some breathing room.

- Follows: Don't lean forward into him. Settle back into the frame. Not so much that he's struggling to hold you, just enough to establish a solid connection.

- Leads: Don't slouch or round your shoulders downward, as this makes it difficult for your partner to hold onto your frame, or rather, your lack thereof. Instead, keep the frame somewhat open and expansive.

- Leads and Follows: Don't pinch, squeeze, or crush your partner's hand. The ideal is a somewhat firm frame with firm arms, but soft, comfortable hands. Avoid both "jellyfish arms" or "vice grip hands."

## Line of Dance, Line of Direction, LOD

Most of the waltzes we describe in this book are waltzes in the most traditional sense, that is, dances which rotate and travel around the room. For these dances, it is important to know the recommended ways of traveling around the dance floor.

**Traveling dances travel counterclockwise around the room**, along a circular path called line of dance, or line of direction, abbreviated LOD in both cases. This is not only traditional, but also desirable, because most traveling dances rotate clockwise, and traveling counterclockwise makes this easier.

In a crowded room, LOD is actually many concentric circular paths. In this case, the paths closer to the center are considered the slow lanes, and the paths on the perimeter are the fast lanes. Couples wanting to travel quickly are encouraged to stay along the perimeter of the room, and couples traveling more slowly are encouraged to stay closer to the center. Couples wanting to dance in place are encouraged to dance in the center of the room, which is usually calm, like the eye of a hurricane.

These dance floor conventions are illustrated below.

You will find more tips for navigating around the room throughout this book.

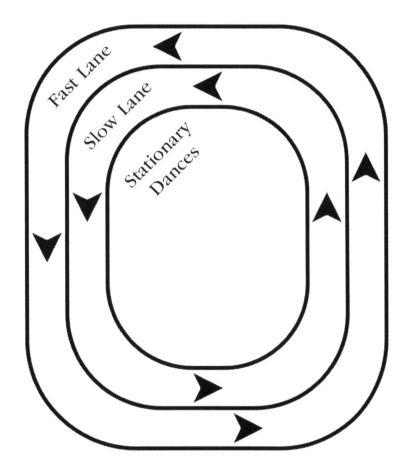

8

# Cross-Step Waltz

Cross-step waltz is the newest social dance form, spreading quickly because it is easy to learn yet endlessly innovative, satisfying for both beginners and the most experienced dancers.

Cross-step waltz travels and rotates like traditional waltzes, but the addition of the cross-step opens up a wide range of playful yet gracefully flowing variations.

## Why Are We Describing Cross-Step Waltz First?

We want dancers to succeed in learning to waltz, mastering the details of technique, partnering, and style. But even more than that, we want dancers to *like* waltzing, perhaps even *loving* to waltz, and cross-step waltz offers the best first impression.

The basic step of cross-step waltz is the easiest to learn. It is also the safest, with the least chance of being stepped on by your partner. Neither box step, rotary, nor Viennese waltz offer this degree of ease and success on the first try. By the end of their first class in cross-step waltz, everyone is successfully turning and traveling around the dance floor.

Then, advanced dancers find cross-step waltz to be infinitely creative, so this dance remains engaging at all levels of experience.

## A Brief History of Cross-Step Waltz

Cross-step waltz evolved in the early 20th century. In 1914, the "Cross Walk Boston" waltz created by Frank H. Norman foreshadowed the cross-step waltz. In the Cross Walk Boston, the Lead crossed his left foot over his right, stepped right with his right foot, and closed left to right. This was then repeated with the right foot. Norman's waltz then went on to other figures. There is no indication that Norman's step evolved into the modern cross-step waltz, but it's an early example of a cross-step waltz.

Cross-steps in general appeared between 1910 and the 1920s in the American one-step (the snake dip), Argentine tango (cruzado, ocho) and foxtrot (the cross step). The early foxtrots were in 4/4 time, but some dance manuals, like Geoffrey D'Egville's 1919 *How and What to Dance* in London suggested that the cross-step "may be introduced into the Waltz," which essentially turned this foxtrot step into cross-step waltz. In D'Egville's foxtrot version of this step, the Lead crossed his left foot over his right on the first count of the musical measure. In the same year, however, Adèle Collier, also from London, described a similar foxtrot "cross step" beginning with the Lead's *right* foot, like today's cross-step waltz. The March 1920 issue of *Dancing Times Magazine* in London reported that in the foxtrot, "The crossing of the feet is popular and effective." Of all the early cross-step dances, this lineage of foxtrot variations is the most likely evolutionary path that became the French Valse Boston and today's cross-step waltz.

After World War I, Americans brought their foxtrot and blues dance steps to Paris, where Parisian dance teachers observed and described the variations. The first descriptions appeared in Parisian dance and music magazines (such as *La Baionnette* and *Musica-Album*) in 1919, then in dance manuals beginning in 1920 (for example, *Toutes Les Danses Pour Tous* and *Les 15 Danses Modernes*). Significantly, most of these French descriptions commenced the dance steps with the Lead's right foot.

Around 1930, waltz tempos were slowed to a walking tempo, about 110-120 bpm, allowing the French crossed-step foxtrot to become a form of waltz, called Valse Boston, which was identical to today's cross-step waltz. At the same time, ballroom dancers in England and the United States developed their own slow waltz variations, but commencing with the Lead's left foot. This gave the cross-step (the "Twinkle" in American slow waltz) a different musical dynamic and momentum from the French Valse Boston, which began with the Lead's right foot.

In 1944, cross-step waltz was demonstrated in the American lindy hop film "Groovie Movie," with the Lead's right foot crossing on the musical downbeat.

The French Valse Boston can still be seen today in southern France and occasionally in Paris. It was revived in the United States around 1995, developed into a social dance form with hundreds of variations, and renamed cross-step waltz. Cross-step waltz has been spreading in the 21st century, is now popular at more than thirty mostly-waltz dance groups across the United States, and has recently become widespread in outdoor parks in Beijing.

*Note:* If this history looks similar to the Wikipedia page for cross-step waltz, that's because we wrote that page.

## Setting It Up

The frame of cross-step waltz is essentially the same as the basic waltz position (p. 4), with several modifications.

As a result of the cross-steps, in which both partners' legs cross through the frame at the same time, cross-step waltz requires a *flexible frame*, with more space between the partners than other waltz forms.

To make the frame more comfortable for both partners, he rests his right palm gently on her left shoulder blade, as opposed to his fingertips reaching her spine in the basic waltz position. This gives a bit more space between partners for crossing feet. Note that while this flexible frame allows for more space to cross through, and will twist slightly back and forth as the bodies aim slightly toward the cross-steps, it is still essential to maintain light push-back pressure in the arms to allow the translation of arm movements to the body.

The stationary version of cross-step waltz generally meanders around one spot on the floor, so in this case, you can set up anywhere you like, facing any direction, preferably away from other couples.

The turning and traveling cross-step waltz travels around the room along Line of Dance (LOD). In this case, the Lead sets up facing toward the outside wall, with the held hands pointing along LOD, counterclockwise around the room.

# Leading Into It

While cross-step waltz is extremely easy to follow on the fly, given the simple mirroring of the feet, it is courteous for the Lead to actually lead the Follow into the primary cross-step, rather than simply dancing off without her.

To lead the Follow into cross-step waltz, the Lead gently guides the Follow to cross her left foot over in front of her right foot and under the held hands, as he similarly crosses his right foot over in front of his left, on count 1. He can do this by leaning slightly toward the held hands and gently guiding her right shoulder slightly forward toward the held hands, just before count 1.

# Dancing Cross-Step Waltz

Cross-step waltz is generally danced to music in 3/4 time between 104 and 120 bpm, with 114-117 bpm being ideal. For recommendations, see "Discography of Waltz Music" (p. 223).

Here is the basic stationary cross-step waltz step:

1: The Lead crosses his right foot over in front of his left foot with weight, while the Follow crosses her left foot over in front of her right foot with weight.

2: The Lead steps side left with weight, while the Follow steps side right with weight.

3: The Lead replaces weight onto his right foot, pulling it back slightly, out of the way, while the Follow replaces weight onto her left foot, pulling it back slightly, out of the way. On count 3, the feet are still slightly apart, not closed together. Think "cross-open-open."

4-5-6: The Lead does exactly what the Follow did, and vice-versa.

Body placement can facilitate this basic step in several ways:

- Face slightly toward the side through which you're crossing on counts 1 and 4. You'll face your partner on counts 2 and 3 (and 5 and 6), before facing slightly toward the other side for the next cross-step.

- Lean slightly toward the side you're about to cross through on counts 1 and 4. This way your feet stay under your body instead of reaching into the cross-step.

- The Lead can assist the Follow's cross-steps by lightly pulling back out of her way, never pushing into her. It is uncomfortable for her to cross over in front when she is being pushed backwards.

# Cross-Step Waltz Variations

Cross-step waltz has hundreds of variations, and many new ones are created each year. Here, we'll cover some of the most essential variations, and later, we'll suggest some more advanced options (p. 159), and give advice on how you can create your own (p. 155).

## Slightly Turning Cross-Step Waltz

As a simple variation, the couple can rotate clockwise slightly during the basic step, usually 90° or less in three counts. For a full 180° turn, see the Turning Basic below.

*Hint:* Pull your right shoulder and right foot back out of your partner's way on the third count. The Lead does this on count 3, then the Follow does it on count 6.

This variation still stays mostly in one place on the floor, without much lateral travel.

## Zig Zag

This variation travels along LOD without rotating.

The Lead travels slightly forward along LOD with the basic step, while he leads her to travel backwards by "over-crossing." Her shoulder pulls back away from the crossing feet, so that her cross-step in front actually travels diagonally backwards, out-running him as he advances toward her. It's as if she's shooting over her shoulder, like Annie Oakley.

*Note:* He does not simply push her backwards. He leads her to over-cross by gently rotating her body even more toward the cross-step.

This creates a zig-zag path which travels along LOD with the Lead traveling forward, and the Follow backing.

## Toss-Across

They dance Zig-Zag, as the Lead casts his partner gently from his right side to his left side, catching her on alternating sides in half-open waltz position (let go of the held hands while maintaining the elbows-side connection). It starts with her on his right side, his right arm below her left, then alternates to her on his left side, his left arm below her right.

*Note:* This can also be done in place, in which case it is simply a more turned-out basic step that switches from one half-open waltz position to the other.

## Orbits
### (Rolling Toss-Across)

This move is usually how we teach the basic 360°-turning, LOD-traveling motion of the cross-step waltz Turning Basic (described below). But it's also a great variation by itself.

It is a Lead's clockwise Toss-Across followed by a Follow's clockwise Toss-Across.

Face forward LOD, with the Follow at the Lead's right side, in half-open waltz position.

Both step forward along LOD with their first feet (his right, her left), on count 1, then the Lead tosses himself across over to her right side, counts 2 and 3. On count 2, he steps back over across LOD in front of her, and on count 3, he pulls his right shoulder back against LOD so that he is directly to her right side, both facing LOD. While he does this, she simply takes three steps forward, count 2 slightly between his feet as he comes around. They end up in half-open waltz position on the other side (his left arm below her right).

Both cross-step forward along LOD, count 4, then he gently suggests that the Follow do the same, allowing her to toss herself across to his right side in the same manner, counts 5 and 6, while he walks forward, stepping slightly between her feet on count 5.

*Hint for Leads:* Don't toss her across too vigorously. She's a dancer, not a puppet, so let her dance across without hauling her.

*Hint for Follows:* As he cuts in front of you, continuing walking boldly forward, diving straight into him. Don't swerve away from him to the right, as you might if he were a truck cutting in front of you on the freeway. Swerving will make it harder for him to get across.

*Another Hint for Follows:* Be active in getting across, so he doesn't need to haul you across.

*Hint for Both:* Track your partner's travel and flow with them, instead of focusing on your own footwork.

Repeat, or take any multiple of six forward steps in between turns to rest.

## The Turning Basic

The Turning Basic has essentially the same footwork as Orbits, but you hold your partner in closed waltz position throughout, turning 360° every six steps, traveling continually along LOD.

**This is the fundamental step in cross-step waltz.**

Below is a detailed description of the steps for the Turning Basic.

The couple sets up in waltz position, the Lead facing toward the outside wall, with the held hands pointing along LOD.

1: The Lead crosses his right foot over his left foot along LOD, while the Follow crosses her left foot over her right along LOD.
    *Hint*: Leads, your body is slightly ahead of her, as if crossing a finishing line first. If you're not ahead of her, you'll have a difficult time passing into the outside lane.

2: The Lead steps back across in front of the Follow with his left foot, his legs bridging over across LOD, while the Follow steps straight forward on LOD, with her right foot slightly between his feet. The Lead pulls himself backwards away from her on this step.
    *Hints*: Make sure the Lead's left foot is actually fully across to the outside of LOD, not stepping *on* LOD, otherwise the Follow won't be able to step forward on LOD, and you'll under-turn, spiraling into the middle of the room. For the Follow, as in Orbits, she dives straight into him, not swerving away.

3: The Lead steps side/forward along LOD with his right foot, while the Follow steps side/ forward along LOD with her left foot. He pulls his right shoulder back out of her way.
    *Hint*: At this point, the couple has shifted their orientation, turning 180° while traveling along LOD. He's now on the outside lane, and she's now on the inside lane.

13

4-5-6: The Lead does exactly what the Follow did, and vice-versa

> *Hint*: Leads, look toward your right just before count 4, to help direct her travel in that direction. This is a visual lead, which is more comfortable than a physical lead pulling her in that direction. In other words, he *lets* her dance by on count 4 instead of *making* her dance.

The Turning Basic takes a little while to perfect, but once you have it, it flows effortlessly.

## Navigating Cross-Step Waltz

How do you navigate the turning cross-step waltz around the room?

It is an essential question, given the challenge of weaving in and out of other couples on the dance floor. Fortunately, the answer is quite simple.

In order to turn *right* (to travel out of the circle, toward the outside wall), simply rotate your partner *more*. In order to turn *left* (to travel into the circle, toward the center of the room), simply rotate your partner *less*.

In cross-step waltz, this increased or reduced rotation can happen at any time during the Turning Basic. To travel to the left, replace all of the "LOD"s in the description above with "slightly left of LOD," or replace the "LOD"s with "slightly right of LOD" to travel to the right.

If you consistently find yourself going one way or the other, simply make a correction in the other direction. Beginners, for example, tend to form a "death spiral" in toward the middle of the room. *To get out of this "death spiral," rotate your partner more.*

It goes without saying, but we'll say it anyway: **it is essential for the dancers—most importantly the Lead, but also the Follow—to continually be aware of their surroundings and carefully avoid crashing into other couples.**

As you rotate, scan the room and make a mental map of the dancers around you, paying particular attention to where you are going, and watching out for couples who may soon cross your path.

*Leads: **It is very scary for a Follow to dance with a Lead who is not paying attention**.* It is your responsibility not to crash her into anything. Don't take this lightly. If you crash her, she may quite reasonably not want to dance with you.

*Follows:* Most Leads greatly appreciate a Follow who helps him navigate, in two ways:
1) You can help him steer. When he rotates you more to travel to the right, help him out and rotate him more as well, or vice versa. If he's spiraling into the middle without intending to, you can help by rotating him more.
2) You can help him avoid crashes in his blind spots. If you see an impending crash that he doesn't, feel free to take initiative and guide him away from it, perhaps catching his shoulder with your left hand. If you overdo this, and repeatedly cry wolf when things are relatively safe, he might begin to feel like you don't trust him, but in general, most Leads greatly appreciate the help in a pinch.

Neither of these are "back-leading," but rather using your common sense and your "field sense" to help your partner navigate through a crowd.

*Les Contretems de la Walse, circa 1848*

## Waterfall
### (The Other Turning Basic)

Waterfall is a Turning Basic where the Lead crosses *behind* instead of *in front* on count 4, while the Follow continues to cross in front. The Follow always crosses in front on counts 1 and 4 in both the Turning Basic and Waterfall.

On count 4, the Lead has passed in front of the Follow and is now in the "outside lane" where he steps back along LOD with his left foot, with his partner at his right side, by his right pocket. He then turns to step forward with his right foot on LOD between her feet on count 5, and side/forward with his left foot along LOD on count 6, as usual. He stays with her the whole time, facing her and tracking her. Everything else is the same as the Turning Basic.

Some Leads prefer the Waterfall to the Turning Basic, and dance it exclusively, citing that it is easier and more comfortable to cross back, where there is lots of room, than crossing in front on count 4. Other Leads prefer the elegant symmetry of the Turning Basic. Both are equally good, in our opinion. It's entirely up to your personal preference.

## Follower's Solo (Ochos)

Adapted from tango Argentino, this works in both stationary and turning cross-step waltz.

In the latter case, it's a nice contrast to turn and travel, then stop and play for a while. Be careful, though, because this variation blocks traffic. Do it in the center of the room, or when you're sure that no one will be coming up behind you any time soon.

The Lead stops completely on count 1 and stays put in his crossed step as he continues to lead his partner through a Basic step in place, for one or more phrases of six counts.

*Leads:* Be sure to continue leading her through the Basic step. If you simply stop, and forget to lead her, there's a good chance that she'll follow visually and simply stop as well.

To restart himself, the Lead simply picks up his crossed foot slightly before any count 1, and replaces it into the cross-step on count 1, mirroring her continued cross-step and dancing away into another variation.

*Follows:* Keep the rhythm. In tango Argentino, you can play with the rhythm of ochos, but in cross-step waltz, that quickly gets messy. You have several footwork options, however.

> *The Basic*: Just keep dancing your cross-step waltz step in place.

> *Touches:* Cross your left foot, then touch your right foot to the side without weight, hesitating there until you cross back with that foot and do the same on the other side (cross, touch, pause).

> *Kicks:* The same as touches, except you kick (just bend your knee and lift your foot) behind you on count 3 to the side on where you touched, while turning away from the kick in preparation to cross that foot the other way (cross, touch, lift).

> *Sweeps:* Cross your left foot, then sweep your right foot along the floor from its position behind your left foot, around to the right side and in front of the left foot, sweeping around for counts 2 and 3, and continuing to sweep directly into the cross-step on count 4, to do the same with your other foot (cross swee-eep-cross swee-eep). In Tango, you would keep your toe lightly on the floor through the sweeps, so we recommend that style here as well. "Fire hydrant" position, with your foot lifted off the ground, is usually deemed inelegant.

*Leads:* How do you lead each of these footwork variations? You don't. She gets to pick for herself. You do, however, get to choose when to restart the Basic. If she seems to be enjoying her experimentation, give her some more time. If she seems to be getting bored, move on to something else.

## He Goes, She Goes

A nice, easy traveling variation in four parts (and four bars of music).

Part A (1-2-3): The Lead raises his left arm and walks straight forward under it, passing in front of his partner to the outside lane, and lowers his arm, as the Follow walks straight forward, ending up in the inside lane.
*Leads:* Look forward LOD as you duck under instead of looking back at her, which would visually misdirect the intended direction of travel.

Part B (4-5-6): Walk forward side-by-side, with the Lead's left arm raised forward along LOD, around her shoulder height. During these counts he rolls his left thumb downward, so that his palm is toward her, to make Part C easier.
*Hint for Leads:* Don't forget this part. It is essential for making the feet work out.

*Optional Styling:* Either the Lead or Follow may do a Grapevine step on Part B, instead of simply walking forward. 4: Slightly face toward your partner and cross in front. 5: Step side along LOD. 6: Cross behind.

Part C (7-8-9): He raises his left hand and loops it up toward the left, in front of her head, to lead her into a counterclockwise Follow's Underarm Turn.
*Hint for Leads:* Keep the lead for the turn light and suggestive, rather than forceful and demanding. Imagine that you're tracing a halo over an angel's head.
*Hint for Follows:* Travel with him as you turn, as opposed to stopping and turning in place. With this timing, your feet are set up so you can simply pivot along, each step traveling LOD as you turn, stepping forward, backward, forward.

Part D (10-11-12): He lowers his left hand and sweeps her by in front of him to his right side and catches her in waltz position. This movement flows smoothly from part C.
*Hint for Follows:* Complete a full 360° turn on Part C so that you're facing forward LOD at the beginning of Part D, crossing boldly forward to his right side instead of backing up into waltz position. As a general hint for social dancing, when he turns you a little bit, turn yourself more. Also, keeping your arm directly in front of your forehead as you turn will keep it comfortable, and help you gauge how much to turn.

## He Goes, Frisbee

The same as He Goes, She Goes, except he leads her into a counterclockwise Follow's Free Spin (no hands, she spins alone) on Part C.

To do this, he keeps his left hand low in Part B, and presses into her hand with his as they approach Part C. She presses back into his hand, then spins counterclockwise alongside him with no hands, using the same footwork as He Goes, She Goes. After the turn, they retake the held hands and finish with Part D.

*Hint for Follows:* Travel straight forward alongside him as you Free Spin.

*Hint for Leads:* In leading the Free Spin, impart rotation rather than translation, i.e., don't push her away from you into the center of the room.

*Another Hint for Leads:* As you're catching her hand for Part D, "cross trails" with her, traveling in toward the inside lane as she is crossing in front of you into the outside lane, rather than making her do all of the traveling.

## He Goes, Rollaway

The same as He Goes, Frisbee, except that he also Free Spins, *clockwise*, as she Free Spins counterclockwise.

*Hints for Leads:* Take care of her. Make sure she knows that she's Free Spinning before you spin away yourself. *Don't just ditch her.* And make sure you're there to catch her right after she spins. In addition, make sure you are also traveling as you turn. Follows have more experience traveling while turning, so if you turn on the spot, she'll pass you by.

## Lead's Underarm Turn

Do Part A of He Goes, She Goes, then skip straight to Part D on counts 4-5-6.

This is a great figure anytime, but it is also useful for when you start He Goes, She Goes, then realize that you don't have enough space to safely complete all four parts.

## Waltz Walk

This variation is one of the most impressive there is.

*Leads:* When you find yourself in a tight squeeze, where there isn't enough room to safely rotate, firm up the frame and lead your partner to walk straight forward, aiming toward a less crowded space on the floor. Your partner, along with everyone around you, will be impressed that you chose to protect your partner instead of risking a crash. When it's safe again, recommence rotation on any count 1 by passing in front of your partner into a Turning Basic.

## Want More?

A list of more than 100 cross-step waltz variations can be found on p. 159.

In addition, videos of more than 300 cross-step waltz variations may be viewed on the Waltz Lab website (www.waltzlab.com), and on YouTube by searching for cross-step waltz.

# Six Fundamental Advantages of Cross-Step Waltz

We love all kinds of waltzing. The original German (rotary) waltz, the later left-turn (reverse) waltz, box step waltz, country walking waltz, tango vals cruzado, etc. But we often hear people say that their favorite is cross-step waltz. This is the most common topic of the dance essays written by Richard's students, and they are often specific about the reasons why they like it so much. Zachariah Cassady, director of Waltz Etcetera in Seattle, has written, "Cross-step waltz, my personal favorite, is the best partner dance in the world."

Why? We think that it is easier to innovate if one understands the reasons why.

### 1) Easy to break into innovations.

In most waltzes, a dancer steps directly into his or her partner on count 1, in a closed frame. In cross-step waltz, however, **you can break out of the frame into something creative right at the beginning of the phrase**, because at the beginning of the basic step you're facing forward side-by-side. And in cross-step waltz the Follow is traveling forward on count 1, letting her instantly travel into a variation. In box step waltz she's stepping back on 1, and must wait until halfway through the figure, count 4, to travel forward out of the frame.

There are three distinct ways to innovate in cross-step waltz:

1. Because you're facing forward side-by-side in cross-step waltz, you can travel laterally forward together, borrowing figures like promenade or grapevine from one-step, tango, and foxtrot.

2. Or the Follow can pass by in front of the Lead, or turn under his arm. Or the Lead can do either, thereby borrowing figures from swing and salsa.

3. Or you can stay in the rotating frame and borrow figures like pivots from waltz, polka, and schottische.

   Therefore, you can easily and instantly adapt figures from literally any other social dance form into cross-step waltz.

## 2) Easy to return to the basic step.

An important part of innovating a new variation is exiting out of it, returning back to the basic step. In box step waltz, you have to align exactly, and one partner must step directly into the other. In rotary waltz, he must get in front of her with a carefully placed left foot, as she must step with her right foot exactly in between his feet.

In cross-step waltz you return to your partner's side, without intertwined footwork, which is *much* easier and safer. Even the trickiest figures are easy to recover from in cross-step waltz.

## 3) Easy to match partner's footwork.

The mirrored footwork symmetry and visual tracking of your partner make it easy to foot-fudge to match your partner's steps, in case an experimental step messes up, or if someone accidentally gets off-phase.

## 4) Dual modes.

Some social dances are comprised of one basic step repeated, like the original waltz, traveling around the room. Fans call this "trance-like."

Other social dances are constantly changing figures, like swing, salsa, and tango.

Cross-step waltz can be done in either mode, as the Lead chooses, or as the Lead senses that the Follow prefers. Doing no variations other than the Turning Basic for three minutes can be sublimely satisfying. And a highly active succession of figures can be a blast. Or shifting from one paradigm to the other offers great variety and contrast.

This dual mode also allows the Lead to relax and coast with a Turning Basic if he wants to, without fear of boring his partner, unlike dances like the hustle where he must come up with a new figure every second-and-a-half without a break. This takes a lot of pressure off the Lead. Follows also enjoy the break of serene traveling, instead of constantly being challenged to respond to a new figure every few seconds.

### 5) Closest to Lead-Follow parity.

Cross-step waltz allows the most equal balance between the Lead and Follow roles of any social dance, partially because the basic step is the same in Lead and Follow roles, mirrored. We acknowledge the inherent differences between Lead and Follow, but we like the two roles to be as equal as possible. This symmetry also makes role-reversal (p. 161) easier in cross-step waltz than in any of the other social dances.

### 6) Full range of complexity.

Some dances are easy to learn, like four-count street swing, but remain too easy to hold the interest of advanced dancers. So on a difficulty scale of 1-to-10, the entire range of the dance is only 1 to 4. Other dance forms are so difficult that beginners find them hard to even begin. The difficulty of tango Argentino or west coast swing might range from 4 to 10, with difficulty level 4 feeling overwhelming to a beginner. Cross-step waltz is the best of both, spanning the full range from 1 to 10. Beginners find themselves traveling around the floor successfully in their first lesson, but the most experienced dancers are still challenged at the most advanced levels, years later.

These are six ways that cross-step waltz is *uniquely* advantageous, but there are also other positive aspects of cross-step waltz that are held in common with other dance forms. For instance, there is an undeniable physical pleasure with dances that travel at speed around the floor, with a partner in your arms. Likewise, many people find rotating dances to be particularly satisfying.

## Dizziness

Beginners often get dizzy when they first learn to waltz. Then after a few weeks of waltzing, they acclimate to continual rotation and the dizziness goes away.

In the meantime, if you don't like getting dizzy, don't tilt your head while waltzing. This also means don't look up or down. Vertigo is monitored by the three semicircular canals in your inner ear, and rotation already engages two of them. Adding the third axis of movement by tilting your head can be too much at first.

The better advice is to *enjoy* the dizziness, before it goes away through acclimation. Most young children enjoy the feeling of dizziness ("Turn me upside down and spin me faster!"), so maybe you can recover a bit of that lost pleasure. If you can't, then it's back to Plan A: don't tilt your head.

> "All the dreamers in the world are dizzy in the noodle."
> — Fairy Godmother in *Cinderella*

INDIVIDUAL (*who is not over strong in his head, or firm on his legs*). "D-D-D-D-oes Waltzing—ever—make—you—Giddy? Because, I—shall—be—happy—to—sit—down—whenever—you're—tired!"

GIRL (*who is in high dancing condition*). "Oh dear, No—I could Waltz all Night!"

# Cross-Step Waltz Mixer

### Choreographed by Richard Powers and Angela Amarillas

The Cross-Step Waltz Mixer is a choreographed sequence dance based on cross-step waltz, in which the couples change partners every eight bars (hence the "Mixer").

**Music:** Any cross-step waltz tune with continual eight-bar phrases.

In a large circle, couples do a turning basic cross-step waltz traveling LOD for 4 bars (two full rotations), opening up to face the center of the room with the Follow on the right side, by the end of the fourth bar.

All take hands in a large circle and take a waltz step forward (step-close-close, beginning with his right, her left), for one bar, and back (step-close-close with the opposite foot), for one bar. A sociable tradition is to glance at your next partner-to-be on the forward step and glance at the partner you are leaving on the backing step.

*Note:* The in and out steps are a good opportunity to fix the circle, if there are any spacing issues. If the circle is getting smaller, take larger backing steps to spread the circle out again.

The Lead turns the next Follow (at his left side) under his raised left arm with a counterclockwise (inside) turn: she cross-steps left over right, places her right shoulder forward under the arched arms and turns under counterclockwise while he cross-steps right over left and passes behind her back into her place while facing her (one bar). Counts 2 and 3 are "open-open," tracking your partner.

Then both take a cross-step (his left, her right) toward the outside wall. She passes strongly in front of him and pulls her right shoulder back to take waltz position at the last moment, both facing LOD. This last part is the same as Part D from He Goes, She Goes (one bar).

Repeat from the beginning with this new partner.

*Note:* If there are extra, unpaired dancers who want to participate, they can place themselves between couples and walk along as everyone dances. When the circle forms, they'll steal the next partner. The dancer whose next partner was just stolen then does the same.

**Cross-Step Waltz Rueda** refers to a Cross-Step Waltz Mixer that has different cross-step waltz variations added, lead-follow freestyle, in place of the four bars of cross-step waltz Turning Basic. Salsa Rueda and Swing Rueda are sometimes prompted by a caller. Cross-Step Waltz Rueda is usually improvised, freestyle.

*Notes for Leads:*
1) If you add variations, make sure your partners are comfortably to their place in the circle by the end of the fourth bar. She gets a very brief impression of you. Make it a good one by taking care of her.
2) There is no need to add variations, and many times, she'll actually prefer it if you don't. She'd much rather feel like she's dancing with twenty different attentive partners than feel like she's being put through twenty different wringers. It can be an absolute joy for both roles to experience dancing the simply elegant Turning Basic with twenty different partners in a row.

# Play

For all of our talk about the benefits of waltzing, the real reason people love to waltz is this: it's simply a whole lot of fun, because waltzing—and social dancing in general—is a quintessential form of play.

In fact, historically speaking, dance and play are synonymous. The English *play* comes from the Middle Dutch *pleyen*, which literally means "to dance, leap for joy."

But dancing as play is even older than words, as many animals play by dancing, solo and socially, in a variety of ways. Harbor seals, for example, play by waltzing underwater, holding each other in their flippers as they twirl.

**The fact that social dancing is play is one of the essential benefits of waltzing.**

To speak of the benefits of play is somewhat incongruous, as one of the key characteristics of play is that it is apparently purposeless, or at least done for its own sake. In other words, it's simply fun. Other key characteristics of play include freedom from everyday, "real world" concerns, diminished self-consciousness, and the potential to improvise.

In a society in which children and adults alike are overworked and starved for play, the benefits of play are worth reviewing.

One reason that play is so important is that it is essential for healthy brain development, not only in children, but throughout the human lifespan.

As Kay Redfield Jamison writes in *Exuberance*, play is a vital facilitator, shaper, and motivator which allows the pleasurable practice of improbable twists and turns and creates a wider range of possibilities for future actions.

Stuart Brown, a dedicated play researcher, explains that in play we can imagine and experience situations we've never encountered before, learning lessons and skills without being directly at risk, and making new cognitive connections that find their way into our everyday lives.

As biologist Bernd Heinrich eloquently summarizes, "Play is an acting out of options, among which the best can then be chosen, strengthened, or facilitated in the future."

By exercising and stretching our minds, play prepares us to face the complexities of life in increasingly intelligent and creative ways. It also physically promotes neuron growth and plasticity. (For more on this, see "Dancing Makes You Smarter" on p. 183.)

> "Men do not quit playing because they grow old.
> They grow old because they quit playing."
> — Oliver Wendell Holmes, Jr., Supreme Court justice

One of the most complex aspects of our lives is navigating our web of social relationships. Thus, *social play*, of which waltzing is a paragon, is especially important for our ongoing development. Social play allows us to test our boundaries, trying out new ways of relating to others, while simultaneously building rapport and partnership.

As Marc Bekoff writes of social play in animals, "Animals that play together tend to stay together." And the same is true in human relationships: couples who play together often, engaging in novel and arousing activities like waltzing, have more satisfying relationships than couples who do not. Researchers have also found that playing a physical game with our partner before having a serious discussion leads to healthier communication in that discussion. Perhaps we should start waltzing together before discussing our issues.

The dance floor is a safe space in which we can act out different social options and apply what we learn to our everyday relationships.

Waltzing is a master teacher of life skills, whether it is helping us harmonize our bodies and minds, or helping us harmonize with each other and the world. One of the most essential lessons it can teach us is the importance of a playful state of mind for adapting to the unexpected twists and turns of life. **For in reality, play is not an activity, but rather a heightened state of mind** that some activities, like waltzing, naturally inspire, which we can learn to apply across our entire lives.

## Transcendent Play

Eloquently portraying this superb state of mind in her description of what she calls *deep* or *transcendent play*, Diane Ackerman says,

> Deep play is an absence of mental noise—liberating, soothing, and exciting. Deep play means no analysis, no explanation, no promises, no goals, no worries. You are completely open to the drama of life that may unfold.

> We spend our lives in pursuit of those moments of feeling whole, or being in the moment of deep play.

The dance floor is a perfect place to begin finding these moments.

## Recommended Reading on Play

- *Exuberance: The Passion for Life* (2004) by Kay Redfield Jamison

- *Play: How It Shapes the Brain, Opens the Imagination, and Invigorates the Soul* (2009) by Stuart Brown and Christopher Vaughan

- *Deep Play* (1999) by Diane Ackerman

# Touch

Throughout the history of social dancing, there have been many treatises railing against dance as scandalous, wicked, and downright evil. (Richard has a collection of over one hundred anti-dance books.)

One of the aspects of waltzing most frequently reviled throughout the ages is its encouragement of close physical contact. For moralists of the past, no greater scandal could be imagined than an activity that encourages unmarried youth to touch.

Far from being a contemptible vice of social dancing, however, there is a growing body of evidence that shows that touch is actually one of its primary virtues, especially in a modern society starved for contact, where people are rarely encouraged to touch.

The dearth of touch in our daily lives is unfortunate, as the benefits of caring human touch are clear from the very beginning of life. As Tiffany Field reports, several studies have found up to 47% greater weight gain in preterm newborns who receive touch therapy in the form of light massage, compared to newborns who receive only standard medical treatment, despite identical caloric intake. In addition, mothers who participate in this touch therapy see a significant decrease in postpartum depression, and fathers who participate see a significant improvement in their relationship with their child.

Over the years, touch has increasingly been identified as a basic human need, as studies have consistently shown that caring, consensual touch is associated with a wide range of positive outcomes for physical, mental, and social health for people of all ages, including:

| *decreasing …* | *while improving …* |
|---|---|
| • anger | • attention |
| • aggression | • cognitive function |
| • anxiety | • immune function |
| • blood pressure | • mood |
| • depression | • self-esteem |
| • fatigue | • sleep quality |
| • pain | • social functioning |
| • stress | • quality of life |

Studies have found that significant benefits can come from the simplest touches, like holding hands and embracing, the kinds of touch found most often in dancing. For example:

Holding someone's hand in a stressful situation significantly reduces our physiological stress response, limiting the rise of cortisol in our bloodstream. It helps the most when this person is a significant other, particularly one with whom we have a good relationship, but there is still an observable benefit when the hand belongs to a complete stranger.

And in a study where students were asked to hug as many people as possible, giving at least five hugs per day for a month, their satisfaction skyrocketed compared to those who did not increase their hugging.

**Touch is also an effective form of emotional communication.** Mothers and fathers can recognize their infants, and lovers can identify each other, by touch alone. And even among strangers, at least eight distinct emotions (anger, disgust, fear, gratitude, happiness, love, sadness, and sympathy) can be communicated accurately through touch. In fact, pro-social emotions (gratitude, love, sympathy) can actually be communicated *more accurately through touch* than through other non-verbal mediums such as facial expressions.

Perhaps in part as a result of this, **touch facilitates bonding and cooperation.**

One recent study found that NBA basketball teams whose players touch each other more in the early season score more baskets in the late season than teams whose players touch each other less. The same is true for individual players. Testing for causation, the study found that touch led to bonding and cooperation, and bonding and cooperation led to success.

In *Grooming, Gossip, and the Evolution of Language,* anthropologist Robin Dunbar describes just how important this aspect of touch (and dancing) was for the evolution of human society as we know it.

> Trying to hold together the large groups which the emerging humans needed for their survival must have been a trying business. They are perpetually at risk of fragmenting because of the conflicting interests of so many different individuals, not to mention exploitation by free-riders. As the group's size increases, factions with opposing views develop, and we begin to take sides. … We still find it difficult now.

> Language allowed us to find out about each other, to ask and answer questions about who was doing what with whom. But of itself, it does not bond groups together. Something deeper and more emotional was needed to overpower the cold logic of verbal arguments. It seems that we needed music and physical touch to do that.

**The harmonizing powers of music and touch allow us to bring together, and hold together, larger and more diverse groups of people.**

As psychologist Dacher Keltner summarizes, "the science of touch convincingly suggests that we're wired to—we need to—connect with other people on a basic physical level. To deny that is to deprive ourselves of some of life's greatest joys and deepest comforts."

What this research on touch suggests to us is that far from being an evil of social dancing, the physical contact that it encourages is actually supremely good for us: physically, mentally, and socially. By waltzing, we bestow this multitude of benefits on ourselves, on our partners, and even those around who haven't yet discovered the joy of "touch dancing."

> "Too often we underestimate the power of a touch, a smile,
> a kind word, a listening ear, an honest compliment, or the smallest act
> of caring, all of which have the potential to turn a life around."
> — Leo Buscaglia, author

## Recommended Reading on Touch

- *Touch* (2003) by Tiffany Field

- *Touching: The Human Significance of the Skin* (1986) by Ashley Montagu

# Everyone Is Different

We celebrate the diversity of people, as a part of the beauty of being human. We come from different backgrounds and experiences, with different ages, genders, and ethnicities. Interacting with the diversity of others enriches our lives. We learn and grow from these interactions.

Each *dance partner* is different as well, in a wide variety of ways: different shapes and sizes, different ways of moving, different levels of dance experience, and different paces of learning, with each having learned from different teachers, or from no teacher, just picking it up on the fly from their friends.

The purpose of social dancing is having fun, so we respect and even admire that each of our partners is different. And we *enjoy* adapting to the differences in their dancing.

> "You don't get harmony when everybody sings the same note."
> — Doug Floyd

**We also benefit from these interactions.** As we learn new ways of moving, we grow to become better dancers. In the process of adapting to others who are different from ourselves, **we become a more flexible and adaptable person, increasing our ability to successfully navigate through life in a rapidly changing world.**

There are some ballroom dancers and teachers, however, who disagree with the validity of individuality and personal preference. They feel strongly that theirs is the one and only "correct" way to dance, and that all of the other versions are wrong. They force their partners to dance in exactly their own preferred style, or criticize their partner's dancing as "incorrect."

Why do some dancers and ballroom studios do that? Do they just want to feel superior to others? Is it to make their dancing easier? Ah, that second one rings true.

We acknowledge that it would indeed be easier to dance if all of our partners danced in exactly the same style and knew the same steps and figures. *If* that were possible.

This leads to two questions:

1.  Is uniformity really *better* than the wide range of experiences that we could gain from others?

    Most of us believe that the answer is no, and there are many pages in this book devoted to the benefits of adapting to a wide range of partnering styles and personalities.

2.  Is the quest for uniformity *realistic*? Is it even possible?

    The second question has an even clearer answer: no, a quest for uniformity in social dancing is neither realistic nor possible.

Everyone is different, whether we like it or not. People are going to be who they are. We can accept this, or we can resist it. But fighting this essential fact of life is a recipe for lifelong disappointment and frustration. **How can a one-way-only approach, to an interpersonal dynamic that isn't one-way-only, possibly be true?**

Our adapting to others' styles is also *friendlier* than insisting that our partners conform to our own rules. And it shows our respect for others. This generous attitude is what makes social dancing *social*.

There is another, somewhat paradoxical, benefit of this approach: by acknowledging and embracing each other's differences, the result is often that we are able to see more clearly the things that we share, discovering that we have more in common than we first thought. This is as opposed to the one-way-only approach, in which dancers, by seeking uniformity in their partners, mostly end up experiencing differences.

A large part of dance partnering is the art and skill of adapting to the many differences that we encounter when dancing with others. As you may already know, this process can become one of the greatest joys of social dancing.

"All the lessons of psychiatry, psychology, social work, indeed culture, have taught us over the last hundred years that it is the acceptance of differences, not the search for similarities, which enables people to relate to each other."
— John Ralston Saul, author

# The Three Worlds of Ballroom Dance

Social   Competitive   Exhibition

## What is Ballroom Dance?

"Ballroom dance" usually refers to traditional partnered dance forms that are done by a couple, often in the embrace of waltz position, also called closed ballroom dance position. These include waltz, swing, tango, and salsa.

**Ballroom dance is the overall umbrella term, covering all three forms discussed here.**

As noted before, the focus of this book is *social* ballroom dance, a term that is self-defining as dancing for the purpose of socializing, for fun.

The earliest dance forms ever described in detail (in the 15th century) were partnered social dances. And many of today's performative dance forms, including ballet and jazz dance, evolved from social dance forms that came before. Most social dance forms over the centuries have been danced as couples, but there are also solo and group forms of social dance.

The three forms of ballroom dance are:

**Social** ballroom dance  **Competitive** ballroom dance  **Exhibition** ballroom dance

These three forms share the same historical roots, similar step vocabulary, and music, so the three forms are considered siblings, related by birth. Yes, siblings are known to fight, but they can also be mutually supportive.

Which one is better?

Yes, that question is intentionally provocative, and is easily answered. **All three forms are equally valid**, each enjoyed by their adherents for good reasons. But it is helpful to know **how and why they differ from each other.**

# Comparing the Three Worlds

| Social Ballroom | Competitive Ballroom (a.k.a. DanceSport) | Exhibition Ballroom |
|---|---|---|

What is the essential difference between the three?

The main distinction is that they have **different audiences**.

### *Who* are you dancing for, beyond your own enjoyment?

| Your partner | The judges | An audience |
|---|---|---|

Then, taking a closer look at the differences …

### What are your audience's expectations?

| Your partners want to interact with you spontaneously, for fun, doing steps that are also enjoyable for them. | Judges want to see that the steps and styles are done precisely and correctly, with great flair. | Audiences want to be entertained, often with a preference for beautiful and/or impressive moves. |
|---|---|---|

### What is your attitude?

| Sociable, i.e., friendly and kind. Flexibly adaptive. You value and adapt to styles that are different from your own. | Rigorously correct, with expansive movements. The many styles outside of the official syllabus are usually considered to be incorrect. | It varies widely, depending on the dance form. |
|---|---|---|

### What is your reward?

| The spontaneous enjoyment of dancing with a partner. The satisfaction of becoming proficient in a dance form. Self-confidence. | Competing. Impressing others. Winning. The satisfaction of becoming proficient in a dance form. Self-confidence. | Entertaining or impressing others, enthusiastic applause. The satisfaction of becoming proficient in a dance form. Self-confidence. |
|---|---|---|

*Note:* Everything has an exception. The above categories are generally true, but there are occasionally exceptions in each case.

| Social Ballroom | Competitive Ballroom (a.k.a. DanceSport) | Exhibition Ballroom |
|---|---|---|

### Are there standardized steps and technique?

| Social Ballroom | Competitive Ballroom (a.k.a. DanceSport) | Exhibition Ballroom |
|---|---|---|
| No, standardization doesn't function because each partner is different. You must modify your steps and style to adapt to each partner. | Yes, rigorously standardized, because competitors need to know exactly what technical details the judges want to see. | Usually not. In today's sampling culture (*"been there, seen that"*) audiences prefer something they've never seen before. |

### Is there a standardized style?

| Social Ballroom | Competitive Ballroom (a.k.a. DanceSport) | Exhibition Ballroom |
|---|---|---|
| Absolutely not. You develop your own personal style, different from others. Some social forms like swing, tango, and salsa especially discourage copying other's styles. | Yes, absolutely. You are trained to copy the style of champions before you, working hard to imitate every nuance of that standardized style. | Styles may be unique to the choreographer, thus not standardized. But the performing group usually works on copying and mastering that one style. |

### Is there a fixed choreography?

| Social Ballroom | Competitive Ballroom (a.k.a. DanceSport) | Exhibition Ballroom |
|---|---|---|
| No. You make it up as you go along, often based on what the Follow is doing at the moment, and what occurs to the Lead spontaneously.<br><br>Both Lead and Follow engage in a highly active attention to possibilities. | Yes. Competitors usually perform choreographed routines that they have rehearsed.<br><br>An exception is Jack and Jill competitions, usually in west coast swing and lindy hop, with a partner that one has not danced with before. | Yes. Exhibitions are usually choreographed and rehearsed. Furthermore, group routines often have everyone dancing in unison.<br><br>But improvised exhibitions do exist, especially in swing, tango and blues. |

### Does it require split-second decision-making?

| Social Ballroom | Competitive Ballroom (a.k.a. DanceSport) | Exhibition Ballroom |
|---|---|---|
| Yes, continually, in both Lead and Follow roles. This increases your opportunities for split-second decision-making, increasing your neuronal complexity (see "Dancing Makes You Smarter" on p. 183). | Usually not. Most decisions have been made by others, first in providing a restricted syllabus of acceptable steps, then often in choreographing the routine for you. You work mostly on style, which many dancers love to do. | Not often. Most decisions have usually been made by the choreographers. But that's what performers usually prefer. |

*Note:* To most people, "competition ballroom dance" means DanceSport, so that's the form discussed above. But there are also competitions in west coast swing, lindy hop, blues, salsa, and other dance forms, most of which do not require standardized syllabi or styling.

# A Brief History of the Three Worlds

For the first century of closed-position couple dancing, there was only the first category of ballroom dance: **social**. This was the 19th century, the age of the waltz and polka, when "ballroom dance" meant precisely that: dancing in a ballroom.

An important part of the 19th century ballroom mindset, in both Europe and America, was **selfless generosity**, with an emphasis on enhancing the pleasure of your dance partners and the assembled company. Another emphasis was on **being flexible** and **adapting to your partner**. For most social dancers, this attitude of generosity, kindness, and flexibility has never ceased, and continues to this day.

**Exhibition ballroom dance** came next. Performative social dance forms were occasionally staged in cabarets and Vaudeville at the end of the 19th century, but the performance of social dances for an audience mostly took off in the 20th century. Vernon and Irene Castle were foremost among professional dancers who started to perform social dances onstage, from 1912 to 1915. Fred Astaire and Ginger Rogers surpassed the Castle's fame and influence two decades later, through the medium of film. The tradition of exhibition ballroom dance continues today in films such as "Take the Lead" and Broadway shows like "Burn the Floor."

**Competitive ballroom dance** came last, growing out of the Sequence Dancing movement in the working-class suburbs of London, where hundreds of dancers would memorize choreographed waltzes like Arthur Morris' *Veleta* (1900), described on p. 68. These expanded to include sequenced one-steps, two-steps, tangos, and saunters (foxtrots).

Different populations of dancers in London had different preferences, and by 1914 there was a class division between those who preferred freestyle vs. choreographed dance. The upper classes in London preferred freestyle dancing. The working class in the outskirts preferred sequence dancing, and would hold weekly balls where dancers would gather to learn, memorize, and perform a rapidly growing number of sequence dances.

The next step was **standardization**. The creation and standardization of these sequence dances was controlled by several organizations which appeared at this time, most notably the Imperial Society of Teachers of Dancing. Today's "international style" (i.e. British style) ballroom dancing is overseen by the Imperial Society, which was founded in London in July 1904 for "the fraternal co-operation of properly qualified teachers of dancing in the British Empire for the safeguarding of our mutual interests." The original focus of these organizations was the standardization of steps, technique, and style into only one "correct" version. Competitions didn't arise for another two decades.

A primary motivation of the middle classes is upward mobility. You can raise your position in life through the mastery of skills. The working class ethic embraced the mastery of sequence dances, which led the Imperial Society to create **judged competitions of ballroom dance** in the 1920s, as a way to elevate one's social position through perseverance and hard work. This work ethic is still visible in competitive ballroom dance today.

In the early years of competitive ballroom dance, the preferred English style was natural and understated. To quote the 1923 London dance manual *The Modern Ballroom Dance Instructor*: "All movement is easy, unaffected, which can be so easily ruined by exaggeration. The best dancers are the quietest; they do not flourish their prowess." In other words, early competitions were simply exhibitions of the dance sequences, evaluated by judges, based on the values of polite social dancing.

Then competitions introduced the format of the **elimination round**, where the competition began with a fairly crowded floor, filled with all of the competitors dancing at once. The judges thinned the crowd down to a few finalists: those to be individually evaluated. This change in competition format resulted in a dramatic change in the look of competitive ballroom dance. The dancers had to perform far more expansive movements, to stand out from the crowd. Exaggerated movements and costuming were a matter of survival: either outshine the others or risk elimination.

To this day, these expansive movements remain a distinctive stylistic difference between social and competitive ballroom dance.

## Motivation

In addition to the stylistic differences, the motivations of social and competitive ballroom dance are quite different as well. A U.S. Ballroom Dance Champion recently described the competitive motivation this way: "You must want to go to the very top and be the very best dancer. You must be able to use your time to practice seven days a week without allowing any other influences to interfere."

Some dancers prefer the easy-going social attitude of dancing for pleasure, while others enjoy the process of mastering competitive styling. Either way, it is smart to be aware of the many differences between the forms: technique, styling, standardization, adaptability, attitude, and motivation.

## Your Choice

So, of the three forms, which one is better? It depends on you. Dancers usually have a preference for the one that best suits their personality.

It's important to know the differences, for two reasons:

1) To recognize which form(s) best match your personality. There's an essential difference between social and competitive ballroom dance, and different personalities are naturally drawn to one or the other. Your choice essentially comes down to knowing yourself, and finding the right match for you.

2) To avoid the unfortunate mistake of applying the rules and attitudes of one form to another. This isn't just an abstract differentiation. The repercussions can be serious.

For instance, occasionally a ballroom dancer will pedantically insist that his partner conform to competitive stylistic details at an informal social dance (*"You're doing it wrong. You have to do it my way!"*), resulting in the contradiction of antisocial behavior at a social event. Conversely, socially adapting to your partner's misstep at a competition may eliminate you from that round. Both forms are equally valid, but they have different attitudes. It is important to be clear on the differences.

Some dancers do both social and competitive dancing, or all three forms, and some of them are wonderfully adept at knowing which attitudes are appropriate for each. At a social dance, these dancers are friendly, spontaneously adaptive, and warmly supportive of their partner's differing style. Then they are rigorously correct and expansive when competing. *They understand and respect the differences.*

## Value Others' Truths

Social, competitive, and exhibition ballroom dancers are all united by a love of partnered dance. We may each have our preferences—that's only natural—but there is no need to dismiss or criticize anyone who doesn't share our preferences. Let's save our criticisms for people who are truly doing harm in the world, not for people whose passions merely differ from our own.

# Conditional Learning

Many dancers believe that the best first exposure to a dance form, as well as the best continuing instruction, comes from the most highly specified, detailed, technical, "correct" teaching. We believe this because teachers constantly tell us this. They tell us that they are the experts, that there is only one correct way to do the dance, and that they know all of the exacting details of the One Way. To learn otherwise, they say, will "engender bad habits."

Sound convincing? Those teachers know that this approach sells, because that's what most of us want to hear.

As Harvard psychologist Ellen J. Langer notes, we dislike not knowing with certainty. Given a lifetime of learning in schools that "teach to the test," it is much more comfortable for us to believe there's one right answer we can master. The problem with this belief is twofold: first, there often isn't one "right" answer, especially in social dance. And second, although we tend to seek certainty, we do so at our own risk, as there is great, untapped power in uncertainty.

Langer's research has repeatedly demonstrated that when we're presented with facts as certain, absolute truths—whether in science and math, or music and dancing—we tend to use them thoughtlessly, making bad, inappropriate, or limited decisions. **But when we are presented with the same information in a conditional, uncertain way** (*"maybe it's so, but maybe it's this other way"*), **we process the information, and we use the information, in smarter, more effective, and more creative ways.**

Someone may reasonably argue, "Sure, I can be flexible *after* I learn the basics of a dance, but in that first learning, I want to do it the correct way, with all of the precise details."

But this is where Langer most strongly disagrees. Optionality in that first exposure is especially important.

In one study, for example, novice piano players were asked to practice and perform a simple C major scale, in either an absolute way (memorize this through repetition) or a conditional way (experiment with your style and try new things). Students given conditional instruction **enjoyed the piano significantly more**, and **were rated by experts as better piano players, demonstrating greater competence and creativity**.

Or consider tennis. At tennis camp, Langer was taught exactly how to hold her racket and toss the ball when serving. Everyone was taught the same way. When she later watched the U.S. Open, she noticed that none of the top players served the way she was taught, and, more important, each of them varied their own technique to adjust to their different competitors. The rules we are given to practice are based on generally accepted truths about how to perform the task, and not on our individual abilities or circumstances. If we mindlessly practice these skills exactly as we are taught, it keeps the activity from becoming our own, and prevents us from adapting. Differences between ourselves and our competitors become a problem when we take each instruction as absolute truth. Instead, if we learn the basics but do not overlearn them, we can vary them as we change, or as the situation changes.

That's a key finding of Langer's work—the importance of not overlearning a task. You can clearly see the parallel in social dance, but now adapting to partners instead of competitors.

Langer notes that given the way most people are taught to practice, the idea that "practice makes perfect" is questionable. To which we would add: unless you practice being flexible.

In another experiment, students were taught a new sport, Smack-It Ball, similar to squash, but with small rackets worn on both hands like baseball gloves, in absolute or conditional language ("this is the *correct* way to hold your hand" vs. "this is *one way* you might hold your hand"). After the students played for a while, researchers unexpectedly changed the weight of the ball. Those who were taught absolutely, and had practiced only the one "correct" way, not only dropped the ball (literally), **they often became angry** that something had been changed from the one correct way they had learned. We often see this reaction in ballroom dancers who have been taught absolutely: anger and frustration when they don't experience the only partnering they've been taught to expect.

A Stanford student wrote about her trip home during Thanksgiving break. She had just learned to waltz through a conditional learning process and she loved it, so she was excited to show it to her boyfriend during the break. He had coincidentally learned to waltz, but had been taught in the absolute manner. When she showed him the waltz she loved, he immediately set about correcting her. "NO, your left hand has to be here. No, *here*. No, you must begin on the heel then transfer weight to the ball of the foot on the half-count. No, your posture must be in counter-body sway. No, your have to lean farther back, and look sharply to your left. No, *more*." After a half hour of being roundly criticized, she was in tears. But here's the interesting part: he admitted that he didn't even *like* the waltz. Of course he didn't like it. Langer would attribute that to the absolute process of learning it.

Langer's extensive research has shown that conditional learning is important in *any* field, even math and science. **But conditional learning is doubly effective for social dancing, because the topic itself is so conditional, with situations and partners constantly changing.** An absolute attitude can't function, at least not sociably, in such a conditional environment. How can a hard-and-fast approach, applied to a dynamic that isn't hard-and-fast, possibly be true?

Rather than concerning us, this conditionality inspires us, as Langer's research has shown that when we learn something conditionally, we use the information in smarter, more effective, more creative, and more enjoyable ways.

And more than just being an essential lesson for students and teachers, we see this as a beautiful philosophy for life. We wholeheartedly agree with Gilda Radner, who wrote, as she was facing cancer,

> I've learned, the hard way, that some poems don't rhyme, and some stories don't have a clear beginning, middle and end. Life is about not knowing, having to change, taking the moment and making the best of it, without knowing what's going to happen next. Delicious ambiguity.

On the dance floor and in life, we savor this ambiguity.

## Recommended Reading on Conditional Learning

- *The Power of Mindful Learning* (1997), *Mindfulness* (1989), and *On Becoming an Artist* (2005) by Ellen Langer

# "Lead" and "Follow"

Knowing many dance steps and figures is fun, but the true art of social dancing lies in great partnering, in the nonverbal lead-follow connection between the dancers. And the best partnering is not only a matter of skill, but also of *attitude*.

In writing about "leading" and "following," we first want to clarify that we're not especially fond of the term *"following."* Yes, we often use the term, but it is a bit problematic for two reasons.

## Reason #1: **The Dark Ages of Ballroom Dance**

The less important reason is that for many people, the term "following" still carries a negative connotation left over from the early 20th century.

The *original* ballroom attitude toward partnering was best, as reflected in these quotes from the 19th century:

> "Recollect that the desire of imparting pleasure, especially to the ladies, is one of the essential qualifications of a gentleman. The truly polite man is always mindful of the comfort of those around him."
> — Prof. D. L. Carpenter, Philadelphia, 1854

> "True, genuine politeness has its foundation deeper than the mere conformation to certain rules, for it is the spontaneous and natural effect of an intelligent mind and kindly heart which overlooks annoyances in consideration for the happiness of others."
> — Edward Ferrero, New York, 1859

Unfortunately, the 1920s through 1950s saw the emergence of a particularly disagreeable phase of ballroom dance, when the term *lead* meant "command" and *follow* meant "obey."

Soon after American women won the right to vote, many dance manuals changed their tone, proposing that the man was still the "boss" on the dance floor, while the "weaker sex" had to "submit entirely" to the man. Advice for women was that, "she must not have a mind of her own," and that "you don't have much to say in the matter at all."

But that was a long time ago, the "dark ages" of ballroom dance. Fortunately, we've become more enlightened since then, as friendliness and respect have returned to the dance floor.

## Reason #2: **It Isn't Accurate**

The main reason that we don't care for the term "following" is that it doesn't accurately describe the role.

Women do not follow. They *interpret* signals they're given, with a keen responsiveness that is not at all passive.

As with a language interpreter at the United Nations, a dancer's ability to interpret signals benefits from intelligence and experience. Leads, if you want to make a good impression on your partner, show her that you respect this intelligence and experience. How? If she does something that you didn't intend, recognize that she still made a **valid alternate interpretation** of the signals you gave her. She didn't make a "mistake."

No, don't just recognize it. *Show* her that you know she didn't make a mistake, by flowing along with her during her valid alternate interpretation. She's dancing—try to keep up with her. And smile!

Unlike language translating, interpreting a dance lead can also include the Follow leaving her own stamp of individuality, adding flourishes and flair which her partner admires. Sometimes, she can even invent her own footwork variations that harmonize with her partner's footwork.

## Leading with Perfect Diction

Leads, we probably don't have to state the obvious, but you must give her a clear lead to interpret. Just as a language interpreter can't translate mumbling, she can't interpret a mumbled lead. And *forceful* leading is no more helpful than the shouting of unintelligible mumbling would be. Israel Heaton of Brigham Young University wrote, "When a girl does not react readily to her partner's lead, he should hold her firmer and give a stronger lead." But we disagree.

**Clear leading is the physical equivalent of perfect diction, not shouting.**

Better yet, great Leads have learned to "speak" in a warm, friendly tone of voice in their partnering. Leads, be clear and precise, but also warm and friendly with your leads. And instantly flexible when she comes up with an alternate interpretation of your signals.

## The Follow in Flow

The Follow role is mentally and physically active, often engaged in a state of "flow" (p. 77).

In sports, we admire the players who zigzag brilliantly across the field, completely aware of their surroundings and responding instantly to each moment, rather than those who slavishly follow a game plan that is no longer working. The nimble, intelligent player is in the flow state of *relaxed responsiveness, paying highly active attention to possibilities.* The Follow role does the same, paying highly active attention to possibilities.

## But Don't You Still Use the Term *Follow*?

Yes, we aren't going to change the dance world's use of the terms Lead and Follow, and some dancers take the opposite role, so saying *men* and *women* doesn't always apply. So we use the terms, but we want to clarify what we mean by *following*.

## And Leading?

That has also changed since the dark ages of ballroom dance. The best dancers now know that a part of great leading is following.

We prefer the term *tracking*: he leads a move, then tracks her movement and stays with her. He is perceptive and responsive to his partner's situation, as he watches where she is going, where her feet are, where her momentum is heading, and which steps flow smoothly from her current step. He knows *and he cares* what is comfortable for her, what is pleasurable and fun. He dances for his partner's ability and comfort.

A good Lead clearly suggests an option, which is different from controlling her. He proposes, rather than prescribes, a way of moving. If his partner does not go along with his proposal, he refrains from exerting more power to press her to accept the proposal.

As with the Follow role, the aware Lead also enjoys the *flow state of relaxed responsiveness.* Both roles benefit by paying highly active attention to possibilities. Both remain flexible, constantly adapting to their partner.

The flow state has often been described as *ecstatic.* Social dancers often describe their flow state the same way.

As we dance, we discover opportunities and possibilities which open doors, as opposed to rules and restrictions, which close them. We generously adjust our own dancing to adapt to our various dance partners, rather than insisting that they conform to us. We enjoy the individuality of our dance partners, and we continually modify our dancing to maximize their comfort and pleasure. Doing so enhances our own enjoyment of social dancing.

Once we discover the benefits of this awareness on the dance floor, we find that it applies to our other activities and relationships as well.

# Tips for Leading

*Follows, you will also benefit by reading this,
to learn how you can be a better partner.*

**Frame**

Establish a strong frame, holding your partner with fairly firm arms, but with soft, comfortable hands. Depending on the dance form, you usually want to brace away from your partner with a fairly firm left arm. Avoid both "jellyfish arms" and "vice grip hands."

Lead from the frame of the dance position, from your center to your partner's center, rather than moving your hands and arms around.

Clearly lead the tricky parts, and coast through the easier parts. Firm up the frame before leading a change, lead the change, then relax the frame a bit. Note that the firmness of the lead is an engaged, directed energy, not a tense grappling or stiffness, and that you'll want to ease your partner into and out of these shifts in firmness, never jolting her.

## Tone and Intention

Whenever a step might be unclear to her, as in the first step of a dance, clearly lead her step, e.g., leaning slightly forward for a backing step (as in box step and reverse waltz), leaning slightly to the side for a side step (as in polka), or leaning to the side while gently guiding her shoulder through for a cross step (as in cross-step waltz). On the other hand, where her steps are clear, let her dance. You don't need to lead every single step, just the tricky ones.

Be clear on your intent, leading a moment *before* a step is taken. Your partner needs that moment in order to respond. But note that a lead too early can be confusing as well. Don't worry, you can fine-tune the perfect timing through practice, by paying close attention to which of your leads seem to be a bit too early or too late.

Give signals that are clearly distinguishable from each other. Over time, you'll develop an understanding of which signals can be interpreted in which ways, and find ways of distinguishing one signal from another. When possible, choose signals that are likely to be universally interpretable, which won't require your partners to have learned them in class.

## Turns

When leading an inside or outside turn, keep the hands and fingers soft and comfortable, functioning as a kind of "universal joint." Begin by clearly suggesting the turn, but then coast through it, rather than cranking her around the whole way. Imagine you're tracing "a halo over an angel's head." By this, we mean: circle out and around (or in and around) her head, rather than bringing your hand straight up or straight out to the side. Keep your hand in front of her forehead, rather than pinning it behind her. When the turn is complete, bring your hand back down so she knows it is over. Similarly, when you're not leading a turn, keep your hand low and steady so that she's not always wondering whether she's supposed to turn under, as she might if your hand were held high, or kept moving up and down.

## Position

One of the ideals of leading is placing yourself in the correct position, rather than moving your partner around all the time. Sometimes you have to redirect her movement, yes, but try to find more opportunities to adjust around your partner's position and direction of travel in order to make her path easier and more natural.

## Dance for Your Partner

Visualize where she is going, where her feet are, where her momentum is heading, and use this information to choose steps which flow smoothly from her current step.

Dance for your partner's ability and comfort. Choose dance forms which she already knows or is willing to pick up. Dance for your partner's length of step, not your own. Don't pull her uncomfortably close (for her). If you aren't sure about a new partner's ability and comfort level, it is nice to start off conservatively, using some easygoing figures to calibrate the partnership before progressing to more advanced moves, where appropriate. Don't just immediately throw your new partner into the most difficult move you know (yes, some Leads do that).

Don't lead with more strength than necessary or you might unintentionally be saying to her, "Don't you get it?!" *Let* her dance, don't *make* her dance. The ideal is to lead as lightly as possible while still successfully communicating your proposed moves. As we've noted before, clear leading is the physical equivalent of perfect diction, not shouting.

## Flexibility

Keep a flexible and open-minded attitude. Dance completely in the present moment, ready for any change, resistance, suggestion from the Follow, or different interpretation of your lead.

Dancing is a conversation, not a lecture. The Lead proposes something, then the Follow responds, *then the Lead responds to the Follow's response.*

If your partner interprets your lead in an unexpected way, immediately respond with something that flows with the new momentum, giving the impression, if you can, that her alternate interpretation wasn't a mistake.

When something doesn't work out, smile encouragingly, to let her know that you're still having fun. If you think it might work if you try it again, feel free to try it again. She'll appreciate another chance to follow it. On the other hand, if you don't think it will work the second or third time, move on to something that will be more satisfying for both of you.

Avoid criticizing your partner's dancing at a social occasion. Feedback in a class may be helpful, but at a dance, never say or imply that your partner is dancing incorrectly or following poorly. And refrain from teaching your partner unless she's asked you to teach her.

## Safety

As a Lead, you are responsible for your partner's safety as well as that of those around you. Always be aware of others near you, and realize that other dancers may suddenly stop or change direction. Don't follow other couples too closely, or assume that their path will continue in a certain direction. And never plow into other dancers in order to complete a step or sequence. Everyone—your partner, the other dancers, and even the teacher, in a class setting—will prefer that you stay safe rather than completing a dangerous step. If you are going to stop or change direction, make sure that there are no couples following closely behind you who may run into you. The best dancers dance not only for the pleasure of their partner, but also for the pleasure of the other couples on the dance floor.

## Leading Is Caring

The essence of your leading should be clarity, comfort, ease, style, musicality, pleasure, and the relationship between partners, not complexity, a large repertoire of moves, or showing off. The term "hotshot" is often derogatory, meaning a self-absorbed and careless dancer.

A good partner is like a good lover: considerate and caring, primarily interested in the pleasure of his partner, rather than his own self-gratification.

Care isn't something which you add later, like icing on the cake. It is a consideration which you begin with and retain as you become more experienced.

This isn't an exhaustive list, and not everything can be described in a book. Many suggestions for better leading are specific to a certain dance, and are best learned in class.

Additional tips on leading, with regard to Musicality, can be found on p. 205.

# Tips for Interpreting (a.k.a. Following)

*Leads, you will also benefit by reading this,*
*to learn how you can be a better partner.*

The pointers for effective leading are straightforward and finite. For example, the Lead should signal with enough time for his partner to respond.

**Following is much more complex, because it is essentially a "receive function" instead of a "send function" in communications.** Programmers know that designing a receive function is much harder than designing a send function, because receiving has to be ready for anything, among a vast array of possibilities.

You'll find this to be an enjoyable challenge.

Below, we provide a general overview of the Follow role, along with some more specific tips.

## The Big Picture

When you are beginning to learn improvised social dancing, you might think that following is like taking a multiple-choice exam. It *seems* that you have to guess what your partner is leading, just in time, then dive into what you guessed that figure will be. This sometimes works, but once in a while, you guess wrong and power yourself through a figure that he didn't intend. The resulting mess-up can range from awkward to painful, so guesswork isn't the best approach.

The better approach is to consider the fact that **following is extreme multitasking.**

You may see a *visual* clue to the figure that he's leading. Maybe it's the direction where he's looking. Maybe his leading arm is starting to raise. Maybe it's some indication in his footwork. But you can't watch both his eyes and feet at the same time. So you **watch with a broad peripheral awareness.** When you relax, your peripheral sphere widens further, and you will be able to catch even more visual signals.

Sometimes you're traveling through a crowd of dancers, and you can see where he is probably leading the two of you, into that open space ahead of you, not crashing into another couple. So you use your intuition and "field sense" to help him navigate both of you toward that open space. This isn't back-leading—it's using your intuition and common sense, and your partner notices and *appreciates* your assistance. The smart ones do anyway. Occasionally one will bark at you, "*Who's* leading here?!" and you'll know you're dancing with one of *those* guys (see "Sketchy Guys" on p. 137).

Then, in addition to visual cues, there is sensing and responding to the *physical leads*, primarily through the frame of dance position, but also through your arms and hands.

There is also your sense of **musicality**, your **personal body styling**, and sometimes even **alternate footwork** that harmonizes with your partner's footwork.

Put this all together and that's extreme multitasking!

That sounds like a lot to master, but the good news is that as you dance, your body-mind connection is constantly rewiring, so to speak, just by doing it. As you dance, you improve your *informed instinct*.

Just place yourself in this lead-follow dynamic as often as you can, letting this rewiring happen by itself. You will notice that you are slowly but surely getting better at this, responding more quickly, and more accurately. **The big payoff is that after a while it feels like you're "just dancing," barely aware of the multitasking that's going on behind the scenes.**

Here's a specific piece of advice that works: just move your body in the direction that your informed instinct seems to indicate, as you keep timing with your feet under your body, moving forward, backward, sideways, and turning. This is different from worrying about where you place each footprint, and it's more successful.

As you're doing this, allow yourself to be a little late now and then, in moving through a figure. You'll catch up by the end of the figure, and if not, he'll track you and wait until you're finished before leading something else. If the direction or movement isn't led clearly enough, just keep doing your basic step until it becomes clear, as opposed to guessing like a multiple-choice exam and plowing into that guess.

This advice is especially helpful during dance *classes*. If your partner's lead is not clear, do nothing other than continuing to step in time, or just continue with the basic step. Why? Because your partner is also learning, and he needs to know if his leads should be clearer, or timed a little earlier. So your doing nothing is exactly the feedback he needs to improve the signals he gives you. After that, you'll notice that he's a bit clearer in leading the next figure.

This advice about living in the moment especially applies to the **first split-second of a figure**. For instance, if his hand is just beginning to raise. What does that indicate? Instead of guessing what the entire figure will probably be, just follow the direction of that hand, moment by moment.

This often feels like responding late then catching up, but don't worry. As your body-mind connections develop through experience, the lag time decreases. In the meantime, just keep a calm expression, as if saying, "I'm choosing to turn *this* fast, thank you." Your partner will wait until you're finished, with a smile.

# Specific Tips

## Frame

Establish a strong frame, holding your partner with fairly firm arms, but with soft, comfortable hands. Depending on the dance form, you usually want to brace away from your partner with a fairly firm right arm. Avoid both "jellyfish arms" and "vice grip hands."

Keep your hands and arms solidly connected to your center, so that signals to your hands and arms will be directly translated into your body.

In addition, keep your upper and lower body solidly connected, allowing him to lead you through your body to your legs. In a grapevine, for example, he leads you to cross in front or in back with your left foot by shifting your left shoulder forward or backward, respectively. Without this upper-to-lower body linkage, many variations won't function.

Mirror the degree of firmness in the frame. When the Lead gently firms up the frame before leading a change, gently firm back in response, and be ready for anything.

## Centered Balance

Before taking your first step, stand with some of your weight lightly on each foot, rather than committing all of your weight to one foot, similar to the ready position in tennis. In tennis, you don't know if the ball will be going toward your left or right, so you stand equally ready for either. Likewise for the initial lead in dancing.

Keep your body centered directly under the lead, maintaining your own sense of balance. Your feet will usually fall naturally under your body and the lead, although it may be a good idea to reach back a bit when stepping backwards. In any case, don't worry too much about your precise footwork. Instead, follow with your center, tracking your partner while keeping time with your feet under your body.

## Turns

In following an inside or outside turn, when he turns you a little bit, turn yourself more. While he suggests the turn, you're the one who dances it. To gauge the speed of the turn and to make sure it stays comfortable, keep your arm directly in front of you, rather than to either side or pinned behind you.

## One Thing at a Time

Follow one motion at a time, instead of rushing ahead to guess the entire figure. While following perfectly on time is ideal, a little late is better than early.

On the other hand, if the dance has a repeating pattern or timing of steps, you're responsible for your own basic footwork. Dance your own footwork instead of making him lead every single step. Embody the role of a dancer, not a puppet.

If the lead suddenly disappears, or if you're not sure what's happening, keep stepping in time with the music, rather than stopping. This way, your correct foot will be free and on the correct timing when the lead becomes clear. If you're traveling when this uncertainty occurs, keep traveling with your partner and the flow of traffic until the clarity reappears, rather than standing in place until you understand your partner's intent (yes, some Follows do that).

Interpret each of your partner's signals to the best of your ability, even if you don't know exactly what move he's trying to lead. If it works out, *you* will have learned something: a new move or a new signal that he uses in leading. If it doesn't work out, *he* will have learned something: that he needs to lead that move more clearly, or differently.

## Support

When something doesn't work out, let your partner know that you're still having fun, with a reassuring smile. If you want to try a tricky move again, feel free to let him know. He'll appreciate your willingness to give him another chance to lead it.

Avoid criticizing your partner's dancing at a social occasion. Feedback in a class may be helpful, but at a dance, never say or imply that your partner is dancing incorrectly or leading poorly. And refrain from teaching your partner unless he's asked you to teach him.

While navigation is primarily the Lead's responsibility, he will appreciate it if you help him out in a pinch. If you are going to crash, give him a signal, perhaps with your left hand on his shoulder.

## Receptivity

Relax. The simultaneous multitasking that is required in the Follow role functions significantly better in a state of relaxation. Take a deep breath, exhale, and smile.

Keep all of your antennae open. Expand your peripheral senses and awareness to pick up any possible cues. Do not assume anything in particular will happen. Be ready for anything.

This is not an exhaustive list, and not everything can be described in a book. Many suggestions for better following are specific to a certain dance, and are best learned in a class.

Additional tips for following, with regard to Musicality, can be found on p. 205.

# Box Step Waltz

## (American Slow Waltz)

This is the classic ballroom and wedding slow waltz.

Box step waltz is often the first kind of waltzing that dancers encounter, and for many people, it is the only ballroom dance they know. If you learn it and dance with them, you might just make their day!

Box step waltz is danced to slow waltz music around 86 bpm to 110 bpm. For specific song recommendations, see our "Discography of Waltz Music" on p. 223.

## Setting It Up

The frame of box step waltz is essentially the same as the original waltz position (p. 4). In box step waltz, it is especially important to stay facing each other squarely, heart to heart, and to maintain a firm frame, keeping a constant distance between you and your partner.

To reduce the chance of stepping on each other's feet, the Lead and Follow usually set up for box step waltz by facing each other squarely, slightly offset from each other, to the left, as if their feet were on four parallel railroad tracks. His left foot is on track 1, her right foot is on track 2, his right on track 3, and her left on track 4.

While most waltzes travel around the room along LOD, box step waltz is generally danced on one spot on the floor, so you can set up anywhere you like, facing any direction, preferably away from other couples.

## Leading Into It

While offsetting the feet will help avoid the greater risk of the Lead stepping on his partner's toes, it can still be embarrassing for both partners if he simply steps forward into her without giving her fair warning to step back.

The Lead can give the Follow fair warning of the oncoming step with a body lead. He firms up the frame and leans forward slightly before the first count, giving her time to prepare, and the impetus to step back.

## Dancing Box Step Waltz

1: The Lead steps straight forward with his left foot, while the Follow steps straight backward with her right foot.

2: The Lead brings his right foot forward and steps side right, while the Follow brings her left foot backward and steps side left.

3: The Lead closes his left foot to his right, taking weight on his left, while the Follow closes her right foot to her left, taking weight on her right.

4-5-6: The Lead does exactly what the Follow did, and vice-versa.

*Note:* Box step waltz is usually danced in a smooth style that undulates slightly up and down (down-up-up, down-up-up). As with all waltzes, it is usually more agile to dance up on the balls of the feet, particularly during the count 2-3 side-close, although some traditions prefer to lead with the heel on the Lead's forward step.

## Rotating Box Step Waltz

The basic box step waltz, danced straight forward and backward, is fun, but it is even more fun when you can rotate it, giving you and your partner a different view of the room.

Box step waltz usually rotates counterclockwise.

In order to rotate it, the Lead turns his body slightly to the left, leading the Follow to step diagonally back with her right foot on count 1 as he steps diagonally forward with his left foot (and vice versa on count 4). They keep rotating smoothly counterclockwise throughout the six counts of the waltz. Everything else is the same as the basic.

Box step waltz generally turns about 90° every three steps, half as much as a reverse/Viennese waltz (p. 81). Box step waltz can, however, rotate anywhere from 0° (in which case it's the basic straight forward box step waltz) to slightly more than 180° (in which case it's a slow reverse/Viennese waltz traveling counterclockwise around a corner).

## Box Step Waltz Variations

In box step waltz, the Lead steps forward into the frame on count 1, when the Follow is backing, making it hard for either partner to walk forward into a swing-like or laterally traveling figure. There is a simple fix for this, however, a way to break out of the closed frame of box step waltz, in order to do variations.

The Lead simply waits until the second bar of music, count 4, to exit out of the frame, toward his left.

The two most common box step waltz variations do this: the Follow's Outside Underarm Turn, and the Twinkle (Cross-Step), both of which are taught by most ballroom dance studios.

### Follow's Outside Underarm Turn

You'll want to know this variation because it is often taught in a dance studio's "free introductory dance lesson," and many people only take that first lesson, so this may be all that they've learned. You probably want to be able to dance the only variation that your future partner may know.

1-2-3) Dance the first half of box step waltz. It makes no difference whether it is the rotating version or not.

4) The Lead raises his left hand, forming a raised arch with his left arm, and gently leads her with his right hand to walk toward her right, under his left arm.

5-6) She walks forward, not spinning quickly around, but instead tracing out a large circular path to her right. He walks forward to the right, traveling to meet her on the other side, as his raised left arm arches over her head.

1-2-3) Continue this long six-count journey to meet and take closed waltz position by count 3. Some dancers do a side-close on counts 2-3, as in the basic box step.

4-5-6) Finish the second half of the box step, with the Follow stepping forward with her left foot and the Lead back with his right.

## The Twinkle
### (Cross-Step)

1-2-3) The Lead braces back a little, away from his partner, during the first half of a box step. *Hint:* As she's already stepping back in the basic box step, he doesn't need to push her back forcefully. Instead, he can simply hang back himself and lightly brace away. As he does this, he shifts to the more flexible frame of cross-step waltz (see p. 10), making space under the held hands for their feet to cross through.

4) The Lead crosses his right foot over in front of his left, and leads the Follow to cross her left foot in front of her right, beneath the held hands, as in cross-step waltz.

5-6) Continue with either the basic or turning version of cross-step waltz (p. 11, 13).

*Note:* With this transition into it, you will be dancing phase-shifted cross-step waltz with the primary cross-step on count 4 instead of count 1, which may feel a little bit different to you or your partner.

To exit from cross-step waltz back to box step waltz:

4) Both take the primary cross-step, with the Lead's right, and Follow's left. He gently passes her further toward his left, beginning a counterclockwise rotation as a couple.

5) Both take a side step toward the held hands, as he firms up and squares up the frame into box step waltz style.

6) Close feet together while continuing to rotate counterclockwise.

1) Begin a box step waltz, rotating or straight forward.

*Note:* You can also do these transitions the opposite way, from cross-step waltz to box step waltz and back again, in which case you will end up dancing phase-shifted box step waltz with the Lead stepping forward on count 4, and back on count 1.

# Make Your Own Box Step Waltz Variations!

If you already know any cross-step waltz variations, it is easy to make your own new box step waltz variations by treating the count 4 exit out of the closed frame as the count 1 of a cross-step waltz variation.

*Cautionary Note:* Some dancers, having learned cross-step waltz and its many variations, feel that cross-step waltz is simply a "better" dance for slow waltz music than box step waltz, as it is more varied, and in their view, less "boring." We disagree. We appreciate both dances for different reasons, and encourage you to find reasons do the same. Resist the urge to say to your future partners, who may only know and probably love box step waltz, "I know a better dance." Instead, be happy to dance box step waltz with them, valuing their truth and appreciating their love of this unique and elegant dance form. Later, if they seem like they might be interested, you can ask them if they'd like to learn another kind of slow waltz.

# Reasons to Love Box Step Waltz

Having made such a strong case for cross-step waltz, it is only fair that we do so for box step waltz, presenting a few of the many reasons why we love it.

- It's compact. Box step waltz generally stays in one spot, making it perfect for those tiny, crowded dance floors at parties.

- It's easy-going. Box step waltz is easy to dance even when you're tired from hours of dancing energetic swing dances and polkas.

- It's good for conversation. Given that it is easy-going, relatively stationary, and face-to-face, box step waltz gives you the perfect opportunity to look your partner in the eye and have a lovely three-minute conversation while you dance.

- Classic music. Whether it is "Moon River," "Edelweiss," or the "Tennessee Waltz," there are many classic slow waltzes to choose from, at the perfect tempo for box step waltz.

- Finally, it is worth repeating once more: for many people, box step waltz is the only dance they know. Chances are good that your grandmother, your uncle, or your cousins may know it, and they'll be thrilled if you ask them to dance it with you.

> "There are shortcuts to happiness,
> and dancing is one of them."
> — Vicki Baum, author

# Il Tempo Giusto

For Leads who are first learning to dance, there is inevitably some insecurity about their knowledge of dance moves: "I don't know enough figures yet. I wonder if I'm boring all of my partners." These beginning Leads equate "good dancing" with "flashy dancing" and think "the more moves in three minutes, the better."

Many eventually overcome this insecurity, usually by learning enough moves to feel confident. But there are also some Leads who never do, and continue their never-ending quest for flashiness, seeking to perform a new move every measure.

In our opinion, and in the opinion of many Follows, who talk with us about this as much as anything else, this goal, while common, is seriously misguided.

As Gandhi put it, **"There is more to life than increasing its speed."**

**Similarly, there is more to dancing than performing lots of figures.**

In fact, the simplest dances are often the best: Richard still remembers a cross-step waltz with Angela from more than a decade ago, one of his favorite dances of all-time, in which they only did one figure, the Turning Basic, the whole time. Nick fell in love with Danielle during a similarly simple cross-step waltz.

Generally speaking, Follows tell us they most enjoy waltzes where a large portion of the dance is the basic waltz step—elegantly simple turning—with **musically-placed, neatly packaged, identifiable figures used as embellishments.**

Rather than seeking ever-increasing speed and complexity, we seek what musicians call *il tempo giusto*, Italian for "the right tempo."

There are two different things that we mean by this:

> First, we mean *literally* step at the right tempo, as there are few things more annoying than being off the beat.

> Second, we mean dance at the right tempo *figuratively*, with complexity appropriate to the situation, considering our partner, the song, and the space on the dance floor.

In both cases, *il tempo giusto* is often slower than we think.

This insight is by no means limited to the dance floor. *Il tempo giusto* of life is often slower than we think too, as beautifully illustrated in Carl Honoré's book, *In Praise of Slowness: Challenging the Cult of Speed.*

In it, he profiles people around the world who are choosing to "slow down," and finding that slow is often better. Rather than simply going with the flow and living life at an ever-increasing pace, these people are coming together to "stop and smell the roses," in various aspects of their lives, banding together to form a constellation of "Slow Movements."

The original slow movement, Slow Food, stands for "fresh, local, seasonal produce; recipes handed down through the generations; sustainable farming; artisanal production; leisurely dining with family and friends."

Slow Parenting encourages "more freedom and fluidity in education, more emphasis on learning as a pleasure, more room for unstructured play, less obsession with making every second count, less pressure to mimic adult mores."

Slow Sex … well, you get the idea.

As Honoré notes, joining a slow movement does not mean that you will always be slow. It simply means that you're searching for *il tempo giusto*, and realizing that *il tempo giusto* may be slower than you once thought.

As he writes, **"the slow philosophy can be summed up in a single word: balance. Be fast when it makes sense to be fast, and be slow when slowness is called for."** (For more on being fast, and staying relaxed while you do so, see "Dynamic Equanimity" on p. 55.)

The same is true in both life and dance: **we're not against speed or flashy moves when they're fun, we simply realize that they're not the ultimate goal.**

More important than *quantity* of moves is *quality*: **quality of partnering**, and **quality of life**.

# Musical Markings for Waltz

The topic of the previous chapter was *il tempo giusto*, one musical marking which is relevant to waltzing. But that's only the beginning, and there are many others.

Take a moment to look through this list of musical markings.

**Can you envision each one as a way of waltzing?**

Think of how much fun you could have in an evening of dancing if you expressed one of these qualities in each dance!

Bring this list with you on your next night out. Variety is the spice of life.

- accarezzévole - fawningly, caressingly
- accompagnato - with flexible accompaniment
- ad libitum (ad lib.) - at liberty
- amabile - amiable, with love
- animato - animated, lively
- a piacere - at pleasure
- appassionato - passionately
- armonioso - harmoniously
- brillante - brilliant, with sparkle
- cantabile - in singing style, lyrical and flowing
- comodo - comfortable
- con abbandono - with abandon, exuberance
- con brio - with vigor and spirit
- con calore - with warmth
- con moto - with motion
- con variazioni - with variations
- deciso - decisively
- dolce - sweetly
- espressivo - expressively

- facile - easily, without fuss
- fresco - freshly
- giocoso - with humor
- gioioso - joyfully
- grazioso - gracefully
- intimo - intimately
- legato - smoothly connected
- leggiero - lightly, delicately
- l'istesso tempo - at the same speed
- maestoso - majestically
- mobile - flexible, changeable
- poetico - poetic
- scherzando - playfully
- soave - smoothly
- sognando - dreamily
- tempo giusto - the right tempo
- teneramente - tenderly
- tranquillo - calmly, peacefully
- volante - flying

# Dynamic Equanimity

## Relax and Be Active

Several chapters in this book mention the fact that we usually function better when we are in a state of relaxation. And the health benefits of living a more relaxed and less stressful life are well documented.

## Three Myths of Relaxation

It is helpful to understand three myths about relaxation. That is, it is helpful to know that these myths aren't necessarily true.

### Myth #1 — Relaxation is something that we do later.

We get to relax at the end of the day after working. Or on vacation. Or when we retire.

This implies, of course, that 95% of our life should be spent rushed and frenzied and stressed. We might not come out and say that, but that's the implication. Many of us postpone relaxation until our inbox is empty. Of course it never is.

But some people, and some cultures, have found that relaxation can be how we respond to everyday life. Now, not later. We can carry a sense of relaxation with us, wherever we go, whatever we do. It's important to note that relaxed people can still be super-achievers. In fact, relaxation actually enables creativity.

A corollary to this first myth is thinking of relaxing as similar to sleeping, a kind of periodic rejuvenation. But the benefits of taking a vacation or an extended break just don't last very long. If the purpose of your vacation is to "recharge your batteries" and help counteract another year of stress, forget it. The accumulated relaxation of a few weeks of vacation will be completely wiped out after the first hour back at a high-stress job.

This is why we want to develop relaxation as an ongoing process, not just an occasional refresher. **Relaxation can be a continual state of regeneration, in which we sustain a relaxed, peaceful, aware state of mind all the time.** We can keep a centered peacefulness with us, bringing relaxation into our daily lives, recharging our batteries as we go.

Make your full workday a moving meditation. The ideal is that when you leave at five o'clock, you are as fresh as when you arrived in the morning, if not fresher.

Easier said than done, you say?

Yes, it is. So maybe we need a manageable practice, a first step to getting there. One of the best ways that we know is social dancing. You can experiment with maintaining a calm state of mind through a full three-minute dance, with friends, in a safe environment. Dance can be a transitional step to being able to bring this into our daily life, as a practice to make it more tangible. We mean a practice in the sense of *enacting*, not just rehearsing. Practice makes perfect.

**Myth #2 — Relaxation is passive, quiet.**

When reading the above suggestion about dancing, one might reply, "No, dancing is far too active. When I relax, I want to lay back and chill out."

That is because somewhere along the line our society has equated calm and *slow*.

This isn't necessarily so. It's possible to move quickly *and* patiently, mindfully, moving fast because we've chosen to.

Think back to the last time you felt completely calm and centered, maybe blissfully serene. When was that?

Chances are that in this recalled instance your *circumstances* were calm and stress-free. Maybe your peacefulness wasn't a state that you consciously entered, but was merely a result of being in calm surroundings. That's too easy. We have to live with the fact that life doesn't give us those peaceful circumstances throughout every day.

One of Richard's greatest discoveries in life was that one can remain calm, centered, and relaxed while being highly active, even in the midst of people continually throwing challenges at you. He calls this **dynamic equanimity**. He discovered it through the practice of kendo (the Japanese art of fencing), then in dancing. One can be completely relaxed in the midst of chaos, as the calm eye of a hurricane, maintaining serenity while being highly active.

In dancing, we get to share this actively calm state with a dance partner.

> "Calmness of mind does not mean you should stop your activity. Real calmness should be found in activity itself."
> — Shunryu Suzuki, Zen monk

**Myth #3 — If we relax, our competition will pass us by.**

Some people fear that if they relax, they might become lazy and apathetic, and will suddenly stop achieving their goals. Or they'll be run over by their more aggressive competition.

Don't worry, because the opposite is actually true. Frantic thinking takes a great amount of energy and drains the creativity and motivation from our lives. And a stressed mind isn't nearly as smart as a calm one. **Any success that you have on a frenzied day is *despite* your agitation, not because of it.**

## Practicing Dynamic Equanimity

Maintaining dynamic serenity takes practice. You can't just nod your head, agree that dynamic equanimity would be a good thing, and then expect that this acknowledgement will reduce your stress. We need a practice to integrate this into our lives, first in a controlled situation—

we recommend actively relaxed dancing—then take it beyond into somewhat more stressful areas, like jobs, relationships, even driving your car in heavy traffic.

In driving, some people maneuver with calm ease, while others zoom around with anxiety, tension, frustration, and often anger, if not road rage. This is the same with steering through traffic on the dance floor. It can be stressful if you choose to make it that way, or you can use your time on the dance floor to relax.

Enter that wonderful flow state of relaxed responsiveness, of alert tranquility. Flowing like water, we pay attention to circumstances and listen to our intuition. "This isn't the best time to do this. I'd better go that way." It's being sensitive to circumstances. This is essential in social dancing. And in life.

## Calm +

As we see it, being calm is not life's goal. If that's all we want, why get up in the morning?

Being calm helps us be more aware of life, to function better, to be happier and healthier.

The fuller experiences in life come from the plusses, built upon the solid ground of calm, not from the calm alone. Our focus is on living life, fully, actively, dynamically, without the stress that can cancel out all of those benefits.

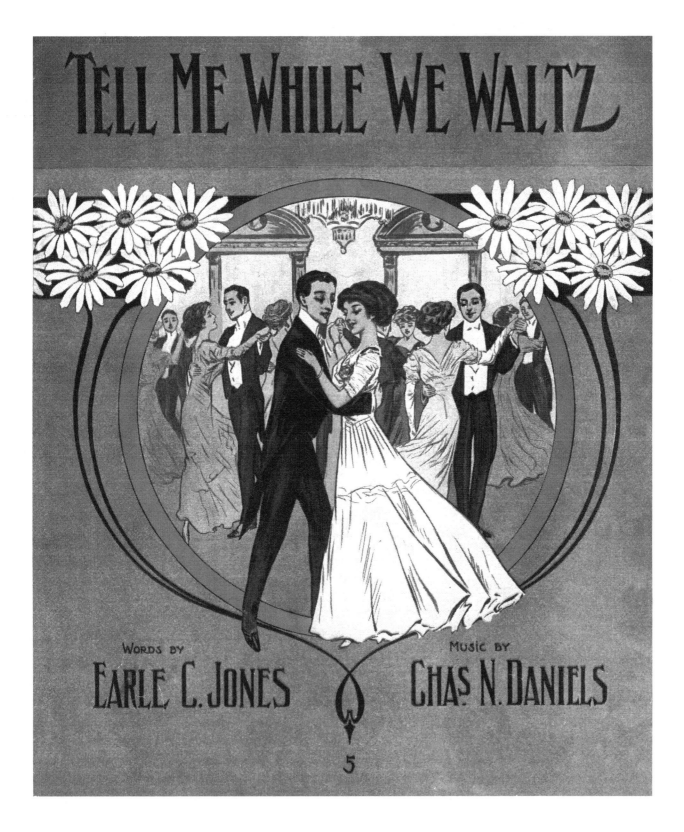

# The Waltz

## (Rotary Waltz, Natural Turn)

This is the original waltz, which has been described in hundreds of dance manuals over the past two centuries.

The original clockwise (natural turn) waltz is often called rotary waltz. This is the waltz of both Johann Strauss I and Johann Strauss Jr.'s eras. The American left-turning box step waltz (or reverse waltz, p. 81) had not yet reached Europe at that time.

Rotary waltz is still very much alive today, healthy and thriving. It has been passed on for generations, and occasionally modified, so there are now different interpretations of the basic step, plus many individual styles, preferred handholds, and postures.

There is *not* only one way to waltz. We support truly social dancing, meaning flexible and friendly. And we also value others' truths. So on this page we describe a few of the most common versions of rotary waltz found in the world today, but without any claim of these being the only "correct" ways to waltz.

Rotary waltz is danced to faster waltz music, from 140 to 190 bpm, with multiple sweet spots, between 144 and 168. For song recommendations, see "Discography of Waltz Music" (p. 223).

## Setting It Up

The frame of rotary waltz is the basic waltz position (p. 4).

As in the cross-step waltz turning basic (p. 13), the Lead faces out of the hall, away from the center, with held hands pointing towards LOD, in preparation. Before taking his first step, he turns one-quarter (90°) clockwise, passing in front of her, in order to build a little rotational momentum before taking his first step.

Does the Lead pull the Follow into rotary waltz (as in cross-step waltz), or push her into it (as in box step waltz)?

Neither. He simply rotates around her clockwise, until he is backing up in front of her, inviting her to step forward into his arms on count 1.

## Dancing Rotary Waltz

1: The Lead turns 90° clockwise, bringing his left foot around in front of his partner, across LOD, and ends up giving weight onto the left foot by stepping back onto it. The Follow turns to her right and steps right foot straight forward, slightly between his feet, along LOD. At the end of count 1, the Lead is backing, like a protective shield, in front of her. *Hint:* Count 1 in rotary waltz is similar to count 2 in cross-step waltz.

2: With his left foot still pivoting in place on the floor, the Lead pulls his right foot back out of her way and gives weight onto it, somewhat behind his left foot, helping him continue to rotate around. The Follow takes a small side-step left along LOD.

> *Note:* His right foot can either share weight with the pivoting left foot, or take full weight. See the "Hint for Leads" below.

3: The Lead replaces full weight on his left foot, continuing to pivot around. The Follow closes her right foot to her left with weight, continuing to rotate. (Or something like this. See "Hint for Follows" below.) By this point, the couple has switched places, turning 180°, while traveling along LOD. Specifically, she has passed by on the inside lane on counts 2 and 3, while he has pivoted around, pretty much in place, tracking her.

4-5-6: The Lead does exactly what the Follow did, and vice-versa.

*Hint for Leads (and Follows on the Second Half):* Don't worry too much about *exactly* where your feet are placed on counts 2 and 3. As long as you:
> a) let her pass by on the inside lane,
> b) continue to rotate, facing her heart-to-heart, and
> c) have your right foot free to step forward on count 4, you'll be fine.

There are many different steps that function here, for example:
> 1) An "assisted pivot" on the left foot where your weight stays on the left foot while your right foot helps you pivot around in place. This is most unique to the original rotary waltz, but certainly not the only option.
> 2) Two steps next to each other wherever they fall as you turn, which is also common.
> 3) A small side-close along LOD, described separately on p. 83.

The same applies for Follows on counts 5 and 6.

*Hint for Follows (and Leads on the Second Half):* There are also several different steps which function for the Follow's count 3.
> 1) A closing step along LOD is usually how it is taught, but
> 2) a tiny, tight cross of right in front of left is quite commonly seen in social waltzing, although dancers often have no idea that they're doing it.
> 3) Not quite closing completely is also fine, as long as you're staying with him.

Most dancers unconsciously vary between these three options as they track different partners who move in different ways. As long as you:
> a) pass by on the inside lane,
> b) continue to rotate, facing him heart-to-heart, and
> c) have your left foot free to back around on count 4, you'll be fine.

The same applies for Leads on count 6.

*Note:* There are still more alternatives. In some waltz traditions, the Lead begins by facing LOD and stepping right foot forward, as the Follow backs up beginning on the left foot, i.e., counts 1-2-3 above are exchanged for counts 4-5-6.

Even with all these hints and notes, we still haven't come close to exhausting the possibilities for functional ways to rotary waltz. For reasons why all of these options are a good thing, see "Conditional Learning" (p. 35).

# Suggestions for Better Waltzing

There are many ways to improve one's waltzing and to be a better waltz partner. Here are just a few suggestions.

- When the Lead backs around with his left foot on count 1, and when the Follow does the same on count 4, step *over across* the invisible line that marks LOD. If you step *onto* that line, you will block your partner's travel.

- Help your partner step over that line by gently sweeping them across it.

- To help your partner sweep you across, allow for some outward tension in the partnership, i.e., don't lean forward into your partner.

- Even better than stepping across LOD, put your *body* across the line by trying to "show your back" to the outside wall. The Lead does it on count 1, the Follow does it on count 4.

- Follows, actively rotate him as much as he's helping you turn. One theory of why some Follows don't do this is because when they were little girls they saw Disney movies and other romantic portrayals of waltzing where it looked like Prince Charming was carrying the Princess like an amusement park ride. These Follows think that's what waltzing is *supposed* to be, with the man doing most of the work. But waltzing is active, not passive.

- You can also help your partner rotate with a body lead, "looking to the right" with your upper body.

- Turn your partner smoothly, as if you are on a rotating platform. If you turn your partner smoothly, your own turning becomes smoother. *Note:* Some people like "emphatic waltzing," with more emphasis on counts 1 and 4, and we appreciate that that can be fun too. But be sure to at least give smooth waltzing a try. We think you'll like it, and maybe even love it.

- For both roles, if your partner isn't getting around enough, scoot yourself around more to help out.

- Think in terms two halves, rather than thinking about all six steps individually. If he gets around on 1, and she gets around on 4, and you're smoothly rotating between those points, that is all that really matters. Focus on hitting those two key points, and everything in between will come together naturally, in some functional version of a rotary waltz.

## Navigating Rotary Waltz

Navigating rotary waltz is similar to navigating cross-step waltz. If you haven't read our notes on navigating cross-step waltz, please refer to them on p. 14, as there are several notes about waltz navigation and safety which are essential for all traveling waltzes.

In order to turn right in rotary waltz (to travel out of the circle, toward the outside wall), simply rotate your partner more. In order to turn left (to travel into the circle, toward the center of the room), simply rotate your partner less.

As in cross-step waltz, this increased rotation can happen anytime during the turn, but in rotary waltz, it is most evident on counts 1 and 4, where you have a clear reference point, i.e., you or your partner swinging across LOD. To travel to the right, swing yourself further across LOD as you are backing around, and help your partner do the same. To travel to the left, swing yourself and your partner less far around.

## Dizziness Revisited

Since rotary waltz spins even faster than cross-step waltz, dizziness can become an issue (again). If you haven't read our notes on dizziness, you can find them on p. 20. The gist is: enjoy the dizziness if you can. Otherwise, don't tilt your head.

## Reasons to Love Rotary Waltz

Having made such a strong case for cross-step waltz, it is only fair that we do so for rotary waltz, presenting a few of the many reasons why we love it.

- It's the original waltz, centuries old and still going. Dancing it, we feel connected with all of the other dancers who have been doing the same steps for centuries in ballrooms and dance halls all over the world.

- There are many versions of the footwork. This simultaneously challenges us to adapt to different styles, and gives a better chance of success in doing so.

- It has a wide tempo range, perfectly comfortable over a range of 50 bpm, from 140 to 190 bpm. And some dance it over an even greater range. Thus rotary waltz is one of the most flexible social dances there is. It also feels slightly different at different tempos, giving it more diverse qualities of experience for the same steps.

- It's particularly conducive to "Dynamic Equanimity" (p. 55). While we could make this case for any of the waltzes, there's something about rotary waltz in particular—that wind-through-your-hair fast but utterly serene and smooth motion that makes experiencing a taste of Dynamic Equanimity more likely.

- Last but not least, it's deliciously dizzying. While this may not immediately seem like a benefit to everyone, as noted before, most children think so, and many adults regain (or have retained) that pleasure.

> "I'd rather waltz than just walk through the forest,
> The trees keep the tempo and they sway in time,
> Quartet of crickets chime in for the chorus,
> If I were to pluck on your heartstrings would you strum on mine?"
> — Owl City, "Plant Life"

# Waltz Variations

Rotary waltz doesn't need variations. It's already perfect as it is. We want to emphasize this, for both beginners and experts. **There is absolutely nothing wrong with—and quite a lot that is wonderful about—dancing the basic step of rotary waltz for three minutes, blissfully spinning with a partner in your arms.**

The basic is all you ever need to know or do. Some Leads do many variations in rotary waltz, while other Leads never do any, and both of these dance experiences can be equally fulfilling.

There are a few rotary waltz variations that are especially satisfying, however, for use as an occasional embellishment by those who do like to do variations.

## The Outside Turn

This move is perfect for Follows who love to spin, as she turns twice as much in these six counts as she would in six counts of regular rotary waltz.

1-2-3: Overturned rotary waltz. Rotate further around than usual, so that the Follow ends up a little more to the outside lane.

4-5-6: With his left hand, he leads her into an outside turn (which is the same clockwise rotation, just more of it) by bringing the hands up in a clockwise halo around her head. She pivots under the arm, staying mostly stationary on the outside lane, ending up ready to step forward between his feet on count 1, as usual. He continues to waltz clockwise, scooting past her on the inside lane to prepare to back around in front of her on count 1. Retake waltz position when facing each other.

Recommence regular rotary waltz on count 1.

*Note for Leads:* She needs some warning that the underarm turn is coming, so start to raise your hands just *before* count 4. If you don't give her enough warning, and her left hand is behind your shoulder, it may get caught there as she turns under. Be sure to notice if her left hand is on your back *before* you lead an outside turn. If it is, use your right hand to leverage her arm off your back before she turns. Protect her arm!

## The Follow's Free Spin

The footwork and rotation is exactly the same as the above.

The only difference is that instead of leading her into an outside turn with his left hand, he leads her into an clockwise free spin by letting go with his left hand and rolling her off of his right arm. As in the Outside Turn, protect her left arm, making sure it doesn't get caught behind your back.

Recommence regular rotary waltz on count 1, catching your partner on the fly.

## The Surprise Swing-Out

This is a variation adapted from the swing out in lindy hop.

1-2-3: Same as above, overturned rotary waltz. He switches from regular palm-to-palm held hands to swing hand hold, tucking his fingers into her palm. This signals to her that something different it coming up, and it makes this more more comfortable because when he releases her to swing-out position, his hand is held horizontally, thumb up, and her fingers hooked on top of his.

4-5-6: He sends her out straight backward at an angle of about 45° to the right of LOD (he mostly just lets go with his right hand and lets her momentum carry her away, smoothly and safely, by maintaining tension in his left arm), then catches up to her by traveling along LOD, retaking closed position and getting ready to back around on count 1. For both roles, track your partner, and keep time with your feet under your body.

## The Shoulder Slide

This is adapted from a variation in very early 1920s lindy hop.

1-2-3: Instead of backing around, he walks straight forward into the held hands, placing her right hand on his right shoulder, leading her around behind his back, and taking her hand again when it passes by his left shoulder. She passes behind his back and around his left side, ready to back around on 4-5-6. She can essentially just keep her usual waltz footwork to do so. He can help reassure her by catching her early as she comes around his left side and swinging her around in front of him so she can back around.

4-5-6: Regular rotary waltz.

## Pivots
### (Canter Pivots)

In the Outside Turn and Follow's Free Spin above, she got to turn twice as fast as usual. Wouldn't it be fun if you could do that together? Fortunately, you can, by dancing Pivots.

In the description of rotary waltz above, to "pivot" means that you have your weight on one foot and you rotate ("pivot") on that foot, which stays in one spot on the floor.

As a figure (in waltz, or other dances like foxtrot and tango), Pivots are a sequence of pivoting steps where you rotate rapidly around each other by alternating between steps 1 and 4 of rotary waltz, pivoting on each step to get around each other.

He backs around, stepping over across LOD, showing his back to the outside wall, while she steps between his feet along LOD. Then she backs around, stepping over across LOD, showing her back to the outside wall, while he steps between her feet along LOD. They travel along LOD, just like rotary waltz. In fact, it *is* rotary waltz, just without counts 2, 3, 5, and 6.

*Note*: At least that's the 180°-turning, LOD-traveling version of Pivots. Pivots can also turn less than 180°, in which case they'll spiral in toward the center of the room. They can even be danced rotating around each other on the spot. In any case, the mechanics (around, between) are the same. The 180°-turning LOD-traveling version of Pivots is the one we'll use here.

Ironically, while the steps underlying Pivots are straight out of rotary waltz, it is actually a little bit tricky to put Pivots back into rotary waltz. But as you'll see, there's an elegant solution.

The problem is that if you simply start pivoting, one step per beat, you'll need to take six consecutive pivots steps before you get back to the correct orientation to keep waltzing in time with the music (or three, if you're willing to shift to the other downbeat). While not impossible, that's *really* challenging, given the faster tempo of rotary waltz.

What most dancers do instead is simply dance fewer Pivots in the same amount of time by varying the rhythm of the steps, using *canter timing*, changing weight on the first and third counts only: 1—3, 4—6.

Thus, Canter Pivots are danced as follows:

1: The Lead backs around, stepping over across LOD, showing his back to the outside wall, while the Follow steps between his feet along LOD. See "Tips for Pivots" below.

3: The Follow backs around, stepping over across LOD, showing her back to the outside wall, while he steps between her feet along LOD. See "Tips for Pivots" below.

4: Repeat count 1.

6: Repeat count 3.

Recommence rotary waltz on the next count 1.

*Note:* On counts 2 and 5, they just continue rotating on the foot they stepped with on 1 and 4, without changing weight.

The above sequence of **four canter pivot steps** will get you back into the correct orientation and timing in order to recommence rotary waltz on count 1.

If instead you do only **two canter pivot steps** before recommencing rotary waltz, you'll then recommence waltzing *on the other downbeat*. This can be useful for fixing your footwork on the fly if you find that you're dancing on count 4 and want to be back on count 1, or if you're dancing on count 1 and want to shift to count 4.

Whether you're dancing on count 1 or count 4, and whether you dance four steps or two, you can also begin pivoting when the Follow is backing around. A nice little four bar sequence which combines both orientations of Canter Pivots (Lead backing, and Follow backing) is: **can-ter, waltz-2-3, can-ter, waltz-2-3**. He's backing for the beginning of the first canter and first waltz, and she's backing for the beginning of the second canter and second waltz. This also gets them back to the correct orientation and timing to recommence waltzing on count 1.

*Tips for Pivots:*

- Face your partner even more squarely than usual, heart-to-heart with parallel shoulders.

- Sink down slightly lower. You'll be more stable with a lower center of gravity.

- Firm up the frame, and hang back in the frame. You'll need that tension in order to …

- Rotate more! Rotate yourself more, and help your partner rotate more, by hanging back in the frame and pulling your right shoulder back, turning your body to the right. For both partners, but Leads especially, use your body to rotate your partner, rather than grappling them with your hands. While Pivots are necessarily physical, comfort is still paramount, and the ideal is have your Pivots feel as comfortable and easygoing as any other figure.

- Leads: Make it extra clear that it's a Pivot. Your first step is in the same place, but everything that comes after is different, so make it clear to her that it's going to be different. Give her as many clues as you can: face her more squarely, sink lower, hang back, rotate more, and maybe give her that mischievous look and smile that says "Pivots!" When you're done pivoting, clearly lead back into waltz by slowing the rotation and returning to a slightly more relaxed frame.

# A Cautionary Note

In the previous waltz chapters, we've noted that it is easy to create new waltz variations, first as a result of the five advantages of cross-step waltz, and second, as a result of box step waltz Twinkle which allows you to import cross-step waltz moves into box step waltz.

While we certainly do not want to discourage you from experimenting in rotary waltz as well, we do want to warn you that it is not quite as easy, and that if it is not done carefully, it can quickly become uncomfortable.

Many Leads try to experiment in rotary waltz by attempting to lead cross-step waltz variations directly, exactly as they learned them in cross-step waltz.

In general, this fails much more often than it succeeds.

The problem is that **cross-step waltz and rotary waltz begin on different feet, and everything you've learned about carefully leading variations at the most comfortable time in cross-step waltz prepares you to lead them at a very uncomfortable time in rotary waltz.** The fact that rotary waltz is faster than cross-step waltz greatly increases the potential for discomfort.

On behalf of the many Follows we've talked to, we ask that you don't throw your partner into something new in rotary waltz unless: (a) you've carefully worked it out beforehand and know that it's comfortable, or (b) you and your partner have an understanding that you are experimenting, in which case, please proceed with caution.

Many other variations which can incorporated into rotary waltz, including:

**Leap Waltz**
**Redowa**
**The Newport**
**Mazurka Waltzes**
(Polka Redowa, Polka Mazurka,
La Koska, La Carlowitzka)
**Hungroise (Heel Clicks)**
and **The Viennese Step**

are described in "Redowa, Mazurka, and More" on p. 147.

Reverse waltz, the counterclockwise turning sister of rotary waltz, is described on p. 81.

Illustration from *A Description Of The Correct Method Of Waltzing* (1816) by Thomas Wilson

# Veleta Waltz Mixer

### Based on The Veleta by Arthur Morris, 1900

Similar to the Cross-Step Waltz Mixer (p. 22), this is a choreographed sequence that you dance with one partner, then change partners to dance it with someone else. This mixer is based on rotary waltz.

**Music:** Any rotary waltz tune with continual eight-bar phrases.

In a large circle, stand side by side facing LOD holding inside hands, Follow on the right.

2 bars: Travel forward along LOD with 6 light running steps (he starts left, she starts right).

2 bars: Facing partners, taking both hands in open position, do a Double Boston sideways along LOD. (He steps side left, closes right to left, and steps side left again. She steps opposite. Double Boston is in canter timing, with the three steps happening on 1, 3, 4.

2 bars: Turning to face against LOD, return to original places with 6 light running steps (he begins right, she left), holding the other hand (the new inside hands).

2 bars: Facing partners, taking both hands in open position, do a Double Boston sideways against LOD, closing up to waltz position by the end of this step (count 4).

2 bars: Do one full turn of clockwise rotary waltz.

2 bars: Do 2 side-draws along LOD (he steps left side, closes right to left, repeats both). These are also in canter timing 1, 3, 4, 6.

2 bars: Do one full turn of clockwise rotary waltz, making sure that the Follow ends up in the outside lane.

2 bars: He raises his left arm to let her turn under clockwise, as she waltzes solo LOD to the right side of the next gent ahead of her. He steps in place to receive the next lady who is progressing forward.

*Note:* This final turn is not the pivoting Outside Turn described in rotary waltz chapter. That happens on the second half of a waltz, 4-5-6. Instead, this is easier, with the Follow simply waltzing forward on count 1 and continuing by waltzing back on count 4.

# Oslo Waltz Mixer

### (a.k.a. Circle Waltz Mixer, a.k.a. Family Waltz Mixer)

This is the most popular waltz mixer in the world, based on rotary waltz.

**Music:** Any rotary waltz tune with continual eight-bar phrases.

**Part I:** All couples take hands in one circle, facing in, Follow to the right of the Lead.

2 bars: All waltz balancé forward and back (forward-close-close, back-close-close), starting on their first feet (his left, her right) swinging the hands forward and back. A sociable tradition is for the Lead to look left and the Follow to look right going forward, opposite going back.

2 bars: Follows pass by the Lead at their right with a Follow's rotary waltz step, falling back into the next opening. She takes two hands with the Lead as she's passing by, then releases right-in-left hands, giving her right hand to the new Lead at her right when in her new place.

4 bars: Repeat the first four bars.

4 bars: Repeat the first four bars.

4 bars: Repeat the first four bars, keeping both hands with the last partner that passed by and turning to face each other, Lead facing along LOD, Follow facing against LOD.

**Part II:** All couples in a circle, two hands with partner, Lead along LOD, Follow against LOD.

1 bar: Side step into center of the circle (1), swing Lead's right and Follow's left in front (2). (*Note:* Some traditions do a simple sideways waltz balancé, 1-2-3, instead of a step-swing.)

1 bar: Side step toward the outside wall (4), swing Lead's left and Follow's right in front (5).

2 bars: Solo canter pivots toward center of the circle, Lead counterclockwise, Follow clockwise. There are three steps, all side steps toward the center, in canter timing (1, 3, 4) (*Note*: Some traditions simply do a walking rollaway instead of canter pivots, turning counterclockwise and clockwise as above, but stepping 1-2-3-4-5.) Re-take two hands.

1 bar: Side step toward the outside wall (1), swing Lead's left and Follow's right in front (2).

1 bar: Side step into center of the circle (4), swing Lead's right and Follow's left in front (5).

2 bars: Solo canter pivots toward the outside wall, Lead clockwise, Follow counterclockwise.

2 bars: Side-close-side (Double Boston) to center of the circle in canter timing (1, 3, 4).

2 bars: Side-close-side toward the outside wall (1, 3, 4), turning 1/4 clockwise and taking waltz position by the end, ready for the Lead to back around in a rotary waltz.

4 bars: Rotary waltz LOD, releasing Follow to the right at the end, taking hands in circle to repeat Part I.

"You'll Win Me If You'll Woo Me While We Waltz."

# My Pleasure

## by Mindy Lange
an essay from Social Dance 2

I looked hopefully around the room. After a few moments, my eyes met his and we walked toward each other. We didn't exchange names or even speak, we both knew what was coming and somehow the anonymity made the encounter more exciting.

He took me by my hand and led me to the corner of the room, causing my stomach to somersault. As he put his arm around me I admired the broadness of his shoulders and savored the sweetness of his smell. Slowly, we began to move, tentatively at first, circling our bodies around each other with the beat of the music. I noticed that his confidence was growing as he pulled me closer to him. His warm hand on my back compelled me to give in to the strength of his arms, but I remembered that it would be more gratifying if I resisted. Reluctantly, I gently pulled away with my body and pushed with my hand. "It's better if we can look at each other," I whispered.

Our bodies moved in sync, rhythmically, our breathing escalated, and the room began to spin faster and faster into a blur of color. I closed my eyes to relish the euphoric sensation of his movements guiding me. I felt like I was the only one he had ever done this with, yet he knew exactly what to do. We moved together as one.

I wished we could continue like that indefinitely, but then, the music faded to silence.

"Thank you," he said.

"It was my pleasure," I sighed.

We parted to search for another waltz partner.

# The Romance of the Waltz

"Never have I moved so lightly. I was no longer a human being.
To hold the most adorable creature in one's arms and fly around
with her like the wind, so that everything around us fades away ..."
—Goethe, *The Sorrows of Young Werther*

"Emma's heart was beating faster when, her partner took her by the tips of his fingers ...
then everything began ... skirts swirled out and rustled against each other ...
Everything was turning around them ... the hem of Emma's dress flared out against
her partner's trousers ... he looked down at her ... she raised her eyes ..."
—Flaubert, *Madame Bovary*

"To be fond of dancing was a certain step towards falling in love ..."
—Jane Austen, *Pride and Prejudice*

"The waltz never quite goes out of fashion;
it is always just around the corner;
every now and then it returns with a bang ...
It is sneaking, insidious, disarming, lovely ...
The waltz, in fact, is magnificently improper ..."
—H. L. Mencken

# Mindsets

In sharing the lessons of this book with the world, there is one particular obstacle that we often run into. We'll be talking with someone about the benefits of dancing, when they'll stop us and say, "I admire what you're doing. But I'm sorry to tell you, *I can't dance!*"

Ironically, this statement is a perfect illustration of one of the potentially life-changing ideas we want to share with you: the power of holding different mindsets.

## Fixed vs. Growth Mindsets

The person who says to us, "I can't dance," is revealing that they hold what Stanford psychologist Carol Dweck calls a *fixed mindset*.

People with fixed mindsets believe that certain kinds of abilities—whether the logical and linguistic abilities required to pass exams, or the physical, musical, and interpersonal abilities required for social dancing—are fixed from birth.

"You're either smart or you're dumb, and you either can dance or you can't."

Not everyone believes this, however. Those who hold a *growth mindset* believe that these abilities are not entirely fixed, but rather that they can change and grow. According to those who hold a growth mindset, these abilities can, and must, be developed.

## Performance vs. Mastery Goals

As a result of these differing beliefs about ability, people with different mindsets tend to adopt different goals.

People who believe their abilities are fixed tend to adopt a goal of *performance*, focusing on *demonstrating* their fixed abilities by showing off and outperforming others.

Those who believe their abilities can grow, on the other hand, tend to adopt a goal of *mastery*, focusing on *developing* their growing abilities by taking on new challenges and learning.

## Self-Fulfilling Prophecies

As explained in *Mindset*, Dweck's book summarizing her decades of research on the subject, a fixed mindset leads to a desire to look smart. Therefore, someone with a fixed mindset has the tendency to avoid challenges, to give up easily, to see effort as fruitless, to ignore useful negative feedback, and to feel threatened by the success of others. As a result, **those with a fixed mindset often plateau early and achieve less than their full potential.**

A growth mindset, on the other hand, leads to a desire to learn. Therefore, someone with a growth mindset has the tendency to embrace challenges, to persist in the face of setbacks, to see effort as the path to mastery, to learn from criticism, and to find lessons and inspiration in the success of others. As a result, those with a growth mindset tend to reach ever-higher levels of achievement.

**In this way, the mindsets become self-fulling prophecies: those with fixed mindsets see their abilities plateau, and those with growth mindsets see their abilities grow.**

> "There are two kinds of people. One kind you can tell just by looking at them as what point they congealed into their final selves. It might be a very *nice* self, but you know you can expect no more surprises from it. Whereas the other kind keeps moving, changing. ... They are *fluid*. They keep moving forward and making new trysts with life, and the motion of it keeps them young. In my opinion, they are the only people who are still alive. You must be constantly on your guard against congealing."
> — Ursula DeVane in *The Finishing School*

## Developing a Growth Mindset

Fortunately, as Dweck and her colleagues have demonstrated in studies of a wide range of abilities—in school, business, sports, and art—a growth mindset can be learned and taught.

People who are introduced to the growth mindset idea tend to shift from fixed to growth mindsets, and as a result, dramatically improve their abilities.

Likewise, people who are introduced to *environments that reinforce mastery* are more likely to adopt a growth mindset with mastery goals, and challenge themselves to greater heights. Environments that reinforce mastery **encourage self-direction and intellectual risk-taking** and **discourage evaluation and competition**. The social dance hall is a great example.

Importantly, these shifts in mindset tend to persist, even when people leave these mastery environments and return to their regular working environments. This shows once again that what we learn on the dance floor can sneak home with us to improve the rest of our lives.

## I Can't Dance ... *Yet*

When potential social dancers tell us they can't dance, what they really mean to say is that they can't dance *yet*. The only problem is that they forget the *yet*.

And while you, reader of *Waltzing*, may not have this particular problem, we hope that this greater understanding of mindsets will help convince your friends who "can't dance" to join you. We also hope that this will help you apply your growth mindset universally, pursuing all of the challenges that interest you, whether in painting, science, or public speaking.

## Recommended Reading on Mindsets

- *Mindset: The New Psychology of Success* (2008) by Carol Dweck

# Conscious Competence

## by Dean Paton
### Seattle, WA

Here perhaps is a more useful way to approach the pleasant discipline we call "learning to dance." Instead of picturing the classes you take as a linear sequence—say Waltz 1, 2, 3, & 4 —imagine yourself in an evolutionary process called the learning cycle, four distinct stages through which all human beings progress whenever they learn anything new.

The first is **Unconscious Incompetence**. In this stage you have little experience or skill. In fact, you're likely quite bad, but because you don't know how truly bad you are, you don't feel bad, and your self-esteem isn't crippled. Yet.

True damage to self-esteem, and to the false confidence that coexisted with the bliss of ignorance, often occurs in the second stage of learning: **Conscious Incompetence**. As your awareness evolves into this stage, you begin to realize how little you know. Perhaps you notice how impossible it seems for you and your partners to do much of anything smoothly. You certainly convince yourself that practically everyone at every dance or class is so talented that they'd never think of dancing with you. You may well flee the dance early, and might even avoid such terrifying places of public exhibition for weeks.

In truth, Conscious Incompetence is a vital step in the learning cycle. For once your exaggerated sense of self-loathing finds an equilibrium, you have the chance for some valuable self-assessment. You can begin to determine your strengths and weaknesses, and from this sense of where you really are you can begin to focus on strategies for improvement. Much learning occurs here.

As your skills get better and your body works with your mind to integrate new steps and moves into your dancing, you evolve into stage three: **Conscious Competence**. This is an enjoyable and exciting stage for most people, because they not only start seeing themselves as good dancers, they realize how much they have learned. Others tell them how enjoyable they are to dance with, now that they've reached a certain competence, so a reborn confidence repairs their self-esteem.

Nevertheless, dancers in the Conscious Competence stage spend much of each dance thinking about what move to execute next, and how to balance the effort required to choreograph the next eight bars with the excitement of connecting with their partner. Brains occasionally go on overload, and feet may still get trampled, but in general, Conscious Competence is an enjoyable stage. Most people spend considerably more time here than in the first two stages. It is also a plateau where many dancers choose to remain.

True mastery isn't attained until the fourth stage of learning: **Unconscious Competence**. This is the place where there is little or no difference between what the body has practiced to perfection and the mind has learned. You no longer think about your frame, or what move comes next. In fact, you don't think much (about the moves, at least). Instead, you're free to enjoy the moment and genuinely connect with your partner. Those who manage to reach this level of mastery are sought-after, indeed revered on the dance floor.

The trick is in the getting there. Anyone who dutifully proceeds through Waltz 1, 2, 3, and 4 is pretty much guaranteed to reach stage three—Conscious Competence. After a year of so, you'll dance comfortably with most partners and have a good time. To achieve mastery, however, you may well have to abandon the linear approach. Give up the convenient notion that simply by progressing through a prescribed sequence of classes you'll end up a great dancer. When we think linearly, we tend to think in terms of quantity instead of quality, or we make alienating comparisons: I want to learn more slick moves; I'll only dance with partners at my level; she's better than I am (or I'm better than him). The trap here is that you risk becoming a dance snob, a stylized technician with the moves of Fred or Ginger, but the heart and soul of Schwarzenegger's *Terminator*.

When you dance with someone who has achieved true mastery, you know it within a few seconds. These partners allow you to look and feel grand, not better than you are, but as good as you can be. You connect. You'll want to dance with them again and again. Such mastery is an art form, a gift they give to each of their partners.

You can choose mastery, just as you can choose to stay at stage three. Both options are valid. If you opt for mastery, however, part of the prescription is to start seeing each class not as a step in a finite sequence, but as a timeless opportunity for learning. So what if you've taken Waltz 2 three times? Take Waltz 1 again. And again and again. What you learn will not necessarily be an expected part of the curriculum, but as you guide a less experienced dancer toward new confidence and grace, as you forget about your own footwork and simply enjoy moving with your partner to a new level of competence, your own dancing will transport you to a place of uncommon joy, and you will learn far more than you ever learned the first time through. About dancing, and about yourself.

# Flow

In the 1960s, Hungarian psychologist Mihaly Csikszentmihalyi (pronounced "chicks send me high") was studying the creative process in painters when he was struck by the observation that "when work on a painting was going well, the artist persisted single-mindedly, disregarding hunger, fatigue, and discomfort—yet rapidly lost interest in the artistic creation once it had been completed." With this observation, he set out on a lifelong quest to understand these activities: activities which were *intrinsically rewarding*, and didn't require fame or money to motivate them.

By interviewing chess players, rock climbers, dancers, and others who engaged in their chosen activities primarily because they enjoyed them, Csikszentmihalyi discovered that their real motivation was an experience, a powerful optimal experience which he called "flow," based on the metaphors of flowing water he often heard in his interviews.

## Characteristics of Flow

Flow, which is the same across lines of culture, class, gender, and age, as well as across kinds of activity, is an intensely satisfying state which is generally characterized as follows:

- Intense, focused awareness of action in the present moment
- Merging of action and awareness
- Loss of reflective self-consciousness
- Fading away of worries and distractions
- Distorted sense of time
- Increased sense of control, agency, response-ability
- Harmony of experience, of thought, feeling, desire, and action
- Experience of the activity as intrinsically rewarding

While we're not self-consciously aware while we're in it, after experiencing flow, we describe it as optimal, an experience we'd like to have again, perhaps as frequently as we can.

Csikszentmihalyi estimates that 85% of us already know flow, if perhaps by a different name: athletes are "in the zone," musicians are "in the groove," and flowing programmers are "wired in." And most of us who know flow probably wish it happened more often.

## Conditions for Flow

Fortunately, Csikszentmihalyi has discovered that certain conditions are especially conducive to generating flow, and although we cannot ever guarantee it, we can create situations that make it much more likely.

Below are the essential conditions of flow. Flow is most likely when all of these are present.

1. *Clear Goals:* Our goals in the activity are clear, along with any rules of the "game" we are playing.

2. *Immediate Feedback:* Our successes and failures are readily apparent, enabling and challenging us to swiftly adapt.

3. *Stretching of Abilities:* Our skills are fully engaged in challenges that comfortably stretch our abilities. Specifically, we are using above-average skills to face above-average challenges. This condition is illustrated in the figure below.

*Note:* An important implication of this third condition is that the best moments in life are often some of our most active moments. For more on finding fulfillment in these moments, see "Dynamic Equanimity" on p. 55.

### Quality of Experience as a Function of Skills and Challenges

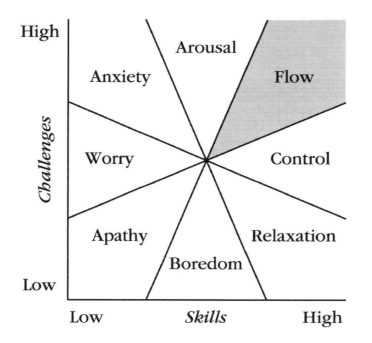

## Waltzing as a Flow Activity

In his book *Flow,* Csikszentmihalyi writes that "a broad range of activities rely on rhythmic or harmonious movements to generate flow. Among these dance is probably the oldest and most significant, both for its universal appeal and because of its potential complexity. From the most isolated New Guinea tribe to the polished troupes of the Bolshoi Ballet, the response of the body to music is widely practiced as a way of improving the quality of experience."

**One of the reasons we love to waltz is that waltzing is a quintessential flow activity.**

First, waltzing has *clear goals*: to turn around the room with a partner and have as much fun as we can while we do so. The "rules" of the social waltzing are also simple and clear: do whatever is safe, comfortable, and fun.

Second, waltzing provides *immediate feedback.* As the primary metric of social waltzing is satisfaction, and we can readily feel this in ourselves, and sense it in our partner's face and body, we have the necessary feedback to adapt on the fly.

Third, waltzing continually *stretches our abilities,* providing unlimited opportunities to use our growing skills to master ever-increasing challenges. For beginners, basic cross-step waltz provides this, while experts may find it in more advanced waltz figures. Whether it is in learning new figures, perfecting old ones, inventing something new, or adapting more skillfully to every partner, there are opportunities for growth at every skill level.

Comparing the conditions of waltzing and flow, it becomes obvious why many people frequently experience flow on the social dance floor. It's also, we'd venture, one of the reasons we all come back, song after song, week after week. We are seeking optimal experience through dance.

And through the lens of flow, it also becomes obvious why, on an otherwise debaucherous Friday night, hundreds of Stanford students will forgo the buzz of beer and grinding to play with perfecting their waltzing. The flow that can result is a much better high.

## Flow to Grow

As Csikszentmihalyi notes, flow is more than just a natural high. *It's also a powerful force for personal development.* In seeking the high that comes with flow, we are continually incentivized to learn new skills, and face and master ever greater challenges.

Suppose, he writes, that a person is in the area marked 'Arousal' on the graph. This is not a bad condition to be in. In arousal a person feels mentally focused, active and involved, but not especially strong, cheerful, or in control. How can we return to the more enjoyable flow state? The answer is clear: by learning new skills. Or look at the area labeled 'Control.' This is also a positive state of experience, where one feels happy, strong, satisfied. But one tends to lack concentration, involvement, and a feeling that what one does is important. So how do we get back to flow? By increasing challenges. **Thus, flow encourages us to grow.**

*Note:* Although it was implied above, it is worth noting again, this time explicitly, that "increasing challenges" in this context doesn't necessarily mean mastering more complex variations in the more difficult dance forms. That is certainly one good way of increasing challenges, but there are also increasing challenges to be found in the practice of every skill we discuss in this book, including dancing for your partner, dancing musically, dancing improvisationally, and many others.

## Flowing Through Life

Waltzing is our (and perhaps your) favorite way to flow, and we hope to see you flowing across the dance floor soon. We also hope you'll bring the conditions of flow—*clear goals, immediate feedback,* and *stretching of abilities*—to the other aspects of your life as well, to find even more fulfillment in all of your endeavors.

> "May what I do flow from me like a river,
> no forcing and no holding back,
> the way it is with children."
> — Rainer Maria Rilke

## Recommended Reading on Flow

- *Finding Flow: The Psychology of Engagement in Everyday Life* (1997) by Mihaly Csikszentmihalyi

- *Flow: The Psychology of Optimal Experience* (1990) by Mihaly Csikszentmihalyi

- *Creativity: Flow and the Psychology of Discovery and Invention* (1996) by Mihaly Csikszentmihalyi

- *The Evolving Self: A Psychology for the Third Millennium* (1994) by Mihaly Csikszentmihalyi

# Reverse Waltz

## (Left-Turn Box Step Waltz)
## (often referred to as "Viennese Waltz")

The original 19th century waltz, called *valse à trois temps* by many dance masters at the time, only rotated clockwise. In the 1840s, the newer *valse à deux temps* allowed counterclockwise rotation, but many dancers found it difficult to do, so it never caught on.

Thirty years later, during the 1870s, the "New Waltz" was created, reportedly in Boston, Massachusetts. This was essentially a box step waltz that rotated 360° (clockwise or counterclockwise), every six steps.

This new waltz was much easier to reverse, so it largely replaced both the *valse à trois temps* and *valse à deux temps*, eventually spreading to Europe.

## Setting It Up

The frame of the reverse waltz is almost identical to the basic waltz position (p. 4), although many teachers emphasize that the shoulders should be even more squared or parallel than in rotary waltz.

In reverse waltz, *the Lead usually begins by facing forward LOD*, instead of facing out of the hall as in the original rotary waltz and cross-step waltz.

As in the rotating box step waltz, the Lead gives the Follow fair warning of the oncoming step with a body lead. He firms up the frame, begins to turn her counterclockwise, and leans forward slightly before the first count, giving her time to prepare, and the impetus to step back with her right foot.

## Dancing Reverse Waltz

1: The Follow steps back with her right foot, diagonally toward the center of the room, as the Lead steps with his left foot forward slightly between her feet, along LOD.

2: The Follow takes a small side step left, along LOD, as the Lead takes a large side step right, along LOD, passing by on the outside lane.

3: Both close their trailing foot (her right, his left) up to that side step, taking weight. In one popular version, the Lead tightly crosses his left over in front of his right, taking weight on this crossing step.

4-5-6: The Lead does exactly what the Follow did, and vice-versa.

Reverse waltz works best if the Follow attempts to place (or "aim") her back toward the center of the room on count 1. She can also help square up the frame by slightly twisting to her left as she places her back into the center, which will help launch him by on the outside lane. Because her left shoulder is directly connected to his right through their arms, she can help him get around by pulling that shoulder back.

The Lead can assist her, of course, by helping aim her back in toward the center, getting around on the outside lane, and aiming his back into the center on count 4. But if he tries to help her by twisting to the left, as she does, he'll twist out of the frame. Thus, the Follow's role is particularly crucial in reverse waltz. This is one of the many reasons we love it.

As reverse waltz turns counterclockwise, and dancers also travel around the room counterclockwise, getting around the corners actually requires a turn of more than 360°, which can be a nice challenge. Beginning reverse waltzers don't like the corners, intermediate reverse waltzers are okay with the corners, and experienced reverse waltzers *love* the corners.

## Navigating Reverse Waltz

Navigating reverse waltz is similar to navigating cross-step waltz and rotary waltz, only reversed. If you haven't read our notes on navigating these other waltzes, please refer to them on p. 14, as there are several notes about waltz navigation and safety which are essential for all traveling waltzes.

In order to turn right in reverse waltz (to travel out of the circle, toward the outside wall), simply *rotate your partner less*. This is as opposed to the clockwise waltzes we've previously discussed, where to travel to the right, you turn your partner more. In order to turn left (to travel into the circle, toward the center of the room), simply *rotate your partner more*.

As in rotary waltz, this increased rotation can happen anytime during the turn, but is most evident on counts 1 and 4, where you have a clear reference point, i.e., you or your partner swinging across LOD toward the center of the room. To travel to the left, swing yourself further across into the center of the room as you're backing around, and help your partner do the same. To travel to the right, swing yourself and your partner less far around.

If you consistently find yourself going one way or the other, simply make a correction in the other direction. Beginners, for example, tend to spiral outward toward the outside walls. To avoid running into the outside walls, rotate your partner more.

## Dizziness Revisited

Beginners in reverse waltz often find it to be the most dizzying of the waltzes, even after they've lost their clockwise-turning dizziness in rotary waltz. If you haven't read our notes on dizziness, you can find them on p. 20. The gist is: enjoy the dizziness if you can. Otherwise, don't tilt your head.

## Right-Turn Box Step Waltz

When reverse waltz is directly reversed, it becomes right-turn box step waltz.

The difference between this and the original rotary waltz (p. 59) is subtle, since both rotate clockwise. Here's the right-turn box step waltz.

1: Facing against LOD, the Lead steps back with his left foot, toward the outside wall, as the Follow steps with her right foot forward, slightly between his feet, along LOD.

2: The Lead takes a small side step right, along LOD, as the Follow takes a large side step left, along LOD, passing by in the inside lane.

3: Both close their trailing foot (his left, her right) up to that side step, taking weight.

4-5-6: The Lead does exactly what the Follow did, and vice-versa.

*Note:* Right-turn box step waltz is often begun with the Lead facing LOD, as with the left-turn box step waltz, except he now steps forward with his right foot on count 1, i.e., you commence with count 4 as described above. We've described it this way to maintain the tradition of the Lead starting on his left foot and the Follow on her right foot, as many dancers prefer.

The main difference between this and rotary waltz is in the Lead's second step, count 2.

For the second step of rotary waltz, the Lead pulls his right foot back out of her way and gives weight onto it, somewhat behind his left, as the left foot pivots in place. As counts 1-2-3 of rotary waltz are essentially a pivot on the left foot for the Lead, he doesn't travel much during those three counts.

For the second step of the right-turn box step waltz, the Lead steps side right, traveling along LOD. On count 3, he closes his left up to his right foot, taking weight. Thus he travels along LOD during all three counts.

The same applies for Follows during counts 4-5-6.

The "other half" of the waltz step (the Follow's 1-2-3 and Lead's 4-5-6) is essentially the same as rotary waltz, simply taking a slightly larger side step on count 2 or 5.

Rotary waltz and right-turn box step waltz each have their own unique benefits:

- Right-turn box step waltz lets you to travel a greater distance along LOD in the same number of counts, allowing more effortless *translational speed* as you travel around the room.

- Rotary waltz, on the other hand, travels less translationally, but is easier to rotate faster than the right-turn box step waltz, allowing more effortless *rotational speed* at faster tempos. In fact, at high speeds, rotary waltz can be thought of, and can feel like, four easy movements, pivot-step-step-step (slooow-quick-quick-quick) whereas right-turn box step waltz always feels like six discrete steps, and can get a bit frenetic at higher tempos.

*Another Note:* Although rotary waltz and right-turn box step waltz are subtly different, they are also compatible with each other. One partner can be doing one step as their partner is doing the other, without any problem. All that really matters is that they stay together and track each other. They are also basically equivalent in terms of doing variations, as in the transitions between right and left turning below.

# Transitions Between Right and Left Turning Waltz

Once you know both clockwise and counterclockwise turning waltzes, it is fun to transition between them on the fly.

## From Clockwise Waltz to Counterclockwise Waltz:

1-2-3: Regular rotary waltz. He backs around, setting up to face LOD on count 4, as usual, as she passes by on the inside lane, preparing to back around.

4-5-6: He "backs the lady" for three steps. He takes three steps straight forward LOD starting on his right foot, leading her to take three steps straight back starting on her left foot.

1-2-3: Begin reverse waltz. He leans in and turns to the left, leading her to step back diagonally toward the center of the room with her right foot on count 1, as he steps forward, slightly between her feet.

It helps if he doesn't let her cross over to the right side of LOD on counts 4-5-6, otherwise, he'll have a difficult time swinging her back to the left into reverse waltz. Instead, he lets her smoothly decelerate up to the centerline of LOD, and then smoothly accelerates her back away from the centerline.

## From Counterclockwise Waltz to Clockwise Waltz:

1-2-3-4-5-6: Regular reverse waltz. They simply reverse waltz, and set up to face LOD on count 1, as always.

1-2-3: He "backs the lady" for three steps. He takes three steps straight forward LOD starting on his left foot, leading her to take three steps straight back starting on her right foot.

4-5-6: Begin the second half of a rotary waltz. He leans in and turns to the right, leading her to step back toward the outside wall with her left foot on count 4, stepping forward between her feet. Counts 5 and 6 are the regular 5 and 6 of rotary waltz.

1-2-3-4-5-6: Regular rotary waltz, starting with the Lead backing around on count 1.

Again, it helps if he doesn't let her cross the centerline of LOD during the transition.

In addition, note that this transition ends up with you starting on the second half of rotary waltz after you back the lady. Many Leads learning this transition jump the gun and try to go straight to backing around after he backs the lady, which doesn't work. Unlike the Rotary to Reverse transition, which feels like it happens immediately, the Reverse to Rotary transition feels like a longer journey.

It's also worth noting that both of these transitions also function, in a similar fashion, if the Lead backs himself for three counts when he's facing against LOD. In fact, this is historically how waltz transitions were done, as you can't "back the lady" when she's wearing a dress with a train, which ball-gowns often had in the 1890s. Today, however, most people use the "back the lady" versions, as it is safer for the Lead to see forward as he's transitioning.

# Reverse Waltz Variations

As with rotary waltz, reverse waltz doesn't need variations. It's already perfect as it is. See our note about this perfection in rotary waltz on p. 63, and our cautionary note about inventing waltz variations on p. 66, which is even more true in reverse waltz.

In fact, reverse waltz is often the only variation used during waltzing, as it's a bit of a challenge in itself. And it provides a beautiful balance to the clockwise waltz. This simplicity is one of the many reasons we love it.

There is, however, one reverse waltz variation that is so satisfying when it works that it's worth reviewing here for those who may have learned it in class. You probably do need to learn it in class, but if you want to try to work it out yourself from the description, we won't stop you. Just be sure do it carefully.

## The Inside Turn in Reverse Waltz

This is the equivalent of the Outside Turn in rotary waltz (p. 63). She turns twice as many times in these six counts as she would in six counts of regular reverse waltz.

1-2-3: Overturned reverse waltz. Both do a reverse waltz, ending up ready for him to back around as usual, but further around, backing a little more to the inside lane than usual.

4-5-6: With his left hand, he leads her into an inside turn. This is the same counterclockwise rotation, just more of it, led by bringing the hands in between their faces. She pivots under the arm traveling straight down LOD with open reverse pivot steps. He continues to rotate to face LOD for the next count 1 as usual, but with his feet mostly in place (he steps, but doesn't travel), out of her way on the inside lane. As soon as he sees her back come around, he places his right hand on it to stabilize her in waltz position again, as she raises her left hand to place it back on his shoulder (being careful not to smack him in the face). Thus he rotates her back into waltz position. They end up with him facing LOD, her against LOD, as usual.

Recommence regular reverse waltz on count 1.

*Note for Leads:* The Follow is traveling LOD with open reverse pivot steps on counts 4-5-6. That's a very active movement, which takes experience and practice for her to achieve. So don't spring this move on a novice waltzer. It is much easier to follow an outside turn in rotary waltz than an inside turn in reverse waltz. Save this latter variation for more experienced partners.

## Reasons to Love Reverse Waltz

Having made such a strong case for cross-step waltz, it is only fair that we do so for reverse waltz, presenting a few of the many reasons why we love it.

- It turns counterclockwise, which makes it feel unlike any of the other waltzes. You see your partner and the room spinning in a different way. And you get to feel dizzy again, even after you've lost your clockwise-turning dizziness.

- It's one of the simplest, smoothest variations of rotary waltz. While waltz variations that break out of the frame can be fun, there's something especially satisfying about being able to vary your waltzing spontaneously by simply reversing the direction of rotation.

- Although the concept and steps are simple, dancing reverse waltz is still quite a challenge. After mastering the basics of cross-step waltz, box step waltz, and rotary waltz, mastering even the basic step of reverse waltz is an above-average dancing challenge. Thus, it's a wonderful opportunity for finding "Flow" (p. 77).

- It gives even greater responsibility to the Follow role. While cross-step waltz may be the most equal dance in terms of partnering responsibility, the Follow has a bit more responsibility in reverse waltz, which gives her a chance to show how active she is.

# Viennese Waltz

We are often asked, "What is Viennese waltz?"

The answer? That depends. What decade, and where? The term *Viennese waltz* has been used in different ways over the years.

1) The Viennese waltz of the Strauss Era in Vienna was very close to rotary waltz. The turning box step, or "New Waltz," had not yet reached Europe at that time.

2) Most ballroom dance studios today define Viennese waltz as a fast reverse waltz, perhaps in International (i.e., British) style with pelvic contact and counter-body sway.

3) Some ballroom dance studios define Viennese waltz as a choreographed pattern of intricate steps, some with syncopated timings that one's partner must know.

4) If by Viennese waltz one means waltzing as done at balls in Vienna today, it is mostly a mixture of the original clockwise and counterclockwise waltzing (essentially the Rotary and Reverse Waltz as described in this book), with lots of individual variety in styling, handholds, and distance from one's partner.

*Note:* To further confuse things, people often use the term Viennese waltz to refer to different kinds of waltz music as well. Some use it to refer to a waltz by a traditional Viennese composer, such as Johann Strauss (I or II). Others broaden it to include contemporary songs written in the style of waltzes from the Strauss Era. And some use the term to refer to any waltz of an appropriately fast tempo for competition Viennese waltz, around 180 bpm.

> "If there exists a form of music that is a direct expression of sensuality, it is the Viennese Waltz."
> — Max Graf, music scholar

In the social dance world, reverse/Viennese waltz is danced to rotary waltz music, often at the slower end of the tempo range, which makes it easier to complete the tricky counterclockwise rotation. For specific music recommendations, see "Discography of Waltz Music" (p. 223).

# Trust

While most dance forms are relatively safe, others involve non-trivial risks, like the polka, and the accelerating waltz (a waltz which accelerates to over 300 bpm).

Sometimes we face these risks with dancers we know and whom we've danced with for years. But other times we face them with complete strangers, people we've never met before, people we may never see again. At a social dance, we do this repeatedly, for hours.

We let these strangers into our space, embracing us closely and leading us into an asteroid field of spinning bodies, **trusting** that they will have our backs. And in social dancing, we mean this literally, as there's half of the room that only they see. We trust that our partner won't step on our feet, or lead us to crash at breakneck speed. We trust that they won't scoff when we stumble, and that they'll be there to catch us if we fall. And our partner trusts us to do the same.

Dance is so effective at building trust that Dacher Keltner writes: **"Dance is the most reliable and quickest route to a mysterious feeling that has gone by many names over the generations: sympathy, agape, ecstasy, _jen_; here I'll call it trust. To dance is to trust."**

Imagine a world as full of trust as the dance floor, where trust and trustworthiness are universal. A world in which we can walk down any street in any country in the world at midnight, and rather than fear for our lives and quickly cross the street as the shadowy figure approaches on the sidewalk, we can relish the opportunity to meet someone new, and interact with a fellow human being. A world in which, if we feel so inspired, we can take each other hand in hand and dance for a moment under the moonlight, knowing that we both have each other in our hearts.

We're sure this sounds wildly, hopelessly utopian, but in a society where one-quarter of our fellow citizens report that they have zero friends that they trust enough to confide in, and where two-thirds report that they have two or fewer such friends, where the percentage of Americans who think people can generally be trusted has fallen twelve percent in the past thirty years, and trust in social institutions has seen a similar decline, rebuilding our trust is more than a dream. Rebuilding our trust is a realistic need.

The good news is that trust can be easily built. Partners who succeed in a game of trust—like waltzing—quickly build rapport and begin to treat each other like old friends.

On a neurochemical level, feeling _trusted_ increases levels of **oxytocin**. Increased oxytocin in turn leads to feeling _trusting_ and being _generous_, creating to a positive feedback loop of trust. Increased oxytocin also leads to bravery. When we face a fearful situation with our oxytocin levels elevated, we are less likely to freeze up, maintaining our ability to move forward and confront our fears.

The bad news is that communities which support face-to-face trust interactions aren't as prevalent as they used to be, as Robert Putnam famously chronicled in _Bowling Alone_. But by dancing, we're helping to fill the void. We're building trusting relationships, reweaving the raveling social fabric, and renewing our stocks of social capital.

Dance alone may not solve all of our problems, but we've yet to find a better way to start.

# Dancing as a Dream State

Everyone has their own pet theory of what dreams are, and what they mean. With due respect to Jungian dream analysis, current dream research shows that most dreams are a meandering path woven into a story by the "interpreter" function of our brain. This meandering path is sometimes based on our life, and occasionally nudged into new directions by the random firing of neurons.

Dreams usually begin with a seed based in our real life, maybe something that happened that day, but we rarely recall how our dreams begin. **The interpreter function of our brain then fabricates the next step in the dream from the previous moment.** It is like driving down a winding road at night-time. You can only see what's in front of your headlights, with no idea what's around the next bend. **In dreams, what's around the bend simply doesn't exist yet.** Your dreaming mind fabricates the next part as you get to it.

That's why one of the most common dream scenarios is that you suddenly have an exam that you didn't know was scheduled and for which you hadn't even begun to study. Or if you're a dancer, you find yourself on stage in front of an audience, to perform a choreography that you've never learned.

The reason why these dreams are so common is because your dreaming mind truly didn't know it was coming. It hadn't arrived at that bend yet. *Of course* you didn't know about it.

## Following as a Dream State

In this respect, the Follow role in improvised social dancing is similar to a dream state. You can only see what's in front of the headlights, so to speak, at the moment. The next moment is still around the corner, unknown.

**For Follows, understanding the significance of this analogy will actually improve your dancing.**

When first learning to dance, some women approach following as if it were a multiple-choice exam, trying to guess which figure her partner is leading, just in time, even trying to out-guess what he will lead next. There are inevitably some misinterpretations, as she occasionally launches herself into a guess to find out that it was actually something else.

Instead, following works out much better if you stay in the moment, split-second by split-second, as you go through each corner. Just keep stepping in the timing of the dance and stay with him. Enjoy the winding path.

## Leading as a Dream State

Then some men discover that this same approach works in leading. Beginners often think that leading means *planning* what to do and when, in advance. And indeed it begins that way, maybe for the first year or so. Then one day the Lead notices that he's planning less, and spontaneously being with his partner more. His "informed instinct" has improved to the point where he can sense where her momentum is going, and he stays with her, *going through that corner without a plan in mind*, discovering … with her … where it will go, as in a dream state. The result often flows better than a plan that he came up with in advance. It's fun to discover the path together.

## Your State of Mind

The fact that dreams are partially shaped by the random firing of neurons does not mean they are meaningless, or impersonal. How you **respond** to these dream scenarios is *very much* you. Do you respond to that unexpected exam with confidence, or with dread? That usually depends on your response to life in general.

Dreams can sometimes be scary. But since you're awake when you're dancing, you have some control over your response. Each dance figure begins with the first step. Just take that first step, with no idea of where it will go next, but with confidence that you'll figure out what to do when you get to that next corner. Through practice, this process slowly increases your confidence, as experience increases the frequency of success. Confidence follows success, as you'd expect.

In dancing, it also works the other way around, for both Follows and Leads. Your success in dancing improves by *beginning* with a confident attitude, being assured that **if it doesn't work out one way, it will work out another way.** With this approach, you'll enjoy dancing more, and so will your partners. They'll quickly see that you're having fun, with a more confident air, and that you trust that they'll work things out well, one way or another. Your partner will sense and appreciate that trust and ready-for-anything attitude.

They say that in life, you become what you practice. You can practice dancing through winding paths in the safe environment of the dance floor. Then you can apply this approach to your other activities, with confidence.

"If to dance is to dream,
then make your dreams come true."
— Anonymous

# We Have Options

An anchor of personal sanity in life is the ability to clearly differentiate between what we *want* and what we *need*. With this clarity, we can be firm about what we need, while being flexible, detached, and good-humored about what we merely want.

## Flexibility

Some genres of dance have been accused of being rigid and inflexible in their attitudes toward dancing, supposedly valuing rules and restrictions over flexibility and sociability.

We don't agree that this is necessarily an attribute of any particular dance *genre*. We'd rather propose that there are rigid and flexible *individuals*, in all camps. We know flexible and open-minded dancers within every discipline, including ballroom, ballet, and historical dance. On the other hand, we have also met individuals in every discipline who seem incapable of differentiating what is optional from what is necessary. The latter impose on their partners— or their friends—to follow their wishes as if they were needs, forcing others to conform to their own restricted palette of options.

If two people are going to dance in each others' arms, some mutual agreement is necessary.

And rather than arguing about whose values are correct, we can go *more than halfway* toward seeing the other person's point of view, or seeing if we can adapt to their style. This approach leads to a richer experience, while learning something new, and being friendlier at the same time.

## Options vs. Imperatives

Leading a partner through a social dance can be a wonderful exercise in differentiating what is necessary from what is optional.

As we mentioned in our pages on partnering, leading is *proposing* a certain way of moving, not *prescribing* it. When our partner does not go with the proposal, we refrain from exerting more power to press our partner into compliance. Considerate leading is about accepting someone as an individual with their own will and goals, not evaluating our own will and goals higher than theirs.

Of course, once in a while, an imperative lead (or back-lead) is necessary to prevent a collision. While dancing, we differentiate between what is necessary and what is optional.

## The 80% Rule

A good approach to social dancing is to be happy if 80% of the dance moves work out okay. Even settling for less is fine, but the point is to not expect perfection, either in one's partner or in oneself.

Furthermore, we note that it is in that other 20% that *learning* happens. We become better dancers, while discovering new dancing possibilities, during the 20% of the time that things didn't go as we expected.

Plus we're so much happier with this approach, not berating others (or ourselves) for not complying 100% with what we want.

## Always?

Does this apply to all of life, or all kinds of dance? No. There are some arenas in life where our options are limited, such as surgery, or the mechanical maintenance of a 747, where only one correct procedure exists for each situation. The wise surgeons and mechanics are able to differentiate their strict workplace requirements from the rest of their lives, but problems arise for the few who unconsciously carry this "one-way-only" attitude into their personal lives, and for their friends, who find this inappropriate.

Competitive and exhibition dancing has a similar restriction of options, which is necessary and understandable when a panel of judges is scrutinizing every move. Once again, the wise dancers make a clear differentiation between the needs of competition versus social dancing, and do not try to impose competitive attitudes upon those outside of that highly specialized discipline.

Fortunately, the realm of social dancing is wonderfully optional. We constantly discover opportunities and possibilities, which open doors, as opposed to rules and restrictions, which close them. We generously adjust our dancing to be compatible with our various dance partners, rather than insisting that they conform to our own tastes. We enjoy the individuality of other dancers, and continually modify our dancing to maximize their comfort and pleasure.

These reminders of the benefits of flexibility, exemplified by our dancing, help us maintain a healthy outlook on life.

# Be Here Now

In order to succeed on the social dance floor, we need to be attentive, aware, engaged, and present, *mindful* in the here and now, sensing the music, sensing ourselves, sensing each other, sensing the room, all at once, all the time.

Thus, one of the life skills we can hone on the dance floor is the essential practice of *mindfulness*, which can simply be defined as moment-to-moment awareness and remembered through the simple phrase "be here now."

There are two ways we can become more mindful on the dance floor. First, we can attend to specific aspects of the dance: really hearing every beat and every phrase, really feeling our feet caress the dance floor, really sensing every signal from our partner. Psychologists call this *focused attention.*

Alternatively, we can open up and take it all in: the music, our bodies, the whole room, at once. This is called *diffuse attention,* or *open monitoring.*

## The Benefits of Mindfulness

By dancing more mindfully, and attending to the present, we are better prepared to make the most of each moment, to the mutual benefit of our partners and ourselves.

In addition, we prepare ourselves to make the most of life. Studies have shown that regular mindfulness practice actually **rewires our brains, improving our ability to pay attention.**

Mindfulness can also have physical benefits: **reducing stress, soothing pain, strengthening our immune system, and heightening our senses.**

And while the effects of long-term practice are particularly dramatic, at least one study has documented **measurable benefits after just two hours of cumulative mindfulness practice.**

Perhaps the most compelling reason to dance and live mindfully is that **we simply have more fun when we do.**

In a recent study, Harvard psychologists Matthew Killingsworth and Daniel Gilbert set out to test the ancient hypothesis that "happiness is to be found by living in the moment."

To do so, they created an iPhone app which pinged thousands of people at random times during their waking hours to ask them three questions: "How are you feeling right now?" "What are you doing right now?" and most importantly, "Are you thinking about something other than what you're currently doing?"

In the process, they learned three essential lessons.

First, they learned that **our minds wander a lot**: at least 47% of the time. As Gilbert puts it, this means that when we look down a crowded street, "half the people aren't really there."

Not only is this a bit scary, it's also a bit sad, because the second lesson they learned is that "a wandering mind is an unhappy mind." Generally speaking, **people whose minds were wandering felt significantly less satisfied than those who were fully engaged in the moment**. Even pleasant daydreaming was no more satisfying than being mindful.*

Amazingly, this was true across all activities, even the least enjoyable. This means that we are generally more satisfied when we are fully present for even the most begrudged tasks than when our mind is wandering away from those tasks.

Finally, they learned that our degree of mindfulness is a better predictor of our satisfaction than the nature of the activity that we are engaged in. Thus, **becoming more mindful of what we're doing in the moment can often be a more effective way of improving our mood than changing what we're doing in the moment**.

We do think it is worth noting, however, that each of the five most enjoyable activities reported in the study—making love, exercising, conversing, playing, and listening to music—has something in common with social dancing!

By fully engaging in the present moment, either by focusing on one aspect of the moment, or broadening our awareness to everything in it, we can train our brains to become more attentive, and make the most of every moment of our lives.

We just need to remember to *be here now*.

> "All that is important is this one moment in movement.
> Make the moment important, vital, and worth living.
> Do not let it slip away unnoticed and unused."
> — Martha Graham, dancer

## Recommended Reading on Mindfulness

- *Fully Present: The Science, Art, and Practice of Mindfulness* (2010) by Susan Smalley and Diana Winston

- *Coming to Our Senses: Healing Ourselves and the World Through Mindfulness* (2005) [and others] by Jon Kabat-Zinn

- *Peace Is Every Step: The Path of Mindfulness in Everyday Life* (1991) [and others] by Thich Nhat Hanh

- *Mind Science: Meditation Training for Practical People* (2001) [and others] by Charles Tart

- *One Moment Meditation: Stillness for People on the Go* (2007) by Martin Boroson

---

* *Note:* The point of the Harvard study, and the point of this chapter, was to reinforce the message of the next chapter, that "the worst thing is to have lived, but missed it." Neither the study nor the chapter should be interpreted to mean that pleasant daydreaming is always a bad thing. If you get pleasure, or creative insights, or any other benefit from daydreaming, we're glad. So do we. In the end, the advice of the study and the chapter was simply that we're more satisfied when we're fully engaged in what we're doing. When you're dancing, dance, and when you're daydreaming, daydream. Just don't daydream while you're trying to dance.

# The Worst Thing Is To Miss It

A woman was interviewed in a Stanford study of women surviving, or not surviving, cancer. She mused philosophically:

> You know, the worst thing in life isn't to die.
> The worst thing is to have lived, but missed it.

This is one of the Big Picture awarenesses of life.

**Here are six ways that we can miss something:**

- Judging it negatively and pushing it away.

- Taking it for granted, not really seeing it.

- Not absorbing it as deeply as we can. Not being as open and receptive as we can be.

- Comparing the present moment to a better one in the past, and finding the current moment disappointing.

- Believing that all will be better in the future, but the present moment isn't there yet.

- Dismissing something with a sampling mentality. "Been there, done that."

This topic is not the same as wanting to be happy all of the time. It isn't about being a Pollyanna. It's about having a sharp and clear perception of what **is**. If the event that we are perceiving is negative, like a social or political injustice, then yes, we also need to experience that, for what it is.

But it's harder to see what is *good* in life, and in people. Our culture gives all too much encouragement to disapprove, complain, and reject.

This chapter describes a few ways to help counter our natural tendency to miss a lot of our lives, including the time we spend dancing.

## Critical Attitudes

Our teachers are anyone we have found who is alive and receptive to the moment, anyone who has the ability, talent, or attitude to appreciate what's good in art, life, and people.

Dale Stevens was one of Richard's teachers, although Mr. Stevens didn't know it. He was a film critic in Cincinnati. He was usually able to point to a wonderful aspect of a film he just saw. A film might have some shortcomings, but he would point out character nuances or effective cinematography or sheer expanses of beauty. He would help his readers get more out of their movie-watching experience. He helped his readers appreciate films more.

This is the opposite of the more typically critical efilmcritic.com, which was originally titled "Bitchslaps from Scott Weinberg" (which is what most of his reviews were). Many critics think that finding faults is what a professional critic must do.

It is all too easy to us to be influenced by critics' disapproving attitudes, so it takes some independence to have a receptive approach to life. Others might even think you're being too enthusiastic about life, but it's your life, not theirs. They are the ones who have become bitter cynics, missing most of their life by pushing it away. You can go in the opposite direction. But it takes practice, to make receptivity a habit.

## Comparative Thinking

Looking more closely at this dynamic, what is the essential process of the disdainful film critic? Comparative thinking is a part of it, usually comparing the film they watched to the best films they have ever seen, and being disappointed that their current experience pales in comparison.

Let's say we have a glass of wine. Do we simply enjoy that it tastes good? Or do we evaluate it as not one of the best wines we've had? If so, we just changed a potentially positive experience into a disappointment. We missed it. It's the same with food. Is it tasty and nutritious and comforting? Or is it not the best version we've had?

Our choice of attitudes affects both our receptivity and our enjoyment.

Now if it actually tastes bad, or if an experience is painful, that's different. Then we acknowledge that fact. But many people push away something good because it is not *as* good as a better version they've once had.

Some do this with their possessions. "My phone isn't the best version anymore. I'm unhappy." It's even worse if we do this with people, instead of appreciating their good qualities. On the dance floor, you can be disappointed that you don't have your favorite partner in your arms, or you can find ways of appreciating the partner that you do have for who they are, and not missing that moment.

You can be disappointed that the DJ isn't playing your favorite dance, or tune, or that the tempo isn't your preferred tempo. Or you can find aspects of the experience to enjoy and appreciate. It's your choice. You can let all of these experiences into your life, or you can push them away.

We can turn around the nosedive that our culture puts us into, and start heading back up. We can consciously intend to miss less of life, and of people, and appreciate more.

## Pushing It Away

An even more fundamental way that we miss something is pre-judging that we don't like that kind of thing, and pushing it away. It's too easy to only like what we already like, and to want to hear what we already believe. One of the best ways to expand our life is to be open to new thoughts and experiences.

Even worse, we could push something away simply because it's *not the version that we already know.*

A visitor from another country once complained endlessly about everything and everyone that he encountered in America. Then he paused to explain, "Well, how can I be expected to like something that I don't already know?!" Needless to say, he was very unhappy with life and with people in general, even back home.

The more possibilities that we are open to, the richer our life becomes.

# Eschatology

Eschatology (from the Greek *eschaton*, meaning the end of time) is the fairly common belief, held by various cultures for millennia, that everything will be better in the end, when everything that is imperfect will finally be made perfect. This of course presumes that it is not good now. The problem with eschatology is that the good days are always deferred to the future. All goodness, enlightenment, justice, and healing will come *later*. Not today, but when we get there. When we get to the Promised Land, when our ship comes in.

One way that we often do this to ourselves is when taking **dance classes**. We can spend hours in class feeling that someday we'll be good at this, but at the moment we're not there. But we *are* there, in the middle of an enjoyable process, with both body and mind fully engaged, with a partner in our arms. What could be better? Relish these moments.

# Double Whammy: Perfectionism

Wanting something to be perfect combines the worst aspects of comparative thinking *and* eschatology.

This is different from wanting to improve upon something. Better is better, but perfect is usually impossible. Chasing after perfection is a prescription for unhappiness and frustration.

Artists know that there can be beauty in the imperfect. And the imperfections are often more interesting than the flawless version.

# Sampling Mentality

Another way that we often dismiss something genuinely good is to complain that we've seen it before, or something like it. "Been there, done that!" We've become a sampling culture, bored with something after we've sampled it once.

Some film critics panned Pixar's *Cars* because its story was similar to *Doc Hollywood* and *Mr. Smith Goes to Washington*. C'mon, this is a kid's movie, and *Doc Hollywood* was twenty years ago. *Mr. Smith Goes to Washington* was seventy years ago. How is that supposed to disappoint today's kids? And besides, what is that repeated story line? It's a story about appreciating the people in front of you instead of pursuing fame elsewhere. Is it so bad to be reminded of that once every twenty years? Some critics thought so.

If something seems overly familiar, try to find a fresh way to look at it, perhaps from a new perspective. What else can you notice about it? Develop ways to look afresh at what has been taken for granted or seen before. Look for the extraordinary in the ordinary. But also appreciate the ordinary.

Sometimes it's as simple as reminding ourselves that just because we have seen something before doesn't mean that it is any less important. If something is a good thing, take a moment to appreciate its positive value.

> "If I were to begin life again, I should want it as it was.
> I would only open my eyes a little more."
> — Jules Renard, author

## Selfish?

To play the Devil's Advocate, we can ask: is this a selfish approach to life, focusing on our own experiences and wanting them to be richer? No, and this distinction is important. It isn't selfish because a large part of our life is how we interact with people, since we're social animals. And the result of fully and completely experiencing someone is as good for *them* as it is for us.

Do you know about the 100 Blessings? This Jewish tradition encourages us to make a hundred blessings a day. That's a lot of blessings! By the time the effect of one blessing starts to fade, we're already blessing something else.

But what does this mean, blessing?

By blessing, we mean the act of recognizing, affirming, and re-appreciating. When we bless something or someone, we become more aware of them and acknowledge that this thing or person is good.

When we bless our food, for instance, we acknowledge its value to us and give thanks for the pleasure and nutrition it provides. When we bless a person, we see them, admire them, and wish them well. We make a direct connection with them and bring them into our sphere of consciousness.

People *like* to be blessed. We don't call it that, of course, but that's what fans seek when they ask celebrities for autographs. To be acknowledged, even in such a small way, is a powerful thing.

We don't need to be famous or powerful to share our blessings. We each have the power to share an emotion with other human beings. We can brighten their day, or we can make them feel bad, by how we interact with them. When we shine our love on them they feel good, and we in turn benefit because they reflect love back to us. In the act of blessing, we are blessed.

This clearly relates to the two-way interaction of dance partnering. And being in a dance community. Or any community.

## Acceptance

A part of the process of appreciating something is refraining from pushing it away. It's intentionally accepting more of life, especially that which we can't change. That's acknowledged in the Serenity Prayer, as some people call it.

> Give us the grace to accept with serenity the things that cannot be changed,
> courage to change the things that should be changed,
> and the wisdom to know the difference.

Note that acceptance is given first priority, over changing, and also note the specification of things that *should* be changed. It is sometimes tempting to be a busybody, meddling in others' affairs, trying to change them to fit the way we think they should be. But maybe their behavior isn't something that *needs* to be changed. Maybe we can say to ourselves, "I don't have to catch that ball," and let others be themselves, including the way they like to dance.

## Stress!

Acceptance also de-stresses our life. Many books have been written about the harmful effects of stress in our lives, and ways to reduce stress, but the aspect we want to mention now is that more frequent acceptance of people and events significantly lowers our level of stress.

The tiniest disagreement or glitch in our plans can be made into a big deal if our goal, conscious or unconscious, is to have everything work out in our favor. But life is rarely exactly the way we want it to be, and people often don't act the way we would like them to.

Moment to moment, there are aspects of life that we like and others that we don't. There are always going to be people who disagree with us, people who do things differently, and things that don't work out. If we fight against this principle of life, we'll spend most of our life fighting hopeless battles, and generally be unhappy with life.

What we are doing, if we choose to live life this way, is allowing others' behavior to stress us, which not only throws us off-balance and makes us unhappy, but is a genuine health risk. A large body of scientific evidence links stress to cardiovascular disease, a suppressed immune system, impaired memory, and irrational decision-making.

Our response to this might be, "But I can't help it! My job is stressful! This relationship is stressful!"

**No, stress isn't what happens to us, even though it often feels that way. Stress is how we respond to what's happening, and we do have some control over that.**

Here's a specific suggestion that works:

Each time that we say to ourselves, "OK, I can live with that," is a victory over stress. We can retain a relatively calm peace of mind, and can continue to operate with all channels open. The other version is, "OK, I can live without that."

If you can't, then you can't. But you'll likely surprise yourself by how often you can say "OK, I can live with that," and be quite happy with the outcome. **And this way you end up stressing other people less at the same time, helping them be healthier as well.**

This response also makes you smarter. Saying "OK, I can live with that" can be an automatic first response, like an instantaneous defuser, which prevents negative emotions from hijacking your mind. You've probably had an experience of doing or saying something stupid while being in a state of emotional hijacking, usually anger. **Your calm mind is much smarter and**

**wiser**. You can always re-appraise a situation, *if* you've succeeded in retaining your mental clarity in the present moment.

Reducing our stress level is important for our health, but to return to the main topic, acceptance is also one of the best ways to miss less of life.

**Dancing** is the perfect place to practice being fully aware, observant, receptive, and open-minded, valuing others' truths, even if they're different from the way we think, and the way we like to dance. Don't miss what the experience has to offer.

## A Seventh Way: Not Showing Up

After all of our best intentions to be more aware and receptive, and not miss the moment, it's all for naught if we don't get up out of our comfortable chair. It's all too easy to feel lazy and want to stay home. And it's easy to say, "I'm too busy." But As Lao Tzu wrote, "Time is a created thing. To say "I don't have time,' is like saying, 'I don't want to.'"

You can read these many chapters on the multidimensional benefits from waltzing and social dancing. You can agree with them. But nothing will improve unless we get up, go out and do it, including going out dancing. Be more active. Show up more often. The worst thing would be to miss it.

# Some Days Just Suck

Noticing what's good in life and appreciating our blessings will turn most days into better, richer experiences. Our attitude and awareness can even turn down days into positive ones. But despite our best intentions, some days are just irredeemable. Everyone has their ups and downs.

So we're having a bad day, and we feel miserable. What could be worse?

Yes, you guessed it. Feeling bad about feeling bad.

We don't want the life-improvement suggestions in this book to make you feel even worse about the times when you just can't turn things around. We don't want you to feel like a failure when you can't find the bright side of a difficult situation.

So we have a few suggestions to help deal with the occasional down day.

## Enjoy It

OK, that sounds weird. But some people have discovered a comforting solace in melancholy. If they play a musical instrument, they use their deep funk to create more deeply moving music. Or an abstract painting, or a dance. Not everyone can do this, but it's worth a shot.

During the Romantic Era, in the early to mid 19th century, prolonged bouts of melancholy were valued as an essential experience.

Tango historian Julie Taylor describes another valuable form of melancholy: *el mufarse.* El mufarse is a surrender to the feelings of anger and sadness, in a ritual that might involve sitting alone at a table with a cup of coffee or liquor, sipping it slowly while contemplating the totality of one's misfortunes and underlying bad luck … and *enjoying* oneself. Upon hearing this description, people either feel that it doesn't make any sense, or else they shake their head affirming, "Oh yeah, I've been there."

Note that this was from a tango historian. Mufarse is one of the many moods of dancing tango. When you are deep in the state of mufarse, there is solace in movement with another, to melancholy music. You can even dance the blues in waltz time.

> "Dance, when you're broken open.
> Dance, if you've torn the bandage off.
> Dance in the middle of the fighting.
> Dance in your blood.
> Dance, when you're perfectly free."
> — Rumi, poet

Many people can't find a way to enjoy their bad days, however, so here are some more practical suggestions.

# The 80% Rule

Many of our chapters suggest that we can apply lessons that we learned in dancing to everyday life. One lesson was to be happy when our dancing works out 80% of the time (or less), instead of searching for perfection.

We recommend applying this 80% rule to life. Bad days happen, so when one comes along, **we can see it as our expected quota of bad days**, not as a personal failure to see a positive side. Don't feel bad about feeling bad.

> "The problem is not that there are problems.
> The problem is expecting otherwise,
> thinking that having problems is a problem."
> — Theodore Isaac Rubin, psychiatrist

## A Valuable Contrast

If all of our days were blissfully happy, we would acclimate to bliss, turning an outstanding day into a typical one. In order for a day to be outstanding, it has to stand out against something worse. We need to experience life's occasional pain in order to fully appreciate its beauty. So when you're having one of those days, think of it as a useful recalibration of your life, an experience that will make your good days even better by contrast.

## A Buffer of Positives

Sometimes a day goes so badly that we feel that things will never get any better. Or someone upsets us so much that we completely forget their positive qualities.

One of the reasons that we want to soak in our good experiences, and more deeply appreciate the beautiful aspects of life and people, is to have a larger and stronger store of positives burned into our memory. This way, when we're feeling a bit hopeless, we will have been pre-reminded that there is hope.

To clarify, we're not talking about building up a reservoir of positive *feelings* to nourish us on a rainy day. That often doesn't work. On bad days, our emotions are sometimes so deep in the red that it seems impossible to access any positive feelings at all. So we look to our rational side to save us.

Deeply appreciating the positive qualities of life and people (and ourselves) is *consciously* reminding ourselves of what is good. These are *objective* notes that we take for ourselves, and they're stored in our rational mind. We may be feeling hopeless on that down day, but our rational mind will speak to us through the fog, assuring us that it will get better, or that this is our expected 20% quota, or that this bad experience will make the next day seem great by comparison, or that the person making us angry isn't really that bad.

**More is better.** The more that we can appreciate about our lives (and our friends, and ourselves), the easier it will be to weather the occasional bad day.

# Polka

## Polka and the Mid-19th Century Dance Craze

The polka was developed in Prague around 1830 as an expression of native Bohemian culture during the Czech National Revival movement. In 1840, the Prague ballet master Raab traveled to Paris to exhibit Bohemian national dances, including the polka, on stage at the Odéon Theatre. During the previous year, the polka had enjoyed successful debuts in Vienna, Berlin, and St. Petersburg, and the reception was especially favorable in Paris. Carlotta Grisi and Jules Perrot danced the polka at the Paris Opera; Eugène Coralli and Marie Vollet performed it at the Variétés. Upon each viewing, French audiences grew fonder of the polka, and by 1842, the dance began to spread from stages to the public dance gardens, where off-duty ballerinas went to dance with their patrons. The following year, a few couples began to exhibit the polka at private salons and soirées, then in the famous Winter Season of 1843-44, the growing interest in the polka suddenly accelerated into a dance craze: *polkamania*.

The waltz had preceded the polka as the prototypical turning couple dance, but during the first three decades of the 19th century, Western European and American social arbiters widely considered the waltz to be too intimate for public display. However, the new polka was so ebullient and good-natured that it couldn't be considered lascivious. Paris quickly became fascinated with the new step, now as a social dance for the ballroom. News of the Parisian polkamania quickly spread to England and the United States, resulting in a similar wave of popularity in the same year. As in Europe, talk of the polka overshadowed politics for many Americans. Some believed that the unknown Tennessee governor James Polk won the race for the Presidency in 1844 primarily because his name was fashionable that year. An English humorist doubted that Polk was even his real name, implying that it was an adopted pseudonym to capitalize on the American polkamania.

The polka revived the ballroom after the relatively quiet 1830s, and dancing was once again thrust to the forefront of social activities. The newfound passion for social dancing led to an appetite for more steps to enjoy. The rousing galop from the late 1820s was revived, often becoming the last dance of a ball, and the mazurka, which had not gained a large following during the Regency era, was also revived, and now became the ultimate saltatorial experience for advanced dancers. Mazurka waltzes were created by Parisian dancing masters who combined the old waltz with various Polish and Bohemian steps, providing further challenges that the more adept dancers could master. As enthusiasm mounted, variety was added by the schottische and redowa. More significantly, the 1844 **polkamania led to a wider acceptance of the waltz**, once society acclimated to the closed embrace of turning couple dances.

Just before 1860, a change in women's fashions changed the way the polka was danced: the hooped crinoline (hoop skirt) replaced many layers of soft petticoats. Bouncy dances like the polka caused women's skirts to sway out of control, occasionally exposing an ankle. The polka was quickly modified into the smoothly turning two-step, which became the new way to polka through the turn of the 20th century.

The polka never died out, and has spread around the world, evolving into many regional forms.

*This brief history is from an article Richard wrote for the Grove Dictionary of American Music.*

Polka is danced to music in 4/4 time (or 2/4 time), from 104 to 124 bpm, with a sweet spot tempo of 114. For song recommendations, see "Discography of Waltz Music" (p. 223).

## Setting It Up

The frame of the polka is the basic waltz position (p. 4).

As in cross-step waltz and rotary waltz, the Lead faces out of the hall, away from the center, with held hands pointing towards LOD, in preparation.

As the first step is a side step, it is easy to lead into: simply lean in that direction and go. In some traditions, the polka starts with a preliminary hop on the second, rear foot before that first side step.

## Dancing the Polka

Many dancers learn to polka on the fly, picking it up as their partner leads (or back-leads) them through it. But for the scholarly type, here's a written description:

1: The Lead slides his left foot along LOD while the Follow slides her right foot along LOD.

"and": The Lead closes his right foot to left with weight along LOD while the Follow closes her left foot to right with weight along LOD, both beginning to rotate clockwise. She pulls her right shoulder back, making space for him to get ahead of her and back around.

2: The Lead backs around in front of the Follow, stepping across LOD with his left foot, and showing his back to the outside wall, as in the first step of a rotary waltz. Likewise, the Follow steps straight forward with her right foot along LOD, slightly between his feet, as in the first step of rotary waltz.

"and": Small hop on Lead's left and Follow's right as the couple finishes the 180° turn in preparation to repeat with opposite feet, dancing over the elbows. *Note:* This really is a *small* hop. The purpose of the hop is simply to facilitate the turn, not to get airborne.

3-and-4-and: The Lead does exactly what the Follow did, and vice-versa.

Altogether, it goes "slide-close-turn-hop."

*Counting Note*: The counts above could just as effectively be named "1, 2, 3, 4" instead of "1, and, 2, and," if that's easier for you to conceptualize. But in practice, polka is usually counted as "1, and, 2, and."

*Style Notes:* 1) Some like to dance the polka in an extremely exuberant fashion, bounding across the dance floor. Others prefer a more subdued and smoother style. Both can be quite satisfying, in our opinion. But be sure to give the smooth version a try. 2) Some like to lean into each half of the dance, leaning toward the hands when dancing over hands, and towards the elbows when dancing over the elbows. 3) There are many different ethnic styles of polka dancing that can be found in immigrant communities throughout the U.S.

# Dancing the Two-Step

**Two-Step** is the smoothest version of the polka, with floor-polishing sliding and closing steps, and no hop at all.

# Dancing the Galop

The earlier, late 1820s galop is also similar to polka, but with many slide-closes in a row, occasionally flipping around with a turn-hop as in polka to continue with the other foot. It can be incorporated into polka by simply inserting more slide-closes in one direction. This is usually done in the form of a Four-Slide Galop, but any multiple of four works nicely.

**Four-Slide Galop:** Where polka has two slides (one slide then a turn), a Four-Slide Galop has four slides (three slides then a turn), i.e., "slide-close-slide-close-slide-close-turn-hop."

*Leads:* When leading a Four-Slide Galop during polka, or any of the other footwork variations described below, be especially clear in signaling where her next step should go: are you continuing to slide-close along LOD, or are you turning and hopping? In addition, make sure you're clear on this distinction yourself. A Four-Slide Galop has three slide-closes straight along LOD, then you clearly step back around on count 4. Either slide straight along LOD, or step boldly across LOD, but not somewhere in between. Between those two points is your partner's foot. Don't be too early or too late in turning.

*Follows:* Don't worry. Just keep doing what you're doing unless he clearly leads otherwise. The polka/galop distinction is one that can easily start feeling like a multiple-choice exam if you let it, which makes this an especially good opportunity to consciously practice the alternative, focusing on interpreting moment-to-moment instead.

# Polka Variations

In the 19th century, the ebullient polka had many appropriately ebullient variations.

Here are a few of our favorites.

*Note:* In the following descriptions one "polka" or one "bar" is the equivalent of "slide-close-turn-hop," i.e., a half turn. A "full turn" or "two bars" is twice that.

**Promenade:** Polka forward in open side-by-side promenade position. The Lead's right arm is around the Follow, often with his left hand on his hip.

**Vis à Vis:** The Lead's right hand takes the Follow's left hand. Polka one bar face-to-face along LOD, then swing the hands forward and polka one bar back-to-back along LOD. Swing the hands backward and repeat.

**Underarm Turn:** From closed position, he leads her into a Follow's Outside Turn in the outside lane, in the space of one full polka turn. She turns under his arm with her usual polka step, while he promenades beside her. This also works as an exit from Vis à Vis.

**Pas d'Allemande**: Take right hand in right hand. Do the Underarm Turn under right-in-right hands.

**Crossed-Hand Polka:** From right-in-right hands, offer left hands below, hold hands close to your hearts, and polka around.

**Coquette (Love Chase)**: The Follow escapes from her partner and polkas solo, traveling straight forward or turning, while the Lead pursues her. They eventually rejoin and recommence paired polka.

**Pursuit**: One dancer polkas backwards while the other advances, in closed waltz position.

**Reverse Polka:** Polka, rotating counterclockwise. The Lead still begins on his left foot, from the inside lane. You can smoothly transition between clockwise and counterclockwise polka by "backing the lady" (Pursuit), as in the transitions between rotary and reverse waltz (p. 84).

**Pivots:** Four pivot steps together in closed position, rotating two full turns in the space of one full polka turn. The same footwork as Canter Pivots on p. 65, but in even timing "1-2-1-2." These are often smooth pivot steps, but they can also be hopped pivots as in Schottische (p. 123), if you find that easier or more fun.

**Esmeralda:** Four-Slide Galop, turning on the fourth, then one full turn of polka, turning a total of 540°. Repeat opposite, dancing it over the elbows.

**Six-Slide Galop:** Six slides, turning on the sixth, then polka once, to complete one full turn.

**Bohemian (Heel & Toe):** Heel-toe along LOD (1-2), turning polka (3-and-4), repeat opposite, followed by four turning polkas. "Heel" means straightened leg extended to the side, heel down on the ground, toe raised. "Toe" means toe to the floor, close to the supporting foot, knee slightly bent.

**Cross-Step Polka:** She takes four slides while he does "step-hop-cross-hop" then polkas, turning together at the end. Then she does the cross-step part while he takes four slides.


Many other variations that can be done in Polka time, including:

>**Leap Waltz**
>>**Redowa**
>>>**Waltz Galop** (and **Ripple Galop**)
>>>>**Hungroise (Heel Clicks)**
>>>>>and **Hops-Walzer (Ecossaise Walzer)**

>>>>>>are described in "Redowa, Mazurka, and More" on p. 147.


> "Some people march to a different drummer—and some people polka."
> — Los Angeles Time Syndicate

# Bohemian National Polka

This choreography by Richard Powers is based on research by the Czech dance historian František Bonuš (1919-1999). It is intended to portray the steps and forms of the original 1830s national style of polka from Bohemia, a decade before polkamania swept the world.

Professor Bonuš' long and complex collection of figures was intended for stage performance by a professional company. Richard's choreography is still challenging but is a social form danced for pleasure.

**Music:** Josef Strauss' "Feuerfest Polka" at 104 beats/minute (slower than modern polkas). An especially good recording is by the Cincinnati Pops Orchestra on the CD "Ein Straussfest." Often mistakenly assumed to mean "Fire Festival Polka," "Feuerfest Polka" actually translates to "Fireproof Polka." It was composed by Josef Strauss, a civil engineer, for a staff party of the Wertheim company, celebrating the completion of their 20,000th fireproof safe. The clang of forge hammers and anvils is thus a fitting tribute. The choreography is perfectly matched to the music, so whether you're learning the choreography from this description, or trying to remember what you once learned, you can let the music guide you.

*Note: One bar of music equals the time of two walking steps or one polka step.*

## Introduction

Taking hands (his right, her left), honor partners: 1) Step back away from partner, he to the inside of LOD, she to the outside. 2) Close feet together, stand tall and look at partner, both perpendicular to LOD. 3) Honor partner (she pliés, head still raised, as he inclines slightly forward, flat back, bending at the waist). 4) Rise and face LOD.

# 1. Promenade

Position: Side-by-side, both facing LOD, lady on the right, taking inside hands, raised to chest height. Man's free left hand is akimbo (on his left hip). Lady's right hand holds skirt down, or may also place free hand akimbo. This convention of free hand placement is kept throughout.

Take two low, somewhat heavy but silent polka steps (slide-close-slide-hop) forward, beginning outside feet.

Walk forward two elegant slow steps.

Rock forward on outside feet, honoring partner, then rock back on inside feet. This is a brief acknowledgment, not a full bow.

Repeat this four-bar sequence a total of four times. On the last repeat, replace the rocking steps with two more walking steps, man leading the lady into the next position.

# 2. Chassez In and Out

Half-close into open waltz position (elbows side connection, no held hands), Lead facing along LOD, Follow against LOD. Her left hand may be at the nape of his neck.

Chassez into the center (slide-close-slide), chassez back out, turning a quarter clockwise so that the gent faces out of the room.

Take two turning polka steps to revolve 3/4 of a turn, still without taking hands.

Repeat the 4 bars.

Take hands palm-to-palm in closed waltz position and chassez in and out as before, but turn 180° clockwise on the second bar, getting the man in position to back around for the following pivots.

Turn as a couple with four slow pivot steps (two full turns). Take each step with a heavy down-up undulation. Some dancers find hopped pivots easier to do.

Dudacka (doo-**dahtch**-ka) Polka: Chassez in (slide-close-slide), look toward the outside wall and stamp outside foot to that side, without taking weight on that foot, looking down toward the stamp. Chassez out rotating a quarter clockwise and stamp along LOD without weight.

Take one complete turn of polka, making sure the Follow ends up in the outside lane. Then cast away from partner, walking around in a tight circle four steps (he to his left, she to her right), to meet again. *Note:* This cast away happens mostly in place, rather than progressing forward along LOD.

# 3. Pivots and Polkas

Quickly take waltz position upon meeting and pivot four slow steps as before, traveling LOD.

Polka two bars (one full turn).

Repeat the four bars (four pivots, one full polka turn). End with the man facing LOD, placing his partner to face him.

*Note:* Remember that pivots and polkas have different starting orientations. The Lead is backing in front of the Follow at the beginning of pivots, and he is facing out of the hall at the beginning of a polka. Therefore, the second polka step in this section must be overturned to segue into pivots.

## 4. Redowacka
### (ray-doe-**vahtch**-ka)

Position: Drop both hands to face partner at a close distance. Man's (and possibly also lady's) hands akimbo.

The lady backs against LOD as the man advances LOD with the opening sequence of steps: two polkas, two walks, and two rocking steps in place. Twist the body with the steps (not in opposition) during the polkas, and twist somewhat during the rocking steps. The walks are straight forward and back, without twisting.

Lady backs the man with the same steps. Always begin with man's left and lady's right foot.

Take hands in waltz position. Repeat the two twisting polkas, but then pivot two full turns with four slow pivot steps, traveling LOD. *Note:* On the second polka, be sure to turn halfway so that he is backing around in front of her for the first pivot step.

Repeat the two twisting polkas backing the lady, pivot once around with two steps, then he turns the lady under by raising his left (her right) arm as she polkas (not pivots) under with three quick steps right-left-right. This gains her left foot free for the next section.

## 5. Chassez and Polka Tremblante

Push off from the held hands into: both chassez to their left side (slide-close-slide), and chassez back to the right side, without touching partner.

The lady does two Polka Tremblante steps turning to her left, traveling LOD. Polka Tremblante is a polka with small steps where the body bounces down and up with each step and hop. Meanwhile, the man walks forward four short steps, clapping boldly four times.

Repeat chassez and polka tremblante pursuit.

The man drops strongly to one knee (either one) and claps 15 times (eight plus another seven) as the lady does seven polka tremblante steps in a large counterclockwise circle around him. He watches her as she encircles him. The lady only travels 3/4 of this circular path, ending on the outside of LOD, facing him. He rises to face her as he claps the last time and as she steps two steps in place right-left (to gain her right foot free for the next part).

## Transition

Taking closed waltz position, polka one full turn (2 bars) and cast away with four steps, as done at the end of Part 2.

## Repeat from the Top

Take inside hands (on the anvil hit) and repeat parts 1 (without the intro), 2 and 3 only.

## Final Honors

1) Release from waltz position, keeping his left (her right) hand, and step back away from partner. 2) Close feet together, stand tall, and look at partner. 3) Honor partner. 4) Rise.

# Stay Young, Go Dancing

*"Stay young, go dancing."*
— Death Cab for Cutie

This is more than just a catchy lyric. It's also an essential fact of life.

By some accounts, time stands still while we're dancing. It is estimated that for every mile we walk in our lives, we add about twenty minutes to our life expectancy, which is around the time it takes to walk that mile.

It seems there really is a fountain of youth. It goes by the name of *physical activity*.

In a recent review of the medical literature, Harvard researchers found that burning 1,000 calories each week through physical activity—equivalent to about two to five hours of dancing, depending on the dance—is associated with a 20 to 30% reduction in risk of death from all causes, protecting against four of the ten leading causes of death in the U.S.: heart disease, cancer, stroke, and diabetes.

Other studies have shown remarkably similar results, and revealed that **the largest benefit comes to people who shift from no physical activity to moderate levels thereof**. Higher levels of activity provide additional, if somewhat less dramatic, benefits, but just getting up and moving is the most important step.

Interestingly, studies have found that time spent sitting is an independent risk factor for disease which cannot be undone by increasing our activity. Instead, it requires that we spend less time sitting. It is recommended that we get up and move—or dance—at least once every waking hour.

The benefits of moving are not purely physical, however.

**Like many aspects of social dancing, moving can also improve our mood**. And it can do so quite dramatically. In a recent controlled experiment involving people who were clinically depressed, **physical activity (30 minutes on three days a week for four months) was just as effective at reducing depression as the most commonly prescribed antidepressant.** Physical activity took effect more gradually than the pills, but in the end, worked just as well as a treatment. In fact, it was later found to be even more effective, as only 30% of the active remained depressed six months later, compared to 52% of those on pills, and only 8% of the active suffered a relapse, compared to 38% of those on pills.

Even for those who are not clinically depressed, the mood-boosting effects of moving are impressive. In a study of healthy college students, just ten minutes of moderate physical activity was enough to significantly increase their vigor while significantly decreasing fatigue, confusion, and overall negative mood, compared to ten minutes of rest.

Other studies have shown that while only a moderate amount of activity is required to achieve these benefits, they often last for a long period of time. For example, one study of women taking an aerobics class found not only that their mood was elevated after the class: their mood had still not returned to pre-class levels when they were surveyed again a full twenty-four hours later.

**As a result, studies comparing different methods for raising our spirits have shown that physical activity is the single most effective mood booster we know.**

Beyond lengthening our lives and boosting our mood, moving through dance can also make us smarter, as physical activity deeply engages the brain, and primes it for learning and creativity. Educators have long known that movement enhances cognition, in several ways.

For example, in one recent study, students learned vocabulary words 20% faster after running, as compared to rest, and retained significantly more of these words over time.

Another study found that performance on a creative task also improved significantly after running, as compared to performance before running or following rest.

In addition, as we note in "Dancing Makes You Smarter" (p. 183), when social dancing was compared to other leisure activities as a potential method for warding against dementia, it proved more effective than any other method tested, with **frequent social dancers experiencing a 76% reduction in dementia risk**. The fact that freestyle social dancing requires split-second rapid-fire decision-making, and integrates several brain functions at once, makes it the perfect activity to improve our mental abilities at any age.

In order to stay young, happy, and healthy, the advice is clear: get moving, go dancing.

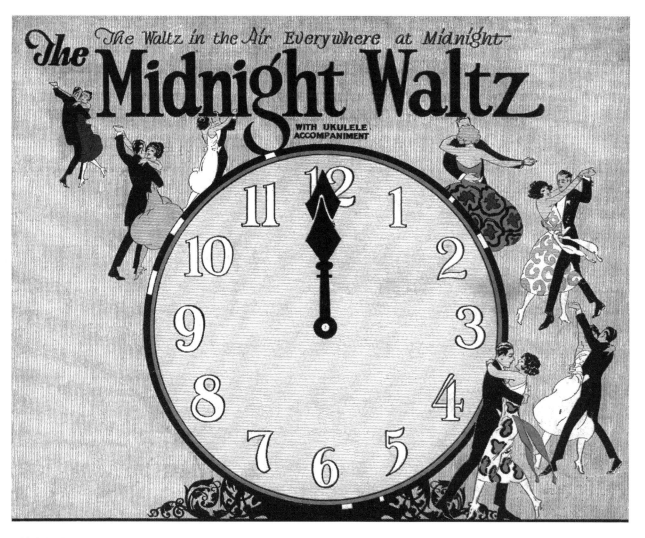

# Love Thy Neighbor

The commandment to "love thy neighbor as thyself" is prominently featured, in some form or another, in every major religion, as well as most major ethical philosophies.

Whether in this form, or in the form of the Golden Rule, "do unto others as you would have them do unto you," this commandment is probably as close as we will ever get to universal advice for being a good person, and fulfilling our purpose here on Earth.

But it's hard, isn't it? How is it even possible to "love thy neighbor as thyself"?

Maybe it depends on how we define love. Our culture holds no consensus on what love is. Ask three people and you may get three completely different answers.

Sometimes love is defined as especially liking something or someone. "I love that song!" But when we think it through, that's probably not what this commandment means.

Many people confuse love with wanting or needing someone. In particular, "really, really, please-oh-please" wanting someone can feel like love. But that's certainly not what "love thy neighbor" means. The great religions and ethical traditions of the world surely had something more generous in mind.

Over the centuries, philosophers and psychologists have found eloquent ways of defining a more generous kind of love. Some, like psychologist Carl Rogers, define love as *unconditional positive regard*. That seems to be headed in the right direction.

One of our favorites is from Robert Heinlein's *Stranger in a Strange Land*:

**"Love is the condition in which the happiness
of another person is essential to your own."**

Yes, that rings true.

It is still not easy, to place such importance on the happiness of another, but it is an ideal that we can aspire to. By that we mean that it's okay if we don't reach 100%. Every step in that direction helps make the world a better place.

This is also the essence of great dance partnering. The ideal partnering is when the happiness of your partner is essential to your own.

You may not have thought of great dance partnering as a form of "love," but now you can. Especially if you feel that your religion has commanded you to.

Who knew that following a commandment could be this fulfilling, or this enjoyable?

"Dancing faces you towards Heaven,
whichever direction you turn."
— Terri Guillemets, author

# The Platinum Rule

Being kindhearted partners in dancing and life, we aspire to dance with our partners as we want to be danced with. We try our best to follow the Golden Rule, to do unto others as we would have them do unto us.

But there's something slightly tricky about this. As we've noted before, everyone is different.

## This Advice May Save Your Relationship
(and in any case, it will improve your dancing)

Someone wise once gave Nick this priceless piece of relationship advice:

**If you want to know how to truly love someone, look at how that person loves, for it is in our loving that we reveal how we want to be loved.**

There are three essential observations underlying this piece of advice:

1) not everyone loves in the same way,

2) not everyone wants to be loved in the same way, and

3) we usually love in the way we want to be loved.

Take Mary and John, wife and husband. In Mary's opinion, spending quality time together with John is the most important aspect of their love. Mary feels the most loving and the most loved when they are spending time together. In John's opinion, showing each other emotional support is the most important aspect of their love. John feels the most loving and the most loved when they are supporting each other's aspirations and celebrating each other's accomplishments.

As you might imagine, a serious problem can arise if Mary and John do not understand each other's styles of loving. "You don't love me. You're always at work!" Mary may exclaim. To which John may counter, "Well, you don't love me either. At least my coworkers celebrated my promotion!"

In reality, John and Mary love each other very much, they just aren't doing it in the ways that show up on each other's radar screens. Mary is looking for more quality time together, and not seeing it, while John is looking for more emotional support, and not seeing it. Of course, on their own radar screens, they each see themselves as a loving partner. Mary's exclamation sounds ridiculous to John, who sees all of the times he showed his love by supporting Mary. Likewise, John's response sounds absurd to Mary, who sees all the times she showed her love by making an effort to spend time with John.

**The problem can only be fixed when John and Mary understand, and take to heart, that essential piece of advice, i.e., when they realize that they have different styles of loving, and commit to loving each other not only in their own loving style, but also in the loving style of their partner.**

John must learn to make more time for Mary, while Mary must learn how to show John more support. Only then will they both truly feel loved. In addition, they'll likely feel even more loving, as each of them will have increased the amount of their actions that one or both of them have imbued with "loving" meaning.

Of course, this also applies to dancing.

Every dancer has a different style, different ways of dancing variations, and different variations that they prefer leading and following. Thus, **even when we have the best intentions to follow the Golden Rule and dance with our partner as we want to be danced with, that may or may not be the way *they* most want to be danced with.**

For example, if John likes spinning more—dancing lots of extra turns and pivots—he may lead Mary into lots of extra turns and pivots. He does so not because he wants to dance them himself, but because he's trying his best to dance for his partner, and he thinks that she'll enjoy the turns as much as he would in her place. But it may actually be the case that Mary gets dizzy easily, and would actually prefer to have fewer turns and pivots. John wants to dance for her, he just doesn't know how yet.

There are several ways we can mitigate this problem.

Before we get to know our partner better, the Golden Rule is a great starting point. But after we've danced with our partner for a little while, we can begin to hone this even further.

To do so, we can follow the above advice, which, translated into the social dance context, might read: **"if you want to know how to dance with your partner, look at how your partner is dancing with you."**

We can tune into the way our partners are dancing with us, because, being the kindhearted partners that they are, they are probably trying to dance with us as they want to be danced with. If they're giving us a firmer frame, we can give them a firmer frame, or if they're giving us a softer frame, we can give them a softer frame. If they're waltzing us smoothly, we can waltz them smoothly, or if they're waltzing us emphatically, we can waltz them emphatically.

**Adapting to our partner in this way, as they simultaneously adapt to us, can be one of the greatest joys of social dancing.**

As we note several times in this book, two partners who both adopt this approach at the same time, dancing for each other and adapting to each other, may end up dancing in a completely new style, one which differs from their natural style, but which may be even more satisfying than their accustomed way of dancing.

Then, in order to get feedback on how we're doing, we can tune into the continuous stream of signals our partners are sending us about their comfort and enjoyment through their physical connection to us, through their facial expressions, and other subtle clues about how they are feeling.

To adapt the philosophy of Joseph Campbell, we can tune into and **follow our partner's bliss**. In doing so, we often find our own greatest bliss too, even if our experience is not quite what we expected.

# The Platinum Rule

As Karl Popper wrote, "the Golden Rule is a good standard which can perhaps even be improved by doing unto others, wherever reasonable, as they would want to be done by." This has been called the Platinum Rule.

Of course, as Walter Terence Stace notes, the Platinum Rule is really just a clarification of the Golden Rule, rather than an entirely new rule. Doing unto others as we would have them do unto us includes taking into account our neighbor's tastes, just as we would like them to take ours into account.

Whether you view it as the Platinum Rule, or simply a clarification of the Golden Rule, it is an essential clarification nonetheless, one that can further improve our dancing and loving.

I NEVER TIRE OF WALTZING — WITH YOU.

*Illustration by Richard Powers*

# Duets

More than one Follow has reported that Edoardo is a wonderful dance partner, especially in cross-step waltz. Years ago, they were surprised to hear the he had only started dancing one year earlier, in Richard's classes. They thought that partnering as attentive as his takes longer to develop.

It does.

Edoardo didn't learn partnering in one year. He plays the piano and developed a sense of partnering over many years of playing duets. He has his favorite duet partners, just as we have our favorite dance partners, and for the same reasons. He loves playing duets with one cellist in particular. The two of them seem to be sharing the same mind when they play. Every phrase, every pause, every breath is matched.

In masterful music partnering, you are completely listening to your partner as you listen to the music that you are playing. You are completely and simultaneously aware of both, not just one or the other.

In addition, you are aware of your partner's limitations. You know when he or she cannot get from one note to the next instantaneously, or can't rip through an arpeggio too quickly, so you hold off a bit for them at these points, as they do for you. Furthermore, you sense when your partner doesn't feel like playing that part as fast, or as loud or as lively as you do.

As Edoardo said, "Music is expression, opening your heart and letting it be free. That's why you never play the same piece the same way. Today you're sad, tomorrow you're happy. You should always be aware of the fact that music may inspire different feelings in someone else. You should respect this just as you respect someone else's ideas."

By contrast, a violinist whom Edoardo plays duets with merely plays the music that is in front of him, apparently oblivious of Edoardo's piano playing. If the piano is approaching a difficult phrase, the violinist charges on nevertheless, leaving the pianist scrambling to catch up. It almost seems that he would rather play solo, unimpeded by a duet partner. Edoardo reported that he felt like saying, "Okay, you don't need me at all. Tell me when you're done and I'll join you again." Perhaps this is reminiscent of some dance partners who act as if they would rather be dancing solo.

Edoardo adds, "We can then go one step further. If the person you're playing with is on your same wavelength, you can come to the point where instinct overcomes reason and you're barely aware of the technical side (assuming sufficient experience, of course). You stop concentrating and you start feeling. You're in intimate contact with the other person. When the cello plays the theme, the piano accompanies and supports the phrase, even with silence. When the piano has a solo, the cello accompanies. When both instruments speak at the same time, partnering really comes into play and none of the two overcomes the other. There's reciprocal respect and attention—both are talking and both are listening at the same time, so that the result is balanced. You breathe together, in equilibrium."

Not surprisingly, out of all the dances Edoardo has now learned and mastered, cross-step waltz is his favorite. Perhaps this is because of its partnering symmetry, where the Lead and Follow are the closest to having mirrored steps and an equal voice, the ideal for perfectly matched duets.

# Dance Poem: Number One

by Zubair Ahmed
a poem from Social Dance 2


Inside the night's circle
Those who would waltz
Gather to hum a 3/4 tune
For a few centuries.

Behind the trees are doorways
To realms where people
Sync shadows
With the music of the soil.

The grass is ours to dance on!
The branches click
Reaching deep into the sky.
The moon is nothing
But a floor.
I am nothing but the moon's slave.

My feet dangle in the wind
As my shoulders turn and fold
Like seaweeds.
We're suddenly alone.
We pivot through the forest
Inhabiting the snow
Moving among the trees.

# Chapter 42

different ≠ wrong

# True?
# Necessary?
# Kind?

Dance partnering is a form of nonverbal communication, so methods for improving our verbal communication often apply to our partnering as well.

Here is some timeless advice:

Before saying something to someone, consider three things:

Is it true?

Is it necessary to mention?

Is it kind?

## 1. Is it true?

This doesn't mean, "Do I believe it?" Instead, it requires stepping outside of oneself and seeing the bigger picture, also considering other people's truths. Is it *really* true, for *everyone*?

This also applies to the nonverbal communication of partnering. Are the rules and styles of your own dancing applicable for everyone, even for partners coming from other traditions or teachers? Re-consider which ones are universal, like the fact that social dancing is sociable and friendly, and which are optional, not necessarily true for everyone.

## 2. Is it necessary?

Have you ever said something hurtful to someone and later asked yourself, "Did I really have to say that?" It's much better to ask yourself if it's necessary to mention something *before* you say it, not after.

As the Lead develops his partnering skills, he learns which signals are necessary to communicate each variation successfully and how much physicality is required, using only the necessary signals and physicality.

In addition, when the Lead proposes a variation, he knows that it isn't necessary for her to interpret his lead in the exact way he intended. If she comes up with an alternative interpretation, he stays with her, instead of treating her as if she made a mistake.

## 3. Is it kind?

Playing Devil's Advocate, one might counter this suggestion by saying, "we can't always be kind. In the workplace, we may encounter a higher priority that preempts kindness." True. But we do *social* dancing. Being sociable and kind *is* the priority. Don't make work out of your pleasures.

This three-part advice is for both nonverbal and verbal communication. Be mindful of it when you converse with your dance partners. And especially with your life partner.

# Schottische

"Ma was delighted with her trip, but she was disgusted with the girls for allowing me to embrace and kiss them—and she was horrified at the schottische as performed by Miss Castle and me. She was perfectly willing for me to dance until 12 o'clock at the imminent peril of my going to sleep on the after watch—but then she would top off with a very inconsistent sermon on dancing in general; ending with a terrific broadside aimed at the heresy of heresies, the schottische."

— Samuel Clemens (a.k.a. Mark Twain), *Letter to Orion Clemens*, March 18, 1861

## Dancing the Schottische

Described below are three basic schottische steps, and three basic schottische styles, followed by many schottische variations.

All of the schottische steps have the same basic timing and weight change pattern.

| | | | | |
|---|---|---|---|---|
| Starting on First (Outside) Foot: | *Step* | *Step* | *Step* | **Hop** |
| Starting on Second (Inside) Foot: | *Step* | *Step* | *Step* | **Hop** |
| | | | | |
| Then Four Step-Hops: | *Step* | **Hop** | *Step* | **Hop** |
| | *Step* | **Hop** | *Step* | **Hop** |

*Note:* A step is a weight change to the other foot, and a hop is a hop on one foot, without changing weight.

Schottische is danced to music in 4/4 time (or 2/4 time), from 74 to 82 bpm, with a sweet spot tempo of 78. For song recommendations, see "Discography of Waltz Music" (p. 223).

## Basic Step #1: The Original Schottische

This is the original mid-19th century (1850s) schottische, rarely seen today except in the performance of vintage schottische quadrilles. It is danced entirely in closed waltz position.

Begin with the Lead facing forward LOD and the Follow facing against LOD.

1-2-3-4: Slow polka step (slide-close-slide-hop) toward the center of the room, no turning.

5-6-7-8: Slow polka step toward the outside wall, turning 180° clockwise to prepare for the Lead to back in front of the Follow, across LOD, on count 9.

9-10: Hopped pivot step (step-hop) with the Lead backing across LOD. Placement of the feet on the step is the same as in the first count of rotary waltz (p. 59).

11-12: Hopped pivot step (step-hop) with the Follow backing across LOD. Placement of the feet on the step is the same as in the fourth count of rotary waltz.

13-14: Hopped pivot step (step-hop) with the Lead backing across LOD.

15-16: Hopped step (step-hop) with the Follow backing across LOD, stopping the rotation in position to begin again, i.e., when the Lead is facing forward LOD, Follow against LOD.

Repeat from the beginning.

## Basic Step #2: The Military Schottische

This is the schottische as it was danced in the later 19th century (1880s). It is still mostly danced this way today, albeit in a different style, as explained below.

Begin with Lead and Follow side-by-side in half closed position (waltz position with the held hands released, so that partners are beside each other), facing forward along LOD.

1-2-3-4: Run three steps forward along LOD (counts 1, 2, 3), starting on outside feet (Lead's left, Follow's right), then hop on outside feet on count 4.

5-6-7-8: Similarly, run three steps forward along LOD (5, 6, 7) starting on inside feet, then hop on inside feet (8), with the Lead turning clockwise on the final step and hop, preparing to back in front of the Follow, across LOD, on count 9. As he comes around in front, they take closed waltz position for the second half of the sequence.

The second half is essentially the same as in the original schottische: four hopped pivots.

9-10: Hopped pivot step (step-hop) with the Lead backing across LOD.

11-12: Hopped pivot step (step-hop) with the Follow backing across LOD.

13-14: Hopped pivot step (step-hop) with the Lead backing across LOD.

15-16: Hopped pivot step (step-hop) transitioning back into half-closed position. The Lead lets go of the held hands and stops his rotation, stepping forward LOD and hopping, while the Follow continues rotating, stepping across LOD and hopping, pulling her right shoulder back to end up at his right side in half closed position.

Repeat from the beginning.

## Basic Step #3: The Walking Schottische

This is a simplified version of the schottische, used historically as the underlying footwork pattern for fancier variations of the military schottische, but now also used by some dance communities as a basic schottische step because it's so much easier without the pivots.

First half (counts 1-8) is the same as the military schottische.

Second half (counts 9-16) is simply four step-hops straight forward along LOD, without turning.

This basic step is danced side-by-side, in half closed or hand-in-hand position.

The walking schottische step can also be combined with the military schottische step, using the former as a way of resting.

## Style #1: Schottische = Easygoing

In the 19th century (and still today in some communities), schottische was a relaxed, easygoing dance. Compared to the faster waltzes, polkas, galops, and mazurkas, schottische was seen as a relatively restful dance.

## Style #2: Schottische = Smooth

The schottische is very much alive in Sweden and Denmark. The Scandinavian style is *very* smooth, without any bouncing. The pivots are also smooth, instead of hopped.

## Style #3: Schottische = Speedy

In other communities, including today's Stanford dance community, the primary value of schottische appears to be *speed*. At a faster tempo, you zoom around the room, and can almost feel the wind in your hair.

At these faster tempos and higher velocities, schottische can easily be one of the most tiring dances of the evening, but also one of the most fun.

*Note:* When pursuing speed in schottische, be careful, especially with the second half, noting that running steps can travel further than pivot steps. For safety and comfort, *decelerate* for the second half, traveling less with the pivots than with the running steps.

As you'd probably guess from our emphasis on flexibility, we appreciate all of these styles.

## Schottische Variations

Schottische variations can vary either the first half, or the second half, or both. Below, we describe some of our favorites of each kind.

### Variations of the First Half

**Cast Away:** Run diagonally forward away from your partner on the first-foot run, then run diagonally forward on the second-foot run to rejoin your partner. Optional clap on count 4.

**Continual Pivots:** Continue pivoting through the first half, i.e., finish the four pivots from the first schottische sequence, then do eight more to fill the entirety of the next sequence.

**Polka Schottische:** Do a slow polka on the first half. In other words, do a turning version of the original schottische footwork in closed position, starting with hands pointed along LOD, and flipping 180° clockwise on the third steps, as you would in a polka.

**Waltz Schottische:** Substitute rotary waltz steps for the running steps: waltz-2-3-hop, waltz-2-3-hop.

## Variations of the Second Half

**Pivot, Underarm Turn:** Two hopped pivot steps (360°) together, then a Follow's Outside Turn in the outside lane. She travels under his arm with two hopped pivot steps while he step-hops alongside her. As usual with outside turns, protect her arm!

**Pivot, Free Spin:** Same footwork as above, but with a Follow's Free Spin.

**Pivot, Rollaway:** Same for her, but he spins counterclockwise as she spins clockwise. She spins with hopped pivot steps while he spins with hopped reverse pivot steps.

**Double Underarm Turn:** With her left hand in his right, he turns her under clockwise two full turns, as she does four hopped pivot steps just as she would when pivoting with him, while he step-hops. You can also substitute free spins, rollaways, or turns for the Lead.

**Wheel:** Wheel around as a couple with step-hops in half closed position, usually counterclockwise. He backs up, she goes forward. Be careful, as this variation blocks traffic.

**Around the World:** With her left hand in his right, he leads her to step-hop forward, then counterclockwise around him as he step-hops in place. This also blocks traffic, especially when combined with a genuflection (he drops to one knee as he leads her to circle him).

**Cross-Body Inside Turn to Pivaloop:** Taking her right hand in his left, a Cross-Body Inside Turn on one set of pivots, then a set of running steps with her on the inside lane, and a Pivaloop to get her back to the outside on the next set of pivots (see p. 160 for this sequence in cross-step waltz). Or do a Pivaloop Around the World, with the Lead running under the raised arms to get her on his left side again, to repeat the Pivaloop.

**Pivot, Underarm Turn to Shadow Position:** Pivot, Underarm Turn as described above, but changing hands to right-in-right above her head to get into Shadow Position (p. 160) for the following figures.

**Shadow Position to Lead's Hammerlock:** He circles their left hands out over her head, turning her clockwise. She turns to face against LOD as he lowers the right hands behind his tailbone, not letting go. He "lassoes" with his left hand to lead her to step-hop forward behind his back, and around to his left side. His right hand is placed in half-nelson position behind his back and his left hand is in front of her, leading her forward.

**Lead's Hammerlock to Skater's Position:** He brings their left hands back, in between them, turning her clockwise, immediately lowering the left hands behind her tailbone then placing them at her left hip, taking right-in-right in front of her. *Note:* Skater's Position is her equivalent of Hammerlock, with the difference that her left hand is at her left hip, while his right hand was behind his back. Both hand positions are set this way to make it more comfortable for her arms, which are likely shorter than his.

**Skater's Position at His Left to Skater's Position at His Right:** He brings their right hands out and over her head to turn her to her left, counterclockwise, until she's facing against LOD, then he leads her to walk forward behind his back to his right side. When his left hand

126

is behind his back, he lets go of it. Then when she is facing forward LOD at his right side, he circles her head counterclockwise again and brings right hands down to Skater's Position at his right side, right hands on her right hip, taking left-in-left in front of her. *Note:* This last variation is essentially a combination of the previous two variations with directions reversed. When you master all of the motions to transition between the positions, you can experiment with shifting between these positions in a variety of ways.

**Mixmaster:** This is like Shadow Position to Lead's Hammerlock above, except that he keeps the right hands high, bringing them to rest by his right shoulder, instead of dropping them low behind his back. Once she has passed behind his back, he brings the left hands to his left shoulder. The body and arm positions of Shadow Position have now essentially been role reversed. To get her back in Shadow Position, he loops the right hands behind their heads and clockwise in front of her, leading her to step-hop across in front of him to his right side, and bringing the hands back to the original Shadow Position.

From right-in-right or left-in-left, you can also take crossed hands in front, for these figures:

**Sweeps:** With crossed hands right over left, he swings her around in front of him to the inside lane during the step-hops, leading her straight forward, then across in front of him, then to face forward again when she's at his left side. Swing her to the outside lane on the next pivots.

**Outside Turn Sweeps:** Give her an outside turn before you sweep her across, leading the turn with the hand on top, followed by the hand below. The turn can be on the first set of four step-hops, with the sweep on the next set of four, or you can use two step-hops for the turn and two for the sweeps in the same set of four.

To get out of any of the right-in-right, left-in-left figures above:

**Face Loop Exit:** The Lead gives her a clockwise turn in the outside lane with the left hands, then combs his right ear with his left hand to drop her left arm on his right shoulder.

**Cast Away Exit:** Alternatively, he can simply disengage the hands entirely, casting his partner away on the running steps and rejoining in waltz position for the pivots.

## Sex Change Schottische
*a.k.a. "Role Reversal Schottische"*

This is a variation which allows for role reversal (p. 161) in schottische, either temporarily (just in the middle of this one figure), or for a longer term. It was brought to the U.S. by a Scandinavian teacher who hadn't quite mastered English, leading to the mistranslation "Sex Change Schottische." Americans found the name charming and kept it.

It begins with the first half of the Military Schottische: run-2-3-hop, run-2-3-hop.

Then, Lead and Follow close up into a modified barrel hold: both partners holding both shoulders, with *both of their left hands on top of their partner's right shoulder.*

They take two normal hopped pivots steps (pivot-hop, pivot-hop, turning 360° total), then, firming up the frame and sinking slightly lower, they do three smooth, quick pivot steps and a hop (pivot, pivot, pivot, hop, turning 540° total).

At the end, they open up (by disconnecting his right and her left arm) with the initial Follow (the new Lead) on the inside lane and the initial Lead (the new Follow) to her right on the outside lane, facing forward LOD.

The five pivot steps get them on the opposite feet, to recommence with their new outside feet. She's now doing the Lead's footwork and he's now doing the Follow's.

Repeat it to give the Lead back immediately, or let her lead for a while, repeating it later.

## Bronco Schottische

This variation, like the Newport it is based on, is rarely seen today, which is unfortunate, because it's a whole lot of fun. This description will assume you know the Newport and Waltz Galop, which you can find described in detail on p. 148.

The entire figure is danced in closed waltz position. Begin with the Follow facing forward along LOD, and the Lead facing against LOD (or turn clockwise before the first step to get there, as in rotary waltz).

1: The Lead leaps straight back along LOD with his left foot, while the Follow leaps straight forward into him with her right foot. They land downward precisely on the count.

2: The Lead leaps straight back with his right foot, while the Follow leaps straight forward into him with her left foot.

3 &4 &5, 6 &7 &8: One full turn of the Newport, with the Lead beginning by leaping backward a third time (leap, side-close, side-close / leap, side-close, side-close).

9 &10, 11 &12, 13 &14, 15 &16: Two full turns of Waltz Galop (4 x "leap, side-close").

Repeat from the beginning.

*Note:* We probably shouldn't mention this, but if you really like turning, you can replace the straight leaps between the Waltz Galops and the Newports with two leaping pivot steps. We also probably shouldn't note that you can reverse it, with counterclockwise rotation.

*Music:* "Bring It On Back" by Corey Crowder works well for Bronco Schottische.

## Last Notes on Schottische

This dance is also spelled Schottisch, and some other countries spell it Scottisch.

There is also another dance called "schottische," the Sweetheart Schottische, a country-western couples' dance in sweetheart (shadow) position. The exact origin of that dance is unknown, but it is likely a modern choreography. If you want to learn that dance, popular among country-western social dancers, there are many descriptions and videos online.

# Four Experiences in Waltzing.

For explanation... the unmusical Reader will consult any Lady and her Piano. —— *Ed. Harper's Magazine.*

SPECIMENS of WALTZING

130

# Style in Social Dancing

In social dancing, we don't imitate one "official" style, but instead develop our own individual style, on the basis of whatever is most comfortable and fun for our partners and ourselves.

As we're developing our own style, we find that it is friendly to adapt to the different styles of our partners, which is also a valuable learning experience.

Here are a few quotations and ideas that we find useful in thinking about this.

In *The Fred Astaire Top Hat Dance Album* (1936), Fred Astaire provides this advice:

> Above all, be yourself! Dancing should be a form of self-expression. Whatever else you may do, don't make the mistake of being an unimaginative copyist. Don't be a slave to steps or routines.
>
> After you have been dancing for a time, you will find that you do the Foxtrot, the Waltz or the Tango just a little bit differently from anyone else. You have developed your own individual style. That is nothing to worry over. On the contrary, there would be more cause for worry if you did not develop a style of your own. Styles in dancing are developed just as inevitably as styles in writing or painting. The dancer without individual style is no more than a mechanical robot.
>
> For ballroom dancing, remember that your partners have their own distinctive styles also. Cultivate flexibility. Be able to adapt your style to that of your partner. In doing so, you are not surrendering your individuality, but blending it with that of your partner.

Dance partnering is a form of nonverbal communication. So when it comes to communicating, which of these is better?

We may have our personal preferences, but in the end, both of these letters are able to communicate effectively.

The different styles of calligraphy are analogous to different styles in dancing. Even when we have a strong preference for one style, we still find that other styles are easy to understand.

Social dancers enjoy adapting to the different styles of their partners, so when the first A dances with the second A, each takes on some of the characteristics of the other's style. It's not only the friendly way to dance, but we also discover new ways of moving.

How about this one?

Well, it is possible to be *too* creative when it comes to dance partnering. An important part of learning to dance is acquiring the basic vocabulary, the steps and figures that most social dances have in common. Some Follows enjoy dancing with especially creative Leads, but only when his signals are comprehensible. So Leads, try your best to give signals that your partner can easily understand, while adapting to your partner's style of dancing.

In *The Dance of Society* (1875), the New York dance master William B. DeGarmo elaborated on adapting to the style of one's partner:

> Gentlemen who acquire a diversified style easily accommodate themselves to different partners. Even among those who possess a diversified style, every one has his individuality. No two persons write alike. A man cannot write his own name twice the same. There is no duplicate in nature. No two persons dance alike. When their movements harmonize, this individuality is not only natural and necessary, but it pleasingly diversifies *le tout ensemble*.

In *Free Play: Improvisation in Life and Art* (1990), Stephen Nachmanovitch describes how this harmonization plays out when two different styles interact:

> I play with my partner; we listen to each other; we mirror each other; we connect with what we hear. He doesn't know where I'm going, I don't know where he's going, yet we anticipate, sense, lead, and follow each other. There is no agreed-on structure or measure, but once we have played for five seconds there is a structure, because we've started something. We open each other's minds like an infinite series of Chinese boxes. A mysterious kind of information flows back and forth, quicker than any signal we might give by sight or sound. The work comes from neither one artist nor the other, even though our own idiosyncrasies and styles, the symptoms of our original natures, still exert their natural pull. Nor does the work come from a compromise or halfway point … but from a third place that isn't necessarily like what either one of us would do individually. What comes is a revelation to both of us. There is a third, a totally new style that pulls on us. It is though we have become a group organism that has its own nature and its own way of being, from a unique and unpredictable place which is the group personality or group brain.

Many students in the Stanford social dance classes have written about adapting your style to that of your partner. Here are two such essays, one from a Lead, one from a Follow.

# Calibration

## by Mike Rodgers
an essay from Social Dance 2
(his thirteenth dance essay)

One aspect of social dancing that has definitely become more integral for me over time is the process of adapting ("calibrating" oneself) to each different partner. As a freshman, when I was first starting out dancing, I would definitely notice that certain dances worked better with some partners than with others, but I could not really discern any rhyme or reason to it. When I took History of Waltz for the first time in the spring of my sophomore year, I started to notice characteristics of my partners' dancing (e.g., "she really leans back," "she hangs on," "she really helps turn me," etc.).

However, more than that, I realized that, as I would dance with a partner, even just for thirty seconds, the connection would rapidly start working better. It was very much like my partner and I were calibrating ourselves to each other. It was as if I had a setting for dancing with Amy, a setting for dancing with Betsy, and a setting for dancing for Carol. (And I'm sure that it was a two way process—Amy, Betsy, and Carol were simultaneously learning how to dance with me.)

Interestingly, this process was, at first, not entirely conscious. Most of the time, I could not really put my finger on what exactly it was that I was doing differently after dancing with a person for a bit. As I've gone on and gotten more experience, some of the adaptations I make to a particular partner have become more quantifiable in words.

After dancing with a person for a bit, you learn how strong of a lead is the right amount to balance between not leaving her guessing and not shoving her around. Similarly, I'm sure that Follows learn to recognize a particular partner's way of leading a particular variation as being distinct from how other partners might lead it.

A further way in which to adapt to a particular partner (and one that is more unique to Leads) is simply by adjusting which variations you lead. A lot of times I can tell by facial expressions what variations someone particularly loves, or sometimes a partner will excitedly mention really liking something I just led. Other times, I'll try a variation two or three times, and it just doesn't work so well, and I make a note that it's one she's not going to feel comfortable with so I probably shouldn't lead it. All of these things are notes that, as a dancer, one stores away for future reference.

Another big observation I've made about dancing is that, whenever I'm dancing with someone and for whatever reason, it's not quite working, the best thing to make it work better is to **completely forget about what my own feet are doing and focus on clearly leading my partner into what she needs to be doing.** Generally, that fixes the problem just fine. And by moving my body wherever it needs to be to give that lead, my feet do something or other underneath me, and nine times out of then, they do "the right thing" since it's the most natural.

Last winter, I was teaching a friend of mine who was a complete beginner how to dance, and the phrasing I used is, **"When you're dancing, you don't move your feet. You move your body, and then you step in time beneath it."**

One of the effects of this calibration is that there end up being two very different appeals for dancing with people you know very well and people that you hardly know at all or are complete strangers. With someone you know well, there is—on top of the emotional connection from being friends—a connection that comes from really knowing how to dance with and for each other. **With someone you haven't met before, walking out onto the dance floor is almost starting off a game. It's a challenge where the objective is to figure out how best to dance for your new partner.**

# Body Conversations

## by Kelsey Lange
### an essay from Social Dance 2

*Note:* Kelsey is Mindy Lange's daughter (see "My Pleasure" on p. 71).
Yes, two generations of students in Richard's classes over the years.

Names are difficult to remember in this class. Each time I turn to a new partner, we introduce ourselves, for the twentieth time or so. Sometimes my partner will remember my name and I can't for the life of me think of his, which leads to a slightly awkward moment when I ask for his name—again.

At the beginning of this quarter, I tried to tell myself that names would be my goal for this class. That quickly faded as the dancing became more complex and engaging. About midway through the quarter, as I greeted another partner who quickly responded with my name, I had the reassuring thought that I at least remembered this partner's face.

As the music restarted, I realized that I also very quickly recognized his dancing style. I could tell by his rather unusual movement of his hips with the lindy-hop turning basic that this partner has a creative spirit, as well as a decent amount of self-esteem. He individualizes all of his dances with his unique style of the slightest added movements.

I try my best to adjust myself to work with his style, responding to his movements. It's so much easier to remember the content of these conversations through body language than that of the small, repetitive, introductory conversations. Over time I get tired of asking for people's names and how they are doing and let myself focus instead on the conversations through dance. As hard as it is to resist the urge to greet him with "Oh hey bendy legs!" I simply smile and try to adjust my dancing to be compatible with his flare. I may not know his name, but I do know quite a bit about his dancing and personality.

> "You can discover more about a person in
> an hour of play than in a year of conversation."
> — Anonymous

# Flexible Doesn't Mean Sloppy

Some of our students were raised in a relatively strict tradition where there is only one correct way to do things. Therefore, their first reaction to the flexibility of social dancing is that it feels sloppy or incorrect. Or they may get the idea that, "there is no correct way to dance."

Compare these two statements:

> "There is no right way to dance."
> "There is no *one* right way to dance."

These two statements, differentiated by a single word, are almost the opposite of each other. The second one is saying, "There are *many* right ways to dance." Yet some people nevertheless have the mistaken impression that there's no right way to social dance.

We want to clarify that there are definitely correct ways to approach social dancing, and they involve precise skills. Flexible doesn't mean sloppy. For instance, partnering techniques are quite specific, and they are constantly fine-tuned. The ability to adapt to a changing situation is a *skill*, one that will save you many times throughout your life.

One student at the Poconos Waltz Weekend, an older German woman, was raised in a somewhat strict one-way-only tradition, and at first she had difficulty with the **combination of two kinds of flexibility**. She was hearing that:

1) there is more than one correct way to do a dance form, and

2) each partner is a bit different from other partners.

When these two variables combined, it seemed like chaos to her—it felt like anarchy—and she was uncomfortable with this at first.

She preferred to have a teacher who told her that there was only one correct version of each social dance. (Which simply isn't true.) And she wanted the teacher to work on the men until each of them danced exactly alike, so she wouldn't have to adapt to differences from one partner to the next. (And that's never going to happen either.)

But as the weekend progressed, she warmed up to both kinds of flexibility. And she came back to the following year's Poconos Waltz Weekend, then to the third, and the fourth. From her initial negative reaction, the combination of these two kinds of flexibility has become her favorite part of social dancing.

Similarly, when we read student essays, we consistently find that the students who are most enthusiastic about this flexibly adaptive approach to life are the ones who came from the *opposite* tradition, initially expecting there to be only one correct answer for anything. They had a larger revelation, and they loved it. Those who had been adapting to alternative paths all of their lives merely saw this as a continuation of their common sense.

The bottom line is that whether your initial response to flexible adaptation is warm or cold, it is a fact of life, in a world that is changing faster than ever before. Many of our students have told us that the instant-adaptation skills that they learned in social dance class not only made them better dancers, but also helped them in their careers.

We want to clarify that our discussion of flexible adaptation is not because we have a personal affinity for alternate paths. We're quite grounded and pragmatic, both having Stanford degrees in engineering.

What we're saying is that when you realistically analyze the dynamics of social dancing, you quickly ascertain that:

1) After many decades of evolution, there are now many different ways to do any given social dance form, not just one. Each style is good in its own way.

2) Each of your partners is different, and you must adapt to their differences in order to dance successfully.

This is simply the nature of the situation. Whether your personal preference is strictly rule-based or highly creative, either way, social dance situations are in constant flux. So is life.

As we mention throughout this book, adapting to changing situations also keeps us engaged in the present moment and more alive.

And we learn more.

And we become a friendlier and more skillful dance partner.

It isn't sloppy.

> "The belief that there is only one truth and that oneself is in possession of it, seems to me the deepest root of all that is evil in the world."
> — Max Born, physicist

# Sketchy Guys

This is a touchy subject, because we don't want to speak dismissively of anyone who loves to dance. However, it's an important subject for the many women who talk to us about "sketchy guys" at social dances, so that makes it worth discussing.

## Who Are Sketchy Guys?

OK, that's a sexist term. So let's clarify that any woman who acts this way is a "sketchy girl." But we usually see more males than females behaving this way on the dance floor.

Sketchy guys are…

### 1) Guys who are physically or emotionally rough with their partners, with a controlling attitude.

A good Lead knows *and cares* what is comfortable for his partner. He wants to lead what is pleasurable or fun for her, as opposed to showing off, or using her as an accessory to his ego.

A considerate man dances for his partner's ability and comfort. Sketchy guys don't.

In *social* dancing, a good Lead clearly suggests an option, which is different from controlling her. He proposes, rather than prescribes, a way of moving to his partner. If his partner does not go along with his proposal, he adapts to her motion instead of exerting more force to press her into accepting the proposal.

But guys, don't be so afraid of seeming sketchy that your leads become wimpy. Signals in leading *are* physical, *comfortably* physical, and your partner depends on feeling clear these clear signals. If the physicality of the lead-follow connection is on a scale of one-to-ten, avoid 0 to 2 (wimpy) and avoid 8 to 10 (physically rough). Anything from 3 to 7 functions, and different dancers have different preferences.

## 2) Guys who correct their partners.

Have you ever danced with one of these guys? Often the first thing he does when he begins a dance is correct his partner: *"You're doing it wrong. You have to do it this way."* Yikes!

The message received by most women is that he's doing this to exert absolute control at the beginning of the dance. It's his way of establishing dominance, saying in effect, "This is *not* a conversation and you don't have a voice when dancing with me, so shut up and do as you're told."

To be fair, this may not be his actual intent. Maybe his teacher gave him the misguided impression that he should correct his partners if they dance differently from the only way he knows. But regardless of his intent, a correcting attitude is disrespectful, so men, be forewarned that if you adopt this attitude, she may reasonably not want to dance with you.

This correcting attitude is usually either: (a) antisocially pedantic (see p. 182), or (b) it demonstrates his inexperience, showing her that he only knows one way to dance, or only one style, or one kind of dance hold. If he thinks, "Oh, I *know* other ways, but they're all wrong," then he's the first version, antisocially pedantic.

A one-way-only attitude is also unrealistic and untrue. Dancers come in different shapes, sizes, and experience levels. Each of our partners may have had different teachers. Or maybe they just picked up dancing on the fly, by diving in and seeing what works. *Different doesn't mean wrong.* When someone has a different style from your own, try to find ways to make dancing functional, friendly, fun, and *social.*

Women aren't exempt from this consideration. When a woman exhibits a correcting attitude, it's just as bad as when a man does it.

*Exceptions:* Correcting is okay, even beneficial, when it's to let your partner know if they're hurting you, "driving dangerously" on the dance floor, or if your partner actually asks you for advice or feedback. Some dancers do request feedback and help from their partners, so if your partner asks for feedback, then yes, it's fine, and even appreciated.

## 3) Guys who try to pick up women on the dance floor.

It's smart to assume that women come to a dance to *dance*, not to find a date. If there's an exception, she'll find a way to let you know, but the default assumption should be that she came to have fun dancing.

**Either way, if she says no to a dance, then no means no. Period. Don't pester her.**

*Note:* Some scenes may be exceptions to the pick-up rule. Some salseros have reported that their salsa club is essentially a pick-up club, and that everyone going there knows this. OK, if that's the understanding at a dance, fine. In any case, the inviolable part of this section is: if she says no, respect her wishes and don't bother her.

## 4) Guys who only want to dance with the cutest women.

And middle-aged men who only want to dance with the youngest women.

OK, everyone agrees that's sketchy. But some women as well as men have the attitude that, "I'll only dance with the cool guys." That's just as sketchy as the male version.

With either gender, that's an attitude from high school, the cruel world where it seems the only attribute that matters is how cute or cool someone is. Most of us mature out of that mindset, and realize that someone can be fun to dance with no matter what they look like, and regardless of their age.

Ever since the 19th century, generosity of spirit included asking overlooked people for a dance. One old dance manual encouraged the gentlemen to "especially seek out the ladies who appear to be acting as adornment to the drapery," a quaint way of describing wallflowers.

## Who *Isn't* a Sketchy Guy?

A man or woman with "emerging social skills" isn't necessarily sketchy. Everyone has to learn somewhere. If you don't know how to respond to someone's social awkwardness, err on the side of patience and encouragement. Smile. They may appreciate your kindness more than you realize!

In addition, some undergraduate students call a grad student sketchy simply because he's older. No, being a different age doesn't make someone sketchy, especially if he's a good dancer and an attentive, respectful partner.

## The Bottom Line

In an age of increasing divisiveness, we should try to be more tolerant and accepting of people's differences. But roughness, criticism, disrespect, discrimination, and predatory behavior are sketchy, and inappropriate at a social dance.

"Kindness is more important than wisdom, and
the recognition of this is the beginning of wisdom."
— Theodore Isaac Rubin, psychiatrist

# Dance for Your Partner

We've said it so many times in this book that it's worth clarifying what we mean by this.

## Altruism and Selfishness

At first glance, it may seem that by saying "dance for your partner," we are asking you to dance *altruistically*. And in some sense, this is correct: in the sense that altruistically means "for your partner's benefit."

But this word is often taken to mean more than this. In the world today, we usually label our interactions in one of two ways: *altruistic* or *selfish*, seen as polar opposites. The implication of this polarity is that many people automatically interpret the phrase "dance altruistically" to mean: "dance for your partner's benefit *at the expense of your own*."

In this sense, we *don't* mean to say dance altruistically, but rather something much more subtle, and important.

What we actually mean when we say "dance for your partner" is that **it is in your benefit to dance for your partner's benefit.**

## Synergy

The confusion arises because social dancing is unique in that it possesses a particularly high degree of *synergy*.

Synergy is a term—proposed by Ruth Benedict and developed by Abraham Maslow—used to describe societies and institutions that are set up so as to transcend the polarity between selfishness and unselfishness, between self-interest and altruism.

**In cases of high synergy, two people have arranged their relationship in such a fashion that one person's advantage causes the other person's advantage, rather than one person's advantage causing the other's disadvantage.**

Anyone who has waltzed will immediately recognize this, because waltzing is essentially synonymous with synergy. We cannot imagine a better example of synergy, nor a better description of the best waltzing. With such a close embrace, and interwoven feet, the advantages of the partners are inextricably aligned.

When you dance for your partner's benefit, you're also dancing for your own.

## Self-Interest Re-Imagined

To put this another way, nineteenth century orator Robert Green Ingersoll wrote that **"the lowest form of selfishness is when one is willing to be happy, or wishes to be happy, at** the expense or the misery of another. The highest form of selfishness is when a man becomes so noble that he finds his happiness in making others so."

Note that in comparing "highest" to "lowest" here, Ingersoll was not making a moral judgment, but rather observing that the highest form of selfishness is actually much more fulfilling than the lowest. Summarizing this succinctly, he wrote simply that "the way to be happy is to make others so."

The Dalai Lama has recently revived Ingersoll's insight, speaking of *wise selfishness* and *foolish selfishness*: "**Being foolish selfish means pursuing our own interests in a narrow, shortsighted way. Being wise selfish means taking a broader view and recognizing that our own long-term individual interest lies in the welfare of everyone.**" In other words, he writes, "If you want others to be happy, practice compassion. If you want to be happy, practice compassion."

This lesson, of the utmost importance today, is easily learned and reinforced on the social dance floor.

## Dancing *With* Your Partner

When two partners take this approach, something truly magical happens.

When both partners dance for the other, the idea of *for the other* stops making any sense. These partners in synergy begin to dance *with* each other.

But even this language understates the transformation that occurs when two partners are truly dancing with each other. The very idea of *each other* stops making any sense, as the partners meld together, becoming something new, dancing together as one.

# Win-Win Practice

## by Daniel Lopez
### an essay from Social Dance 2

I took Social Dance I on the recommendation from an RA, and immediately loved being introduced to such an enormous, amazing community. That appeal has been one reason why I have returned again and again, and tried to be as involved as I can with social dance, because it's a truly fantastic feeling to see familiar faces everywhere I go.

The true appeal of social dance, though, has been, and still is, that it gives me the opportunity to **practice**. I genuinely relish the act of striving for mastery, of learning dances and steps and partnering, and then working long and hard to perfect them.

I love how practicing dance has such a monumentally greater reward than any practicing I have ever previously done, although the violin comes close. With tennis, and with my academic competing, the better I became, the more assuredly it became that my opponents would experience a horrible defeat. This was great for me, but, well, not so good for them.

However, with dance, like with the violin, **the better I became, not only did I have a better time, but my partner also had a better time!** And so now not only did I practice for myself, but also for the hundreds of potential partners out there who might one day have to endure my leading.

Tennis practice, and studying for competitions, rewarded me with medals. But **social dance practice rewards me with smiles**, and I've come to realize that I treasure those the most.

> "I believe that we learn by practice. Whether it means to learn to dance by practicing dancing, or to learn to live by practicing living, the principles are the same. In each, it is the performance of a dedicated, precise set of acts, physical or intellectual, from which come shape of achievement, the sense of one's being, the satisfaction of spirit. One becomes in some area an athlete of God. Practice means to perform over and over again, in the face of all obstacles, some act of vision, of faith, of desire. Practice is a means of inviting the perfection desired."
> — Martha Graham, dancer

# Giving

"In general manners, both ladies and gentlemen
should act as though the other person's happiness
was of as much importance as their own."
— Professor Maas, American dance master, 1871

Throughout this book, we have endorsed the sentiment that the key to dancing well is dancing for your partner.

But the wisdom of this perspective isn't limited to dancing, as Professor Maas was clearly aware. In fact, as we saw in the previous chapter, many believe that this other-regarding approach is not only the key to dancing well, but also the key to a happy, healthy life.

Psychologists have recently confirmed this wisdom, finding that **an other-regarding approach, in which our primary aim is to improve the lives of others, is in fact a superior path to happiness compared to direct attempts to make ourselves happy.**

For example, studies have found that spending money on others is significantly more satisfying than spending money on ourselves.

This fact has been observed in countries as diverse as the United States and Uganda, and throughout the lifespan: even two-year olds, notorious for having trouble sharing, are happier giving away one of their Teddy Grahams than they are to receive several Teddy Grahams in the first place.

In a wide array of studies, psychologists have consistently observed that in general, acting kindly for the benefit of others is a reliable way to feel better ourselves.

**Neuroscientists have recently shed light on the mechanisms behind this, finding that giving benefits to others activates the same reward circuits in our brain as receiving those same benefits ourselves.** In addition, they have found that if we choose *not* to give when we have the opportunity, we feel bad about it and physically stress out, as our cortisol levels rise significantly.

The giving approach also paves the way for a happier, healthier life in the long term.

Teenagers who are more "generative" in high school, demonstrating great givingness, prosocial competence, and social perspective, are found to be **psychologically happier and physically healthier** than less generative peers, when contacted again fifty years later.

At the other end of the lifespan, older adults who are more giving, volunteering for one or more social benefit organizations, actually **live significantly longer** than their peers who do not volunteer.

Interestingly, scientists have also discovered that *giving* material and emotional support to one's spouse, relatives, friends, and neighbors has a much larger health benefit than *receiving* such support, demonstrating that **it really is "more blessed to give than to receive."**

Even just *observing* the act of giving has measurable personal and social benefits. When we witness acts of kindness, we feel an emotion called **elevation**. We feel moved, uplifted, optimistic about humanity, and often report a physical sensation of heart-warming.

Having experienced elevation, we feel inspired to emulate the acts of kindness that we have witnessed, to be a better person, and to do good for others.

And in practice, feeling elevation actually does make us significantly more likely to give to others, both in the moment, and months down the road. It can even lead us to act charitably towards groups we might previously have felt uncharitable toward.

**In witnessing the best that humanity can offer, we are inspired to offer the best that we can too.**

Ask some of the newcomers, or wallflowers, to dance. Dance for the ultimate enjoyment of your partners, adapting to their styles and leading their favorite moves. Help your partners learn something new.

These are just a few of the many ways in which waltzing provides us the opportunity to give. By offering us these chances to give, and opportunities to witness giving, the social dance floor is a powerful catalyst for making the world a better place, one act of giving at a time.

# Recommended Reading on Giving

- *Why Good Things Happen to Good People: How to Live a Longer, Healthier, Happier Life by the Simple Act of Giving* (2007) by Stephen G. Post and Jill Neimark

- *The Power of Kindness: The Unexpected Benefits of Leading a Compassionate Life* (2006) by Piero Ferrucci

- *The Healing Power of Doing Good: The Health and Spiritual Benefits of Helping Others* (1991) by Allan Luks and Peggy Payne

- *How Can I Help?: Stories and Reflections on Service* (1985) by Ram Dass and Paul Gorman

- *Everyone Helps, Everyone Wins: How Absolutely Anyone Can Pitch In, Help Out, Give Back, and Make the World a Better Place* (2010) by David T. Levinson

- *29 Gifts: How a Month of Giving Can Change Your Life* (2009) by Cami Walker

- *The Power of Half: One Family's Decision to Stop Taking and Start Giving Back* (2010) by Kevin Salwen and Hannah Salwen

- *The Life You Can Save: Acting Now to End World Poverty* (2009) by Peter Singer

# Redowa, Mazurka, and More

## (Advanced Waltz and Polka Variations)

These advanced forms of waltzing are best learned in class. The descriptions provided here serve as brief reminders of the steps you may have learned.

Unless otherwise specified, the Lead always begins these steps facing out of the hall, away from the center, in waltz position, hands pointed along LOD, as in rotary waltz.

## Leap Waltz

### (Hop Waltz, Jeté Waltz, Sauteuse Waltz)

As the name suggests, this is simply a rotary waltz with a leap rather than a step on counts 1 and 4. You *land*, downward, on counts 1 and 4, *finishing* the leap on these counts, not airborne. Keep all of the other counts the same (i.e., one leap and two smooth steps, rather than three leaps). The feet touch the floor in the same places at the same times, you simply leap slightly before counts 1 and 4, landing on those counts.

*Music:* "Flora's Secret" by Enya gives a good sense of the feeling.

*In 4/4 Time:* Simply do a Leap Waltz in polka time (1-and-2, quick-quick-slow).

## Redowa

### (Turning Pas de Basque)

An undulating dance that flies around the dance floor, the Redowa is a perennial favorite.

1: The Lead leaps back 90° clockwise around the Follow with his left foot across LOD while she leaps with her right foot between his feet. This is a very short step, almost in place, not a traveling leap. At the end of count 1, he is facing straight back against LOD, and she is facing straight forward along LOD.

2: The Lead extends his right foot straight back along LOD as far as it can reach, as the Follow extends her left foot straight forward along LOD as far as it can reach, taking weight on these feet. They keep their extended legs perfectly straight, so that the extended legs are parallel, hers below his, reaching straight back along LOD. Sink lower on this step, in order to reach farther.

3: The Lead closes his left foot to his right with weight, turning 90° clockwise to face the center of the hall, as the Follow closes her right foot to her left with weight, turning 90° clockwise to face out of the hall. *Note:* The closing foot can optionally cut under the foot it is closing to, taking its place, rather than closing up next to it.

4-5-6: The Lead does exactly what the Follow did, and vice-versa.

*Tips for Dancing the Redowa:*

- Reach *straight back/forward* along LOD on counts 2 and 5. Think "back-back-turn, forward-forward-turn," or simply "straight-straight-turn." *Note:* A side step (second position) on counts 2 and 5 isn't "wrong." In fact, one dance manual describes Redowa that way. But the majority of manuals describe it as straight back/forward (fourth position), and we find it to be even more satisfying this way.

- On a crowded dance floor, it is safer if you bring your foot in and extend it straight backward on count 2 or 5, rather than sweeping it ("ronde de jambe" style) around to the side as you bring it behind you.

- The main traveling action of the Redowa happens on counts 2 and 5. Think "short-long-short." (Which coincidentally is "R" in Morse code, for Redowa.)

- The Redowa oscillates up and down, sinking lower on count 2 to allow the extended legs to reach even farther. (Hypotenuses being equal, lower height means longer base.) Think "up-down-up."

- Although the Redowa oscillates up and down, it doesn't lean back and forth. The upper bodies are perpendicular to the floor the whole time. To correct for the tendency to lean forward when reaching the leg back, and to lean back when reaching the leg forward, lean slightly back when reaching the leg back, and vice versa.

- To help the partner reaching forward (the Follow on count 2 and the Lead on count 5), the partner reaching back can help "shovel their partner under" their back leg, which 1) gives their partner confidence to reach forward, and 2) physically helps them to do so.

- The backing partner pulls the forward-facing partner along LOD, and the forward-facing partner pushes the backing partner along LOD. Think "pull-pull-turn, push-push-turn."

- *The Redowa flies across the dance floor.* Yes, that in itself is a hint. Travel more on counts 2 and 5, and many of these tips will take care of themselves.

*Music:* "Nara" by E.S. Posthumus is a classic song for Redowa, which alternates between smooth rotary waltz and undulating Redowa.

*In 4/4 Time:* Simply do a Redowa in polka time (1-and-2, quick-quick-slow).

# The Newport
## (and Waltz Galop)

More rarely seen than the Redowa, the Newport is just as much fun to dance. When it works, it almost feels like flying.

1: The Lead leaps back 90° clockwise around the Follow with his left foot while she leaps with her right foot forward between his feet, as in the Leap Waltz.

"&": The Lead steps side right along LOD, as the Follow steps side left along LOD.

2: The Lead closes left to right with weight, as the Follow closes right to left with weight.

"&": Repeat first count "&."

3: Repeat count 2.

4 &5 &6: The Lead does exactly what the Follow did, and vice-versa.

*Note:* All of the steps feel like little leaps, light and airy, up on the balls of the feet.

All together, it goes: "back, side-close, side-close / front, side-close, side-close," turning 360° in six counts.

*Note on Timing:* The "&" used to describe this timing is different from the "and" used to describe polka time. It's like a dotted ("swung") triple, as in lindy hop, except that in this case it's a dotted quintuple (1 &2 &3).

*Variations:* **The Three-Quarters Newport**: Do the Newport for counts 1 through 9 (three half turns), then simply waltz for counts 10-11-12. It adds a nice bit of variation to the sensation.

*Music:* "Leaf on Leaf" by Akeboshi has a lovely beat for the Newport.

*In 4/4 Time:* The Newport can be adapted to 4/4 time in one of two ways: take out a side-close (i.e., "back, side-close" in two counts), in which case it is a **Waltz Galop**, or add a side-close (i.e., "back, side-close, side-close, side-close" in four counts), in which case it is a **Ripple Galop**.

*The next footwork variations are often collectively characterized as Mazurka Waltzes. They are especially nice for songs in which every beat is highly accented, like Owl City's "Plant Life."*

# Polka Redowa

*Note:* This is not to be confused with the "Redowa in Polka Time" described above.

This Polka Redowa step is foundational for the steps that follow.

1: The Lead slides his left foot along LOD while the Follow slides her right foot along LOD.

2: The Lead undercuts his left foot with his right foot, taking weight on his right foot where his left foot used to be. The Follow undercuts her right foot with her left, taking weight on her left foot.

3: The Lead leaps clockwise around the Follow across LOD, turning 180° clockwise as he does so. The Follow leaps forward along LOD, turning 180° clockwise as she does so.

4-5-6: The Lead does exactly what the Follow did, and vice-versa. In other words, they repeat it with the opposite foot, dancing it over the elbows.

Easily verbalized and remembered as "slide-cut-leap."

*Notes:* 1) Polka Redowa can be danced with all six steps in sequence, as a dance by itself, or it can be split in halves (half Polka Redowa, half something else), as in the steps below. 2) The

Polka Redowa can also be danced straight forward without rotating. In this case, count 3 is a leap forward.

## Mazurka Step

Though it is usually combined with something else (like the Polka Redowa, as in the case of the Polka Mazurka below), the basic Mazurka step is also foundational.

1: The Lead slides his left foot along LOD while the Follow slides her right foot along LOD.

2: The Lead undercuts his left foot with his right foot, taking weight on his right foot where his left foot used to be. The Follow undercuts her right foot with her left, taking weight on her left foot.

3: The Lead lifts his left foot up, bending his knee to point it along LOD, taking a small hop on his right foot. The Follow lifts her left foot, knee bent, taking a small hop on her right.

This is all performed straight along LOD, with no turning (hence why it is usually combined with something).

Easily verbalized and remembered as "slide-cut-lift."

*Note:* This can also be done with the opposite feet (his right, her left), as in the steps below.

*Historical Note:* There were originally several entirely different steps called "Mazurka Step," but over time this one grew to be so prevalent that it became *the* Mazurka Step.

## Polka Mazurka

A simple combination of the Mazurka Step and the Polka Redowa.

1-2-3: Mazurka Step ("slide-cut-lift"), not turning.

4-5-6: Polka Redowa ("slide-cut-leap"), turning 180° clockwise.

Repeat it all with the opposite foot, dancing it over the elbows.

Easily verbalized and remembered as "slide-cut-lift, slide-cut-leap."

## La Koska

A simple combination of three Mazurka steps and one Polka Redowa, i.e., "slide-cut-lift x 3, slide-cut-leap," turning 180° at the end of 12 counts.

Repeat it all with the opposite foot, dancing it over the elbows.

# La Carlowitzka (La Gitana)

A somewhat trickier combination of gliding, rotating hops with the Polka Mazurka.

1: The Lead slides his left foot along LOD while the Follow slides her right foot along LOD.

2: The Lead hops on his left foot while the Follow hops on her right. (Each of these and the following hops glides forward.)

3: The Lead hops on his left foot while the Follow hops on her right, bringing the rear feet (his right, her left) in towards the leading ankle without taking weight on it.

Over the course of the preceding three counts, the couple turns 180° clockwise.

4-5-6: The Lead does exactly what the Follow did, and vice-versa, turning another 180° clockwise, so that the leading hands are pointed long LOD again.

7-8-9-10-11-12: Polka Mazurka, turning 180° clockwise at the end of 6 counts.

Repeat it all with the opposite foot.

Verbalized and remembered as "slide-hop-hop, slide-hop-hop, slide-cut-lift, slide-cut-leap."

*The following variations are based on heel clicks.*

To perform a heel click, have one foot lifted, then close the other foot toward it in mid-air. The lifted heel is the target for the clicking heel.

# Hungroise
## (Heel Clicks)

1: The Lead clicks his right heel to his left heel along LOD while the Follow clicks her left heel to her right heel along LOD.

2: The Lead steps side left along LOD while the Follow steps side right along LOD.

3: The Lead closes his right foot to his left with weight while the Follow closes her left foot to her right with weight.

4-5-6: Repeat counts 1, 2, 3.

7-8-9-10-11-12: Redowa around all the way.

Easily verbalized and remembered as "click-step-close, click-step-close, re-do-wa, re-do-wa."

*Variations:* If you perform an odd number of heel clicks (each heel click being a three count "click-step-close") in concert with an odd number of half Redowas (re-do-wa), you can repeat the sequence with the opposite foot. For example, "click-step-close, re-do-wa, click-step-close, re-do-wa" or three heel clicks and one half Redowa.

*In 4/4 Time:* Do it in polka time (1-and-2, quick-quick-slow).

## Viennese Step
### (and Hops-Walzer)

This term is sometimes confusing, because it sounds similar to the term *Viennese waltz*, but looks nothing like the Viennese waltz. It was called the "Wiener Walz" in many early (1820s and 1830s) German dance manuals.

*The Lead begins facing forward along LOD, with the Follow facing back along LOD.*

Note that the first half of the step is in canter timing (changes on counts 1 and 3 only).

1: The Lead leaps forward on his right foot while the Follow leaps back on her left foot.

3: The Lead clicks his right heel to his left heel sideways along LOD. The Follow clicks her left heel to her right heel sideways along LOD. *Note*: Of course, after the heel click, the clicking heel returns to the ground. In terms of weight changes, a heel click is like a hop on the clicking foot, although you hop slightly early, to click exactly on the count.

4-5-6: The Lead steps back across LOD with his left on count 4, and the Follow steps forward along LOD with her right, to dance the first three counts of a rotary waltz, turning 180° clockwise to get into position for the next count 1.

*Variations:* Substitute Redowa for rotary waltz on the second half to do an Air Redowa.

*In 4/4 Time:* The Viennese Step is actually easier in 4/4 time, in which case it was called the **Hops-Walzer** or **Ecossaise Walzer**. Leap-click on 1-2, then waltz (or Redowa) around in polka time on 1-and-2.

## Reverse It

For an extra challenge, all of these variations can be reversed, with counterclockwise rather than clockwise rotation. We'll leave you the satisfaction of working out how.

## Cautionary Note

Each of these advanced variations is fun, but none of them are nearly as fun than really dancing with your partner.

If your partner is smiling broadly as you try these, then by all means, go right ahead. But be especially attentive to your partner's reactions, and make sure you're dancing for their comfort and success. "Dance for Your Partner" (p. 141) at "Il Tempo Giusto" (p. 51), even if that means that all you do is waltz or polka, simply and elegantly turning around the room.

# Dancing in the Rain

Whether on the dance floor, or dancing through life, things don't always go as we'd hoped. Perchance we are dancing with a partner who's off the beat, or one who doesn't understand that a waltz turns all the way. Perhaps our partner is perfect, but the dance floor isn't—too sticky, too slippery, or just too crowded for our taste. Maybe the music is less than ideal—too slow, too fast, or we don't like that tune. We will let you fill in your own examples from life.

In cases like this, we have a choice: we can lament these realities and make ourselves miserable, or we can make the most of them and dance, having as much fun as we possibly can. We can try to deny the reality before us, or we can adopt an attitude of radical acceptance, not only living with, but loving our fate.

Let's take a look at how this choice can play out.

Imagine that you are walking two miles home from the library, when all of a sudden it begins to rain—not just to drizzle, but to really pour. You have another mile to walk in the torrent. How will you respond to this "bad" situation?

Let's compare two possible responses.

One response is to curse your luck, and dramatically exclaim how terrible the rain is. "I can't believe it has to rain now! Of course I forgot my umbrella! This is by far the worst day of my life!" You slog home, begrudging every step, while cursing your mistake the whole time in your head, and wishing you were warm in bed. When you get home, you're totally soaked, emotionally drained, and hating life. You crash on the couch, turn on the TV, and blow off everything you wanted to do.

This response, while common, is not inevitable. Let's explore another possibility.

Caught unaware, you have the same first instinct: that this is not an ideal situation. **But, realizing that rain is your reality for a while, and *will be so no matter what you do*, you accept the outcome, and choose to enjoy it.**

You take a deep breath and look up at the sky, feeling the rain caress your face. You pull a Gene Kelly, singing and dancing. Seeing the rivulets of rain on a leaf, you remember that your region is in a drought. "The rain is the best thing that could happen!" you exclaim. You stick out your tongue and taste the cold, sweet drops. You skip home and splash in all the puddles like a kid. When you get to your door, you set down your things, but you are still having a grand time. As you could never be wetter than you are right now, you perform another epic dance in the downpour before thanking the clouds and heading inside. Once inside, you draw yourself a bath, thankful for the reservoir being filled by the rain. You read one of the books that you got from the library, learning all manner of enlightening ideas. After a long soak, you finally get dry, still totally jazzed from your day. You finish your work and even get ahead, before settling into a deep sleep in bed.

In both cases, you get equally wet, but in one case you feel drained, and in the other you feel energized. In the first, the rain ruins your day. In the second, the rain actually improves it.

How can this be?

**The only difference is your chosen response. By accepting your circumstances, you turn your day around.**

Nietzsche wrote of this radical acceptance as *amor fati*, or "**love of fate**."

In *Ecce Homo,* he writes, "My formula for greatness in a human being is *amor fati*: that one wants nothing to be different, not forward, not backward, not in all eternity. Not merely bear what is necessary, … but *love* it."

In *The Art and Practice of Loving*, Frank Andrews asks us to imagine living our lives this way:

> Imagine living the same life you do now, only loving deeply and continually—delighting in the warmth of your morning shower, relishing the smell of breakfast cooking, celebrating with the birds on your way to work, enjoying driving the roadways, feeling bonds of cooperation with your co-workers, cherishing your family members, and deeply appreciating whatever and whoever is at hand. Visualize going through the activities of a typical day while deeply caring about what you are doing, a day in which sensitivity, affection, warmth, and wonder fill the moments."

This is a life we can live if we choose to.

# Creativity

It's fun to learn and dance the classic variations. But it's also fun to create your own.

Here are some tips on being creative and innovating your own social waltz moves. Or anything else you might enjoy creating.

And you almost certainly will enjoy creating. Neuroscientist Kelly Lambert has found that creative activities, particularly those involving movement, activate a special "effort-driven rewards circuit" in our brain, releasing a cocktail of feel-good chemicals like endorphins.

## The Purge Phase

Before attempting to come up with something new, it's useful to **purge** your existing ideas, cross them off your mental checklist and clear your mind. Put your initial hunches out on the table. Try them. Sometimes your first intuitive hunches are ultimately the best ones, after considering dozens more.

## Mix It Up

As Matt Ridley provocatively puts it, **innovation occurs when ideas have sex.**

Thus, the easiest way to create new dance moves is often by borrowing and combining moves from different dances, like putting a pretzel from swing into waltz. Play with a collision of various elements, perhaps far-ranging, from even the least likely sources. See what you can create by borrowing and adapting.

Have you ever been impressed with someone's combination of two unlikely elements in a creative way? A key part of the creative process is breaking away from accustomed patterns of thinking. Ideally, we generate as many alternative approaches as we can, to bring about repatterning, but the hard part is coming up with the unexpected mind-jogs.

Stanford student Lucas Garron developed the Random Dance Move Generator to help stimulate creative dance innovating. It tosses out descriptive enchainments of possible dance moves, then our optimizing skills spot the keywords that seem to be promising and develop them into a new dance figure. For the link to this page, and a YouTube video that shows how to use it, visit: waltzingbook.com/create

## Relax

While trying to come up with these creative combinations, it's essential to maintain a **relaxed** and **open** state of mind.

Studies of creativity have shown that the ideation phase of the creative process (a right brain activity) is actually thwarted by intense concentration (a left brain activity). Instead, creativity requires **diffuse and flexible attention** and **lateral thinking**, which both function best in a state of relaxation.

So take a deep breath. Exhale. Quiet yourself for a moment while relaxing your shoulders, neck, jaw, and hands. Maintain a relaxed attitude, both physically and mentally.

In these periods of relaxation, your "Aha!" moment will be more likely.

# Incubation

Work on it for a while, then drop it. **Let it incubate**. Come back to it again later.

Often the best "Aha!" moments occur after you've stopped concentrating on the problem.

# Editing

An "Aha!" is just the beginning, of course. The real task of creativity is **editing**: **testing** and **refining** your initial ideas by building and playing with various **prototypes**.

In the Marshmallow Challenge—a competition to build the tallest tower which can support a marshmallow on top using only 20 lengths of spaghetti, one yard of masking tape, one yard of string, and eighteen minutes—kindergarteners consistently outperform adults.

This is because while the adults spend the entire time coming up with one "good" idea **in theory**, only to find out that their idea is flawed **in practice**, the kindergarteners spend the whole time building and **experimenting**, trying different things and actually finding out what works and doesn't.

# Beginner's Mind

The kindergarteners in the Marshmallow Challenge also have the advantage of **beginner's mind**, being relatively **unconstrained by assumptions**, which often hinder the creative potential of adults, who think they know better and don't give different ideas a chance.

> "Every child is an artist, the problem is staying an artist when you grow up."
> — Pablo Picasso, painter

Fortunately, beginner's mind is a perspective we can cultivate. In one study, researchers found that simply by asking participants to imagine that they were seven years old, they could put the participants in a childlike mindset, and make them significantly more creative than usual. **Play the role of a kindergartener**, setting aside your adult assumptions.

In addition, **seek out new and diverse experiences**. Not only will this make you smarter (p. 183), but having diverse experiences will help break down your assumptions. Studies have shown that students who have lived abroad tend to be more creative, as are people who integrate multiple social identities, and those who have many acquaintances.

# Teamwork

Diverse perspectives are also an advantage of **teamwork**, which waltzing couples naturally benefit from. The benefits of working in a team are dramatic: in academia, research papers authored by a team are more than twice as likely to be cited than papers with a single author, and more than four times as likely to be cited 100 times.

The most creative teams, researchers have found, are those with **intermediate intimacy**, with close friends and new faces for everyone in the group. Which is a pretty good description of a social dance party.

Within a team, **constructive criticism** is key: brainstorming sessions in which criticism is withheld actually generate *fewer* ideas than if the group members work alone, but sessions with group brainstorming *and constructive criticism* are the most effective. Giving and receiving feedback gets us to **look beyond our own ideas** and think about the new ideas that our teammates are proposing, opening us up to new creative perspectives.

# What's Creative?

Don't worry about the possibility that someone else has already thought of an idea that just occurred to you. Creativity is coming up with something new to you, not something that has never been thought of by anyone in the world.

# How to Create Waltz Variations

The innovation process is similar to sculpting in damp clay.

First, just **rough out the concept** that you want to try. Walk through any version of what you have in mind. Then you can see where it flows and where it jams. And you can see what is comfortable for your partner or not.

Then, **fine-tune your first draft**, like finessing your clay sculpture.

Leads, **be especially gentle** at this stage. Don't force your partner into anything that might be painful, or throw the Follow off balance. And don't make her rotate faster than is possible.

**Ask your partner for feedback** at this first stage. Ask where it could be better.

Here's the simplest three step approach to creating a waltz variation: **Break out of the frame, maintain waltz phrasing,** and **smoothly return to the basic step.**

## 1) Break out of the frame.

The basic waltzes continually rotate in closed waltz position as the couple travels around the room. It's like orbiting twin planets traveling around a sun. Breaking out of the frame (the closed waltz position) means varying that basic dynamic.

- You can both travel forward, not rotating.
- The Follow can travel under the Lead's raised arm, as in swing and salsa.
- The Lead can travel under his own raised arm.
- Both dancers can travel with fancier steps, like Grapevines.
- You can vary the closed Waltz Position with other dance positions, e.g.,
  Open or Closed Promenade Positions
  Shadow (Sweetheart) Positions
  Crossed-Hand Holds
  Follow's and Lead's Cradle Positions
  Skater's Positions

Often, you'll break out of the frame on the first half of the waltz (1-2-3), but you can also break out of the frame on the second half (4-5-6).

## 2) Fit the variation into pairs of 3-count waltz phrases.

A variation will usually be danced to 2, 4, or 8 bars the music, taking 6, 12, or 24 steps.

## 3) Return to the basic step.

An elegantly designed waltz variation will end up in the starting position of the basic step, with your first foot free.

## Other Considerations

The variation should ideally function in freestyle partnering, as opposed to a choreographed pattern that both dancers need to know and practice ahead of time. However, a flashy pattern that requires both dancers to learn and practice it may occasionally be a worthy exception.

The variations should work smoothly and easily for the Follow. Maintain the Follow's momentum (including rotational momentum). Where and how would she naturally step next? Let the Follow continue with her most natural footwork. If someone needs to make a foot-fudge, the Lead usually makes it.

If you introduce fancier steps, ideally continue the basic timing of one step per beat. And if at any time you choose to introduce a different timing, combining slow and quick steps, make that especially clear to your partner.

# Get to It!

Whether it's a new waltz move, or the next Google, we can't wait to see your creative results!

In the case of waltz moves, you can submit them to the Waltz Lab (www.waltzlab.com). Or just post it on YouTube with a clear title and we'll find it. (Something like "Name of Dance - Name of Variation.")

# Concise Compendium of Cross-Step Waltz Figures

These advanced variations of cross-step waltz are best learned in class.
The descriptions provided here serve as brief reminders of the steps you may have learned.
These are just a few of the classics. For hundreds of other variations, see the Waltz Lab (www.waltzlab.com).
A easy way to remember these is to think of the different ways they start (underlined categories below).

**In Place (or Blocking Traffic)**
Straight Basic
   or Slightly Turning Basic
Toss Across (Flip Flops)
Follower's Solo (Regular, A-Frame, or Waterfall)
   with Basic Footwork, Touches, Kicks, or Sweeps
Counter Crosses (Foot Fudge to Cross Opposite)
Hesitating Side Sways (Fred and Ginger Style)
Hesitating Cross-Lunge with Side Step Recovery
Hesitating Tango Dip (Cross, Side Step Dip on 2)
Molinete (Cross-Rock-Rock-Rock-Rock-Step, CCW)

**Basic Traveling (Moving LOD)**
Turning Basic
   or Waterfall (Lead Crosses Behind on 4)
Orbits (CW)
Traveling Toss Across (Alternating CW and CCW)
Zig Zag (Backing Along LOD)
   Pas Titubé (Zig Zag, Lead Crossing Behind)
Waltz Walk (Simple Promenade)
   with Outside Turn* on 4
   Double Outside Turn* on 2
   Splits (to Avoid Rocks in the Rapids)
Cross Swivels (Cross-Step x 3)

**He Goes, She Goes (He Dives Under)**
He Goes
   to Close Up (Lead's Underarm Turn)
   to Walk, Inside Turn* and Close Up
   to Walk, Pivaloop and Free Spin*
   to Walk, Pivaloop Around the World°
   to Make Stuff Up!***
Shoulder Slide and Close Up

**Grapevine (He Crosses Back)**
Three Step Grapevine to Outside Turn*
Six Step Grapevine
   to Double Outside Turn*
   to Grapevine Rueda
   with Inside Turn on 6, Tuck Turn* on 4
Waterfall Grapevine (Starts on 4 of Waterfall)
   to Inside Turn on 1 and Close on 4
   to Inside Turn on 1 and Tuck Turn* on 4

**Traveling Swing Out (Cross Body Lead)**
Traveling Swing Out and Close Up
Traveling Swing Out with Cross-Body Inside Turn
   to "He Goes, She Goes" Exit, usually Pivaloop*
   or Cross-Body Triple Turn and Close Up
Traveling Swing Out to Tuck Turn on Outside Lane*

**Inside Turns (Out the Back Door on 2)**
Inside Turn* to Grapevine Recovery
Double Inside Turn to Double Outside Turn

**Cradle (Inside Turn into Cradle on 2)**
Cradle In, Walk 6n, Outside Turn* on 4
Cradle In, Walk 3+6n, Double Turn* on 2
Chained Inside and Outside Turns°
   Magic Wand (One Handed Chained Turns)°
Cradle Wheel (Lead Backing)
Cradle Lunge on 4 (Up on 1, Outside Turn on 4)

**Pivots (Cross-Pivot-Pivot...)**
Single Pivot and Turn (Cross-Pivot-Pivot-Turn-2-3)* °
   Single Pivot Texas Tommy
Tripled Single Pivots (Cross-Pivot-Pivot-Step x 3)°
   Tripled Single Pivots with an Extra Pivot Turn*
   Reverse Tripled Single Pivots
Double Pivots (Cross Pivot Pivot Pivot Pivot Step)
Single Pivot Transitions to and from Rotary Waltz

**Shadow Position (or Many Other Names)**
He Goes, Outside Turn, and Swing Out Entrances
Crossed Hand Sweeps (with optional Outside Turns)
Skater's, Hammerlock, and Crossed Hand Positions
Mixmaster°
Windmill (or Follow's Turn, or Tandem Free Spins)°
Shadow Flip (Illusion Turn)°
Free Spin (or Turn or Face Loop) Out of Shadow on 4

**Reverse Cross-Step Waltz (CCW Rotation)**
Reverse Turning Basic (or Reverse Waterfall)
Dance it in Regular Waltz Position, or with
   Reversed Waltz Position and Reversed Figures!***
Easy, Zig Zag, or Cross-Body Turn Entrances and Exits

**Role Reversal (Follow Leading)**
Stop and Go to Shift the Beat (or Cross Cha-Cha)
Role Reversed Turning Basic (a variation by itself)
Simply Change Hands, Orbits, or Waltz Lab Entrances

**Jedi Waltzing (No Hands)**
Gypsy (Turning Basic with No Hands)
   or Almost Any Other Figure with No Hands!***

**Transitions to Other Waltzes**
Transitions to Box-Step, Rotary, Reverse Waltz, etc

**Cross-Step Troika (Tripling, for Three People)**
Triangle Trade and Other Figures (see Waltz Lab)

*\* Many additional variations are possible here by substituting turns, free spins, rollaways, and parallel spins.*
*More variations are also possible for all of these by changing hand hold: one hand, two hands, right-in-right, etc.*
*\*\*\* These are variations that open up whole new worlds of waltzing.*
*° These moves can be easily repeated, and the resulting repeated sequence feels like its own variation.*

# Notes for Interpreting the Concise Compendium

*A General Note:* Don't worry whether you know enough of these figures, or enough other figures. It's good that each person knows a different set of moves: it "pleasingly diversifies *le tout ensemble.*"

*In Place (or Blocking Traffic):* Do these in the middle of the room, or when you know there won't be anyone coming up behind you soon.

*Waltz Walk:* Firm up the frame and lead directly forward. This is good for getting through tight squeezes where there's not enough room to rotate through.

*He Goes:* He walks forward under the arch of the leading hands on count 1, to the outside lane. As described in more detail on p. 16, he looks and leads her forward, to avoid misdirecting her.

*Pivaloop:* Pivaloop is an outside turn for her from the inside lane to the outside lane, with her stepping across to the right of LOD with her left foot on count 1. The lead hands come straight down between them to start the outside turn, not into her, and early, so she knows to step across LOD on 1.

*Grapevine:* He crosses back on count 1 while she crosses forward, and they grapevine, parallel shoulders, cross-side-cross, with him crossing back then front while she crosses front then back. Usually three steps or six. Turns happen on count 4 after three grapes, or count 2 after six grapes.

*Traveling Swing Out (Cross Body Lead):* He leads her, with a body lead through his right arm, to cross in front of him to their left, turning her CCW. If there's a cross-body turn, it is on count 2.

*Inside Turns:* He leads an inside turn on count 2 by bringing the leading hands in between them.

*Cradle:* He does the same, catching her left hand with his right as she turns, into cradle position.

*Pivots:* He crosses, then steps boldly across LOD on count 2, squaring up the frame, firming up the frame, sinking slightly lower, and rotating more. Return to a more flexible frame after the pivots.

*Shadow Position:* She "puts her hands up" by her shoulders, and he takes her right hand in his right and her left in his left, standing to either side behind her, not directly behind her. The easiest way in is to turn her CCW as in traveling swing out, taking right in right, then left in left.

*Reverse Cross-Step Waltz:* Footwork is generally the same, just reverse the rotation. Easiest way in is simply to start it on any count 1, but you can also "back the lady" into it with Zig Zag. Reversed waltz position (his right and her left are the leading hands) allows reversed figures.

*Role Reversal:* The easiest way in is simply to change the arms one at a time, but Orbits is an especially nice entrance. Remember to ask if she wants to lead.

*Jedi Waltzing:* Simply do all the figures you know, or anything else that inspires you, *with no hands.* Hands hover near each other, to allow a visual lead, but there's no physical lead.

*Transitions:* There are many ways of transitioning between cross-step waltz and box step waltz, rotary waltz, reverse waltz, and many other waltzes. The easiest way is simply to walk it out. Waltz Walk from one waltz until you're on the feet and in position for another, and begin.

*Cross-Step Troika:* Three people dancing together, or one person (consensually) cutting in on two.

*Combinations:* As we've noted, it's nice to return to the Turning Basic after playing for a while, but while you're playing, it can also be fun to occasionally combine multiple variations, dancing them one right after the other. Some combinations feel like entirely new variations. See what you can invent.

# Role Reversal

Many people enjoy experiencing social dance from the perspective of the opposite role.

There are many reasons for its appeal, and many benefits.

**We want to learn how to dance in the opposite role for at least six reasons:**

## 1) We love dancing.

*All* of it, not just the half that our traditional role allows us.

Role reversal lets us complete the experience by learning the other half.

## 2) It improves our partnering.

We can understand our own traditional role more completely if we learn from firsthand experience what the other role is doing. We discover which partnering techniques function the best, from the other perspective, while also learning, the hard way, which annoying or painful habits to avoid.

Through role reversal, Leads become better at leading and Follows become better at following.

## 3) Role reversal boosts empathy.

Learning the complementary role goes a long way toward gaining an appreciation of our partner's skills, which we often take for granted.

Maybe he thinks, "She has it easy because I'm doing all the work." Then he tries following and discovers that it's challenging to be that responsive, while multitasking in several dimensions, so quickly. He appreciates her skill, experience, and sensitivity much more after trying it.

And vice-versa. "He gets to have all the freedom and all of the fun," becomes, "Wow, that's hard work! The Lead has to think so much and be aware of everyone around us." After trying role reversal, we no longer take our partner's skills for granted.

## 4) Cross-step waltz encourages role reversal.

The symmetry of cross-step waltz makes explorations into role reversal much easier and more successful than in any other social dance form.

Furthermore, cross-step waltz is a new dance, blossoming in the 21st century. New, liberated ideas about exchanging roles accompany a new dance form. Leading does not necessarily equal male, nor following female, at least not to an inquiring mind.

161

## 5) Trying a new learning experience makes us smarter.

Read "Dancing Makes You Smarter" (p. 183) for more on this.

## 6) It's fun!

Read "Play" (p. 23) for more on this.

# First Reactions

Many women think "I hate this" on their first attempt, only because they don't feel very good at it. Then the next day this changes to, "OK, this isn't so bad," followed by "This is fun!" After a few days, guys, you might not get the lead back. So women, if you think, "I hate this" at first, don't worry. You're right on track for an experience that you'll enjoy.

Men tend to warm up to following more quickly, with many finding out that they actually enjoy the Follow role more. Of course, leading is also an enjoyable role, and even after learning role reversal, most men go back to leading most of the time. But a significant number of men, including Richard and Nick, come away with the opinion that the Follow role is actually more enjoyable, because you can get out of your head and experience more.

# Tips for Role Reversal

Here are some tips regarding role reversal.

- New Follows (men) tend to forget to brace their right hand into the Lead's left hand. Follows, brace away from the Lead, no "jellyfish arms."

- New Follows (men) also tend to be bad at "back sensitivity" at first. Make the spot on your back where the Lead holds you as sensitive as possible. Notice where she's trying to "aim" you and respond by turning yourself in that direction, like power steering. Don't make her force you to turn.

- It's harder to hear the music in the Lead role. The simultaneous multitasking of following is primarily a right-hemisphere function, which is also the musical hemisphere. Leading, planning, remembering, and analyzing are primarily left-hemisphere functions, and as a result, the music isn't felt as keenly when dancing in the Lead role, regardless of whether the Lead is a man or woman. So Leads (women), try to pay extra attention to the music to compensate for this. Follows (men), you can help her by keeping the beat with your feet.

- Leading is not the opposite of following. It is a matter of the Lead taking care of one's partner, and the Follow living in the moment without outguessing. Women (Leads), instead of focusing on your own footwork, your new priority is taking care of him. Men (Follows), you're no longer thinking about what the next move will be, but rather, you're mindfully interpreting the signals you're given, in the moment.

- An Exercise: Men (Follows), close your eyes. Women (Leads), protect him from crashes. This exercise usually ramps up leading skills because hearing advice from a teacher isn't nearly as effective as the actual imperative of protecting one's partner. This is also a useful exercise for honing partnering skills in traditional roles.

- You can change roles back and forth while moving. According to some traditionalists, cross-step waltz starts on the "wrong foot" to begin with, so you don't have to stop and foot-fudge when you change roles, as you'd have to do in tango and swing role-reversal. Just keep stepping in time as you exchange roles in motion. Similarly, in rotary waltz and reverse waltz, some traditions start with the other half of the dance. In role reversing these dances, you're not off the music, you're simply shifting to the other timing.

- The Lead usually *gives* the lead over to the Follow. The Follow doesn't grab the lead. This is true for both female and male Follows. When he's following, role reversed, he lets her give the lead back to him.

- It's considerate for the Lead to *ask* her first if she would like to lead. Don't just spring it on her. You can do this verbally, or nonverbally. One way to do it nonverbally is to dance Orbits (p. 12). As they are rotating, he puts his left hand on top of her right shoulder, as he would if he were following, then offers his right hand to her. If she takes it, she's leading. If instead she puts her left hand back on top of his right shoulder and continues orbiting as usual, it's her way of saying "no thanks," because he's back in Lead position.

- Role reversal doesn't need to be women leading men. Men can partner men, and women can partner women, with several benefits:
  1) Women find it easier to lead successfully when dancing with someone who has more experience following (usually a woman), while men can follow more successfully with an experienced Lead (usually a man).
  2) The same-gender ice is broken. From now on, if there are two people standing out without a partner, you can dance with each other.

## A New Adventure

We'll conclude with a thought by tango instructor Nina Pesochinsky:

I believe we all agree that dancing as a Follow is a completely different experience than dancing as a Lead. To be stuck in a role because of one's gender can be confining and mentally oppressive. Therefore, I do not find reversal of the roles to be a game.

When I lead a dance, I do not pretend to be a man, or play this part the way a man would. Dance teaches people an art of conversation that could be translated into everyday life. One person speaks, another one listens. When it is the listener's turn to speak, does the conversation become a game? No.

My favorite dance partner always tells me a story when he creates a dance with me, for me. One day, when I feel creative and skilled enough, I hope to be able to do the same for him. It will be a new adventure.

164

# Eyes Closed

## by Cynthia Shih
(also known as Vienna Teng)
an essay from Social Dance 2

from a letter home, Thursday Oct 30.

My morning was absolutely wonderful.

Thursday mornings start with dance class, where we're currently learning cross-step waltz. I've got a friend named Dan, whom I met last year in Social Dance I. He's also a fellow pre-med, as we discovered later. Anyhow, he was my second partner this morning, and we were cruisin' about the room, gliding along like water, when the instructor said, "Follows, now close your eyes."

So I closed them. It was scary at first. Waltzing involves a lot of navigating, as you may know, especially in a roomful of people going in all random directions. I started worrying a lot about where I was stepping, how far I was turning.

But then I gave up worrying. The person leading me, I realized, knew what he was doing, and all I had to do was attune myself to the signals he was giving me. So I stopped *thinking*, and let a different kind of awareness take over—an awareness that's sharp and responsive. You become acutely aware of the signals you're given, because you rely on them for your every move. Yet somehow you're completely relaxed. *Natural*, if you will. *Effortless*. Not the kind of mindset I have very often.

*Elation*, let me tell you! There's a very pure joy that arises from this sort of thing; when you summon the courage to go blindly into a confusing world, letting yourself trust someone completely, even if it means you might get hurt... going into it with some unshakable faith that this person will guide you, and keep you safe. And when you let go, nothing goes wrong. You keep dancing—maybe flying. Grace and unity and direction, all preserved.

This is what love must be like, I said to myself. This is what religion must be like!

Poor Dan couldn't understand any of this for the life of him. "That was so cool!" I exclaimed when the music stopped, throwing my arms around him in a bear hug and laughing out of sheer happiness. "Wasn't that *amazing*, Dan?!"

He gave me one of those bewildered faces. "Sure, umm... it worked, I guess. I was just doing what I usually do..."

"No, but don't you understand, it *worked*—I was just following you and it *worked*."

"Well, yeah, aren't you normally following me?"

I struggled to explain. "But... but it's really different with my eyes closed. It's this whole different perspective. I guess you didn't have it 'cause your eyes were open..."

Finally he just grinned at me. "Well, I'm happy for you, Cynthia."

So Leads, if you're ever waltzing and your partner closes her eyes, it means she really trusts you. Take it as a compliment.

# Enhanced Waltzing
## Discovering the Lost Art of Receptivity

In learning to waltz, we discover a sublime pleasure that can be shared with a partner.

We also discover the first altered state of consciousness created by waltzing: dizziness. Then, as we continue our dance education, many of us proceed to discover a deeper altered state, which often carries with it a more profound benefit that extends beyond the realm of dancing. Through waltzing, we can discover the lost art of receptivity.

## Inputs

In our culture, we are more often encouraged to focus on what we *do*, and what we *produce*, not on how well we *perceive*. Our *outputs* are valued, not the quality of our *inputs*.

This is unfortunate, because it overlooks the fact that **we need clear, deep inputs in order to replenish our inner resources and motivations and produce high quality outputs.**

Intellectually and emotionally, we are what we eat. We are the sum total of our experiences, different from anyone else's, and we continually draw upon this unique experiential database for inspiration, motivation, and raw materials for creativity and for our enjoyment of life.

When a life experience reaches us deeply, we can think of it as planting a seed deep within our minds, which grows through resonance with similar experiences. These experiential seeds are valuable because they provide a reserve of positive images that future inputs can resonate with, giving our lives a greater sense of **meaning**.

When something feels meaningful to us, that sensation of meaning is often a resonance with these vivid seed experiences. Thus, the more seeds that are active within us, the more likely it is that our future experiences will interest or excite us, and the more likely it is that our lives will feel meaningful. On the other hand, if our reservoir of seeds dries up without being replenished, fewer experiences and ideas will feel meaningful to us. We may enter **burnout**, losing our passion for our profession, or worse, our passion for life.

## Filters

In order for these meaningful seeds to be created in the first place, we need to be open to the multidimensional stimuli of our lives, receiving them as totally and directly as possible.

But that's easier said than done these days. We live in an age of information overload, when everyone is clamoring for our attention, especially in the media and on the Internet. And since our earliest days as students, we've been told to pay attention to everything.

**When we focus our attention, we can only notice a single aspect of something**. The rest of the multidimensional deluge of stimuli is filtered out of our perception, so as not to overload our consciousness with thousands of "meaningless" bits of information. Our rational mind filters out that which is not immediately useful to us, and that which does not immediately fit into our current worldview.

This is our mind's survival tactic. But it's also problematic.

Many life experiences are too complex to survive this filtering. Consider music, for example.

At each moment of music there is a simultaneity of tonal quality, melody, harmonies, harmonics and other acoustic phenomena, chords, rhythmic effects, dynamic interplays, counterpoint, instrumental combinations, cultural flavorings, traditional emotive content, and so on, like a 50-track recording, where each track is a different conceptual layer.

Our analytical, rational mind, with its linear functioning, is not capable of receiving the multidimensional simultaneity of music. If it wants to pay attention to an element of music, to one of those 50 tracks, it must screen out the other 49 in order to clearly follow the one. Given enough time and repeated listenings, our rational mind might be able to re-assemble most of the original composition, one bit at a time. But it still wouldn't "get it." The total effect of those 50 tracks is far more than the compiled list of its components.

In *playing* music, we can create deeply moving music only if we are deeply *moved* by music —now, and continually, not just once upon a time when we were younger. And while single-track analytical listening is an important tool in the musician's toolbox, it often becomes a musician's automatic response to music. The analytical functions dissect and label, replacing the music with *words and ideas* about music. Instead of hearing the music openly and uncritically on its own terms, we now hear our own recognition patterns buzzing away. We describe the piece to ourselves as we hear it. Or outside the realm of music, we find our inner voice describing our experiences—often our best experiences—as if for someone else. This is the sound of our left brain overriding our right, blocking direct nonverbal experience.

The problem is that these analytical responses eventually become so automatic that we cannot avoid noticing these fragmented aspects, even if we try to relax and listen deeply. This is the process that burned-out musicians describe.

Whether or not we consider ourselves musicians, we can't afford to let our mind's survival tactics block off, or filter out, the experiences that we need to nourish and replenish us.

## The Lost Art of Receptivity

So we wonder: is this process irreversible? Is burnout inevitable?

As it turns out, the multitasking *right hemisphere* of the brain *can* simultaneously receive all 50 tracks of experience, so to speak, in their entirety. *If,* that is, it hasn't been closed off by the dominant, analytical left hemisphere.

The question is: are there methods that can help us recover or enhance our receptivity?

Some people have explored *self-hypnosis*—not the old mesmerism, but a lighter, more useful kind. The pendulum is still there, but you hold it yourself, and you sink into a quieter state of mind without the aid of a hypnotist. You close your eyes and become one with the motion. It's the motion, and the relaxation, that are most important.

Self-hypnosis doesn't work for everyone, but those who succeed report that they enter a more receptive place. There is somehow a greater "presence" to whatever happens during this light trance state, which usually lingers after the self-hypnosis session is over. And whatever one experiences in this state is recalled with more immediacy. It feels like the filters have been removed. Experiences are received more completely, and recalled more vividly.

Self-hypnosis is just one technique for opening ourselves up to direct experience. *Meditation* is another. But one of the pervasive myths of meditation is that once our verbal, analytical mind has quieted down, our receptive mind will automatically awaken. Instead, many meditators find that this deeper awareness does not automatically follow, and when the chatter quiets down, they simply get drowsy.

The Chinese art of *t'ai chi* discovered a wonderful solution to this: **adding kinesthetic motion to a contemplative state energizes the receptive part of our mind**. The kinesthetic and spatial cues of body movement activate the intuitive and simultaneous mind just as the rational mind quiets. Like self-hypnosis, *ta'i chi* combines relaxation and motion, except that *you* yourself are the center of motion. This is even more effective.

Likewise, in the 13th century, Sufi dervishes developed *whirling* as their way to reach this actively receptive state through motion.

Here is a quote from Margaret Mullen, chair of the Stanford Dance Division in the 1930s, which describes her experience with whirling, in a dance class with Hanya Holm.

> We begin gently, turning once, twice, a total of ten, then twenty turns. Finally we are asked to keep turning as long as possible. As I whirled on and on … I vaguely realized that I had moved into another world, an ecstatic reality.

> I was "conscious," in the normal sense, of nothing. In my enhanced state, I was conscious of everything. My dripping body had cooled, my fatigue was gone, there was no dizzy giddiness. I was erect, in balance, at ease. I had entered ecstasy. I could turn forever in my single spot.

> The drum beats accelerated, I spun faster and faster. Then they slowed, carefully, deliberately. My body obeyed. At last they stopped and I stood motionless to find myself the only one on the floor. Hanya came toward me, beater in hand, drum quiet. "Yah, Margaret. You know," she said. I did.

## Trance Waltzing

Becoming one with motion has long been recognized as a gateway to deeper states. And waltzing places you, and someone else, in the center of the most totally enveloping motion.

As Goethe wrote of waltzing, "Never have I moved so lightly. I was no longer a human being. To hold the most adorable creature in one's arms and fly around with her like the wind, so that everything around us fades away…"

While waltzing, as we move within this nonverbal, musical, kinesthetic state, the filters of analytical thinking fade away, our experience starts to become more vivid, as we become far more deeply receptive of … of what? The music? Yes, and also this fascinating creature that is right there in front us, in our arms, together at the center of a vast, spinning universe. Talk about altered states of consciousness!

## Tips for Trance Waltzing

Simply rotating around the room with someone doesn't automatically guarantee the opening of new experiential doors If openness to deeper experiential states appeals to you, however, here are some suggestions.

- That wonderful, almost mystical state we just described is unlikely to occur unless you are relaxed. So be as relaxed as you can while waltzing. Breathe deeply, relaxing your face and shoulders. Cultivate a state of "Dynamic Equanimity" (p. 55).

- Avoid an overcrowded dance floor. You don't want to spend the entire time trying to avoid collisions. Stay until the end of a dance, when the crowd usually starts to thin out. On the other hand, as long as the dance floor is safe, the synchronized movement of couples around you can contribute to your finding this state.

- Allow your waltzing to be nonverbal. There is no need to carry on a conversation at this moment. Don't even verbalize to yourself the experience you are feeling. Just waltz.

- One of the challenges of meditation is trying *not* to think of something that you're thinking about. One effective way *not* to do something is to do something else in its place. Try replacing the verbal soundtrack that usually runs through your mind with a *musical* one. Draw the music into the foreground of your awareness and let it sit there, nonverbally, feeling it, rather than analyzing it. It works.

- *Leads:* While trance waltzing, avoid doing the most challenging variations that you may have learned, which require concentration. If you like variety, choose the simplest variations, entering into them with gentle transitions and staying with each variation long enough for it to become an unconscious rhythm. Be aware that your partners are just as likely to enjoy falling into a deeper state, and avoid jarring your partners out of their reverie by throwing them into hot-shot moves.

## Balance

We may be giving the impression that we value opening the doors to direct experience more than we value complex, rational thought, or cerebral music and challenging dances. If we have given that impression, it is only for the sake of balance, in a culture that overvalues our productivity and undervalues our receptivity.

If you have already found this balance, then yes, complex dance music and challenging figures are fun. Do those more advanced variations when you feel like it, and enjoy them. But also try dancing in a relaxed, receptive state. Life needs balance.

Since we don't receive much encouragement to open ourselves to direct experience, we feel a special need to champion our ignored receptive side. Without developing this essential part of ourselves, we cannot be whole.

Since our culture doesn't offer many disciplines to help us reach a state of enhanced receptivity, and since waltzing can be one of the best ways to open our senses through motion, we encourage you to take advantage of the opportunity.

# Inverse Pedagogy
### *Learning dances by observation*

We usually prefer to take classes from the clearest teachers, but what if we had to pick up dances on our own, just from observation?

Throughout the history of social dancing, dancers have watched what other dancers did, then made up their own variations of what they saw. This process of riffing on others has driven the evolution of social dancing forward for centuries, even leading to the invention of entirely new dance forms.

Throughout those same centuries, professional dance masters have complained about dancers picking up dance steps and styles on their own, grumbling that grass-roots social dancers are doing it all wrong. And many of today's dancers have become dependent on teachers methodically breaking down all of the steps and figures.

We're not saying that either camp is necessarily right or wrong. We're certainly not advocating against learning from dance teachers in classes (or from this book). Instead, we recommend developing *both* skills: learning from other dancers via keen observation, while also finessing your dancing in classes.

Unfortunately, one of these two approaches has almost died out today. This is especially unfortunate, because the endangered approach is the one that has driven social dance forward from the beginning.

Fortunately, learning by observation is a skill that can be developed, a skill that can help us continue to learn dances long after the classes are over.

## The Basics

Here are some general suggestions about how to become better at this skill:

✓ Try to figure out if there is a "basic step" to the dance you are observing.

✓ Break down complex, simultaneous components of the dance into single elements such as floor patterns, timing, arms, etc. Focus on one element at a time.

✓ Similarly, see if you can break a longer choreographic pattern down into sequential modules. A long and apparently complex movement may only be a chain of easy elements strung together.

✓ Correlate new material to steps and movements you already know. Note the similarities and differences.

## The Specifics

The following suggestions will likely involve a lot of note-taking on the dance that you're observing. You could take written notes, but we recommend using a digital voice recorder, allowing you to keep your eyes on the dancing. Taking a video is another possibility, but that postpones the analysis to a later time, in a smaller two-dimensional format. The best way to develop the skill of learning by observation is to do it in real time.

Here are some specific details to notice. If the first ones seem too obvious to you, skip down halfway to find the more interesting suggestions.

✓ Which foot does the dance begin on?

✓ Notice any slow and quick patterns. Do the patterns repeat?

✓ Make a note on whether the lengths of each step are large, short, or in place.

✓ If it is a partnered dance, are the Lead's and Follow's footwork similar, opposite, or unrelated?

✓ Is body weight centered, or shifted forward or back or to the side? Notice any body sways or counter-body twisting. Notice hip and lower leg articulations. Are hip motions toward the step, away from it, or circular?

✓ Once the footwork starts to make sense, notice all arm, hand, shoulder, and head movements. Are arm movements angular or circular? Expansive or understated?

✓ Make a note of whether turns are clockwise or counterclockwise. This may be difficult to recall later unless you make a conscious note of it while you are watching.

✓ Make up your own nicknames for step elements, based on whatever they remind you of. This will help you identify them when you see them again.

✓ Ask the dancers what the dance, steps, and figures are called. Ask them to spell the terms.

✓ Don't just watch. Move while observing.

✓ If it is a couple dance, ask them to dance with you. Even if you're terrible at it, this will give you a much better kinesthetic sense of the dance than just watching it will. Ask a somewhat new dancer. They might give you a clearer idea of the basic structure than someone who knows too many variations. But since newbies may possibly have it wrong, dance with several beginners, then work your way up to someone who has apparently mastered the dance.

✓ While observing and dancing, note the differences and similarities between various couples and individuals. Are there different versions of the dance? One core version with individual styles? In any case, note as many of these differences as you can, so as to avoid the naïve assumption that the first version you are exposed to is the only version.

✓ While observing and trying it at the same time, relax. Breathe. Your ability to process large amounts of simultaneous material is greatly enhanced by alert tranquility.

✓ Spend some time just absorbing the dance in a diffuse, unfocused, relaxed mode. Give your right brain a chance to absorb the complete, simultaneous entirety of the dance without your analytical left brain dominating the process, preventing direct experience.

✓ Make a note of what kind of music is being used for this dance. Try to feel the dance's connection to the music. Make a note of the tempo. If you can't guess metronome tempos, compare the tempo to another dance you know. Or use a tempo-tapping app. If you can, find out the name of several songs representative of the dance, so that you'll have something to dance it to later.

✓ Shift between learning modes when you begin to feel fatigued. Shift *before* you become fatigued. Try focused concentration for a while, then drop it and play with the general feel of the dance for a while. Then feel the connection to the music. Then shift back to the footwork.

✓ Work out the dance with your dancing fingers, both while observing and while recalling it later on. Point your hand down and "walk" with your index and middle fingertips on the tabletop. You can quickly learn to approximate most foot and leg placements with these two fingers. It's a quick way to work out steps that you're working on.

✓ Take notes. Write it all down. Maybe learn a notation system. (See the next chapter for one possibility.)

## Overview

✓ What seems to be the appeal of the dance? Is it fun? Flashy? Graceful? Aerobic? What qualities do the dancers seem to be focusing on or enjoying the most?

✓ Be clear on what you want to get out of this dance. Do you want to perfect and perform it? Adopt elements into your freestyle dancing?

✓ Find written descriptions to compare with your observations, for instance, in how-to dance books and on the Web. Look for similar examples on YouTube.

✓ Take many different dance classes, anything that will add variety to your present ways of moving. Get as much dance vocabulary into your mind, body, and eyes as you can. The greater your dance vocabulary, the more likely you'll recognize elements in the dance you're observing.

✓ If you want to further fine-tune your learning-to-learn skills, take classes from teachers who don't teach very clearly, or someone who teaches in a foreign language that you don't understand.

✓ One of the best ways to really understand a new dance is to try teaching it to someone, even before you fully understand it. This helps you observe and pinpoint the missing elements that make a dance work.

✓ When you think you finally have the dance figured out, continue to observe carefully for other stylistic details such as posture, gestures, and partnering, as well as new variations.

✓ Go back a few months or a year later to see if the dance has changed. Go to different settings to see the bigger picture of the dance.

✓ Monitor your own progress in picking up a dance on your own. Notice how quickly you comprehend new material. Check your ability to make quick corrections. Learning how to learn by inspection is teaching yourself. No one else can do it for you. And since this is a multidimensional simultaneous process, there is no better exercise for improvement than just doing it.

# BALS ET SOIRÉES

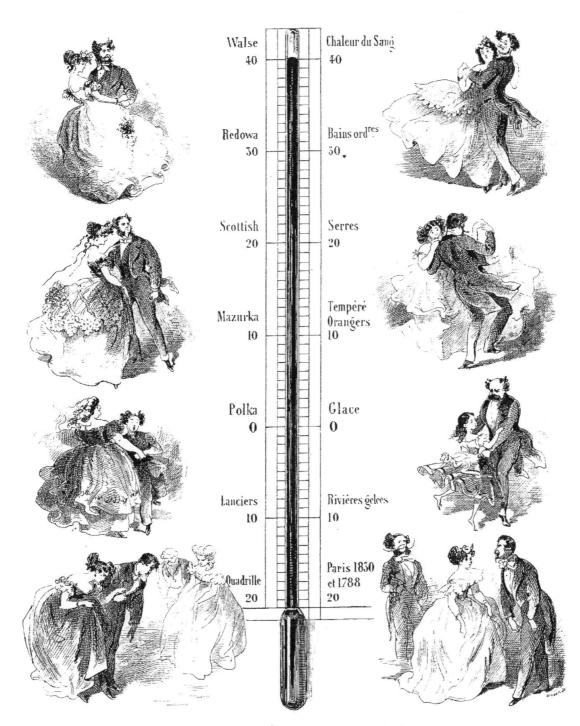

| | |
|---|---|
| Walse 40 | Chaleur du Sang 40 |
| Redowa 30 | Bains ord^{res} 30 |
| Scottish 20 | Serres 20 |
| Mazurka 10 | Tempéré Orangers 10 |
| Polka 0 | Glace 0 |
| Lanciers 10 | Rivières gelées 10 |
| Quadrille 20 | Paris 1850 et 1788 20 |

## LE THERMOMÈTRE DE LA DANSE

174

# Dance Notation

Dance notation systems of the past shared one characteristic. Each one attempted to be as thorough as possible, capable of notating even the smallest gestures, made with any part of the body. As a result, the accumulation of hundreds of symbols made these systems extremely difficult to master. Labanotation, Benesh Notation, and others require years of study.

This streamlined system takes the opposite approach. Since only a few of the symbols—the symbols for the basic steps—are used 95% of the time, it's more expedient to use only those few core symbols. Any details beyond the basic foot patterns (such as *dip, kick, stamp*) tend to be rare, so you can just write out those occasional details in English. This allows quick and easy mastery of the system.

This system is also quick to read and write. With just a little practice you can read a step description as fast as you can dance it, like sight-reading music at performance speed, and you can also jot it down quickly.

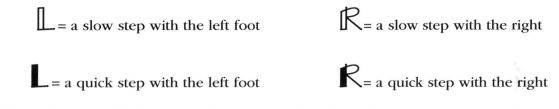

This is analogous to hollow, slow half-notes and solid, quick quarter-notes in music notation.

**Arrows indicate the direction of steps:**

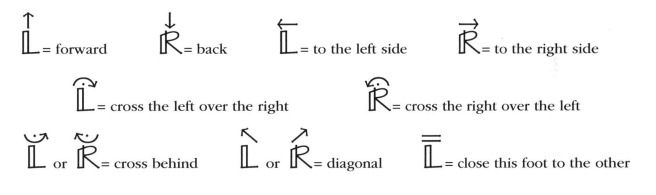

**Dotted arrows indicate placing or pointing the foot without taking weight:**

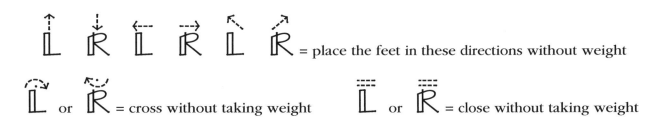

## Turns:

( = turn clockwise, to the right          ) = turn counterclockwise, to the left

(¼ = quarter turn          ½) = half turn

## Examples

How might you represent the cross-step waltz basic (for the Lead)?

Answer:

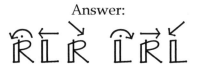

Box step waltz is even easier.

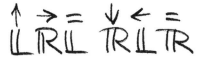

(This example also shows how the notation can be quickly hand-drawn.)

What waltz step does this notation represent, and for which role?

Here's an advanced one, if you want to try it. Recognize it?

It's impressive if you recognized that. Not many people know the Newport (p. 148).

Powers Notation System designed by Richard Powers. Tango Tekton font crafted by David Siegel, designer of the Tekton font. You can draw the symbols by hand on the fly, or you can download the font and learn how to use it at: waltzingbook.com/notation

# Hambo

Hambo is a Swedish folk dance characterized by a turning and traveling step that rotates 360° in three counts (twice as much as a waltz). Hambo music is in 3/4 time between 124 and 132 bpm. See the end of this chapter for specific music recommendations.

There are many different styles of hambo dancing, and many different elements of flair that can be added, such as stamps, and vertical oscillation called *svikt*. The version we describe below is the common denominator of hambo.

First, we will describe the basic hambo step, followed by the most common variation of hambo, which mixes hambo steps and walking steps in a repeated eight-bar pattern.

Hambo is generally danced in barrel hold, with both arms matching the elbows-side connection in the basic waltz position. Both partners hold each other's shoulders, with his arms under hers.

## The Hambo Step — Follow's Part

*Note:* This time, we've described the Follow's part separately, and first, because a) his part is simply her part shifted one count later, and b) we find that her part is easier to visualize.

1: She takes the backing step of a rotary waltz with her left foot, turning clockwise in front of him and stepping over LOD with her left foot to show her back to the outside wall.

2: Without changing weight, she continues to turn (pivot) on her left foot, preparing to face forward LOD for count 3, as she brings her free right foot in toward her left ankle without taking weight. (For the mechanically-inclined, this closing of the right foot to the left increases the speed of rotation by decreasing the moment arm.)

3: She takes the forward step of a rotary waltz along LOD with her right foot (or a forward leap, if she prefers), then pivots around on her right foot to prepare to back again.

Repeat counts 1-2-3.

## The Hambo Step — Lead's Part

His step is the same as her step, except that everything happens one count later.

1: He takes the forward step of a rotary waltz along LOD with his right foot, then pivots around on his right foot to prepare for the backing step of a rotary waltz.

2: He takes the backing step of a rotary waltz with his left foot, turning clockwise in front of her and stepping over LOD with his left foot to show his back to the outside wall.

3: Without changing weight, he continues to turn (pivot) on his left foot, preparing to step forward again with his right foot, as he brings his free right foot in toward his right ankle on count 3 without taking weight.

Repeat counts 1-2-3.

# Hints for Hambo

Although the two steps are pretty much identical, when you shift them by one count and put them together, they seem almost completely unrelated. He's making a weight change on count 2. She isn't. She's making a weight change on count 3. He isn't.

Here are two essential tips for making this odd pair of steps work smoothly together:

1.  Regardless of the step you're on, hambo has a slight downward pulse on every beat. Bounce down-down-down, down-down-down, like you're dribbling a basketball on every count. Unless your partner looks down, they shouldn't be able to tell whether you've changed weight or not. All they should feel is this consistent downward pulse. Bounce down when you're changing weight on the steps, and bounce down in exactly the same way when you're pivoting around without changing weight. The reason for this is that if you pulse unevenly, as you take weight, you will throw your partner into your timing.

    *Note:* In some hambo traditions, there is an added vertical movement, called *svikt,* in which both partners dip down and lift up together in an coordinated oscillation. This is different from, and complementary to, the downward pulse described here.

2.  Regardless of the step you're on, hambo rotates smoothly the entire time. Rotate your partner as smoothly as you can throughout the three counts, so that someone observing only your speed of rotation would have no way of telling what step you were on.

Although it can be danced by itself continuously (and dizzyingly), the hambo step is most frequently seen as part of an eight bar sequence, described below in two parts.

# The Hambo Sequence — First Part

The first part consists of easy walking steps and swinging of the feet.

**First Bar**

Both step on outside foot (his left, her right), count 1.

Both swing inside foot (his right, her left) in front of their outside foot (and back to place), counts 2-3.

**Second Bar**

Both step on inside foot, count 4.

Both swing outside foot in front of their inside foot (and back to place), counts 5-6.

*Note:* The first two bars are called the *dalsteg*.

**Third Bar**

Both run forward three steps, starting on their outside foot, counts 1-2-3.

# The Hambo Sequence — Second Part

The second part consists of one bar of modified hambo, three bars of regular hambo, and one bar of walking steps.

**Fourth Bar**

He simply begins to do his part of the basic step, stepping diagonally forward to the right with his right foot (count 4), turning clockwise in front of her to step back around with his left foot (count 5), and pivoting around on his left foot the rest of the way (count 6). He takes barrel hold as he turns in front of her, and continues with his part of the basic step in barrel hold on count 1.

She steps in place or slightly forward with her left foot (count 4), brushes her right foot forward without changing weight (count 5), and starts her part of the basic step on count 6, stepping (or leaping) forward with her right foot, then continues with her part of the basic step on count 1.

**Fifth, Sixth, and Seventh Bars**

Three bars (three full turns) of the basic hambo step in barrel hold.

**Eighth Bar**

He takes three small steps (right-left-right), either in place or slightly forward, while allowing her to roll open out of barrel hold to half-closed position on his right side and then to inside hands, ready to repeat the sequence from the beginning.

With three pivoting steps (left-right-left), she rolls opens out of barrel hold to half-closed position on his right side and then to inside hands, ready to repeat the sequence from the beginning.

There are many other variations of hambo. If you're interested in learning more, search for hambo on YouTube, and try your hand at learning by observation.

## Hambo Music

- "Trollspolska" (126 bpm) by Laurie Hart & Sarah Cummings

- "J.J's Hambo" (123 bpm) by Daron Douglas and Paul Moore

- "Hambo fran Bonsor" (120 bpm) by KGB

Many more can be found by searching for "hambo" on iTunes or Amazon.

# Welcome Chance Intrusions

Someone once proposed this theory:

Dancers on the East Coast focus on definitions and rules—categorizing, then standardizing the categorization. *Does it belong in this box or that box? Which style is correct?* In East Coast thinking, there is an emphasis on technique, more specifically on defining and enforcing one *correct* technique.

Dancers on the West Coast focus more on the way dance feels—the subjective experience of dancing. How does it impact us? How can we enhance the experience for our partners? West Coast thinking therefore embraces more creativity and flexibility, to adapt to partners who are different from our own style.

Is this theory true?

No, there are far too many exceptions. Many rule-based dancers live on the West Coast, and many adaptive, experience-based dancers live on the East Coast. And the theory ignores the dancers between the coasts.

The geographical division is an oversimplification. We prefer to think of it as a difference between *vertical thinking* versus *lateral thinking*, which can happen anywhere.

## Vertical and Lateral Thinking

These terms were coined by Edward deBono, who wrote that:

- Vertical thinking is selective. Lateral thinking is generative.

- Vertical thinking selects a pathway by excluding other pathways, leading to the jokes about "illegal moves" in strictly ballroom dance. Lateral thinking does not restrict, but rather seeks to open up new pathways.

- *Correctness* is what matters in vertical thinking. *Richness* is what matters in lateral thinking.

- Vertical thinking moves only if there are directions on how to move. Lateral thinking moves in order to generate directions.

- Vertical thinking depends heavily on the rigidity of definitions. It often depends on identifying something as a member of some class or excluding it from that class. Once something is given a label or put into a class, it is supposed to stay there. With lateral thinking, classifications and categories are not fixed pigeonholes, but rather signposts to help navigation.

- **Lateral thinking welcomes chance intrusions.** With lateral thinking one welcomes outside influences for their provocative action.

Welcoming chance intrusions is one of the fundamental components of creative thinking. Lateral-thinking dancers see differences from what they expected to happen as opportunities, not mistakes.

## Word of the Day: Pedantic

Some advice is timeless, like this, from a 19th century dance manual:

"Never be pedantic on a dance floor."

According to Random House Dictionary:

**pedantic** adj.,

1.  characterized by a narrow, often ostentatious concern for formal rules; overly concerned with what are thought to be correct rules and details; marked by a narrow, often tiresome focus on or display of learning and especially its trivial aspects.

2.  narrowly, stodgily, and often ostentatiously learned.

3.  unimaginative, pedestrian.

Etymology: From *ped*, form of *piede*, foot, in meaning of servile follower.

Never forget that social dance is *social*.

## Always?

But lateral thinking isn't better for *all* kinds of dancing. Both vertical and lateral thinking are valid, where appropriate. Rule-based vertical thinking makes perfect sense for competitive ballroom dance, for example. You can't hold a competition unless everyone agrees on the rules.

But one of the strangest mismatches you'll find in the dance world is when someone applies a rigidly vertical thinking attitude to a lateral thinking dance form, like cross-step waltz, lindy hop, Argentine tango, west coast swing, salsa, or blues. Those dances were born and bred in cultures which valued spontaneity, flexibility, and personal variations. The original spirit of those dances is lost if their freedom is replaced by an emphasis on rules and restrictions.

Skippy Blair wrote the following about west coast swing, but she could have been writing about waltz, tango, or any truly social dance:

The most fascinating part of swing dancing is the individuality of the dancers. Stylings are flexible … the style one chooses should be as individual as the clothes one chooses to wear. The only problem that exists in swing is when someone decides there is only ONE WAY to dance it. *[The caps were hers.]*

Welcome chance intrusions, and keep the spirit alive!

# Dancing Makes You Smarter

For centuries, dance manuals and other writings have lauded the health benefits of dancing, usually as physical exercise. More recently, we've seen research on further health benefits of dancing, such as stress reduction and increased serotonin level, with its sense of well-being.

Most recently, we've heard of another benefit: frequent dancing apparently makes us smarter.

A recent study added to the growing evidence that stimulating one's mind by dancing can ward off Alzheimer's disease and other forms of dementia, much as physical exercise can keep the body fit. **Dancing also increases cognitive acuity at all ages.**

The 21-year study of senior citizens, 75 and older, was led by the Albert Einstein College of Medicine in New York City, funded by the National Institute on Aging, and published in the New England Journal of Medicine. Their method for objectively measuring mental acuity in aging was to monitor rates of dementia, including Alzheimer's disease.

The study wanted to see which, if any, recreational activities influenced mental acuity. Some activities, they discovered, had a significant benefit. Other activities had none.

They studied cognitive activities such as reading books, writing for pleasure, doing crossword puzzles, playing cards, and playing musical instruments. And they studied physical activities like playing tennis or golf, swimming, bicycling, dancing, walking, and doing housework.

One of the surprises of the study was that almost none of the physical activities appeared to offer any protection against dementia. There can be cardiovascular benefits of these activities, of course, but the focus of this study was on the mind.

There was one important exception: **the only physical activity to offer protection against dementia was frequent dancing.**

In fact, **frequent dancing was the *most effective preventive measure against dementia studied*, resulting in an impressive 76% reduction in dementia risk**, compared to 41% for frequent crossword puzzle solving, and 35% for frequent reading, for example.

## Neuroplasticity

What could cause these significant cognitive benefits?

In his pioneering work on Alzheimer's, neurologist Dr. Robert Katzman proposed that people become resistant to the effects of dementia as a result of having **greater cognitive reserve** and **increased complexity of neuronal connections**. Similar to education, participation in some leisure activities can lower the risk of dementia by improving these neural qualities.

As psychiatrist Dr. Joseph Coyle explains, "Mentally engaging hobbies may lay down new neural pathways. The cerebral cortex and hippocampus, which are critical to these activities, are remarkably plastic, and they rewire themselves based upon their use."

Our brain constantly rewires its neural pathways, *as needed*. If it doesn't need to, it won't.

# Aging and Memory

When brain cells die and the connections between them weaken with aging, our nouns go first, like names of people, because there's only one neural pathway connecting to that stored information. If the single neural pathway to that name fades, we lose access to it. As people age, some of them learn to parallel process, coming up with synonyms to go around these roadblocks.

The key here is Dr. Katzman's emphasis on the complexity of our neuronal connections. More is better. **Do whatever you can to create new neural paths.** The opposite of this is taking the same old well-worn path over and over again, with habitual patterns of thinking and living.

When Richard was studying the creative process as a grad student at Stanford, he came across the perfect analogy for this:

> **The more stepping stones there are across the creek,**
> **the easier it is to cross in your own style.**

The focus of that aphorism was creative thinking, to find as many alternative paths as possible to a creative solution. But as we age, parallel processing becomes even more critical. Now it is no longer a matter of style, it is a matter of survival, getting across the creek at all. Randomly dying brain cells are like stepping stones being removed one by one. Those who had only one well-worn path of stones are completely blocked when some are removed. **But those who spent their lives trying different mental routes each time, creating a myriad of possible paths, still have several paths left.**

As the study shows, we need to keep as many of those paths active as we can, while also generating new paths, to maintain the complexity of our neuronal connections.

In other words: **Intelligence—use it or lose it.**

# Intelligence

What exactly do we mean by "intelligence"?

You'll probably agree that intelligence isn't just a numerical measurement, with a number of 100 plus or minus assigned to it. But what *is* it?

To answer this question, we go back to the most elemental questions possible. Why do animals have a brain? To survive? No, plants don't have a brain and they survive. To live longer? No, many trees outlive us.

As neuroscience educator Robert Sylwester notes, *mobility* is central to everything that is cognitive, whether it is physical motion or the mental movement of information. Plants have to endure whatever comes along, including predators eating them. Animals, on the other hand, can travel to seek food, shelter, mates, and to move away from unfavorable conditions. Since we can move, we need a cognitive system that can comprehend sensory input and intelligently make **choices**.

Semantics will differ for each of us, but according to many, if the stimulus-response relationship of a situation is **automatic**, we don't think of the response as requiring our intelligence. We don't use the word "intelligent" to describe a banana slug, even though it has a rudimentary brain. But when the brain evaluates several viable responses and chooses one (a real choice, not just following habits), the cognitive process is considered to be intelligent.

As Jean Piaget put it,

**Intelligence is what we use when we don't already know what to do.**

## Why Dancing?

Returning to the leisure activities study, we ask two questions:

1. *Why* is dancing better than other activities for improving mental capabilities?

2. Does this mean *all* kinds of dancing, or is one kind of dancing better than another?

As we just saw, the essence of *intelligence* is making decisions. The best advice for increasing or maintaining our intelligence then, is to exercise our decision-making capabilities as much as we can, involving ourselves in **activities which require split-second rapid-fire decision-making**, as opposed to rote memory (retracing the same well-worn paths), or working on your physical style.

One way to do that is to learn something new. Not just dancing, but anything new. Don't worry about the probability that you'll never use it in the future. Take a class to challenge your mind. It will stimulate the connectivity of your brain by generating the need for new pathways. Difficult classes are better for you, as they create an even greater need for new neural pathways.

Then take a dance class, which can be even more effective. Dancing integrates several brain functions at once—kinesthetic, rational, musical, and emotional—further increasing your neural connectivity.

## What Kind of Dancing?

Do *all* kinds of dancing lead to increased mental acuity? No, not all forms of dancing will produce the same benefit, especially if they only work on style, or merely involve retracing the same memorized paths. Making as many split-second decisions as possible is the key to maintaining our cognitive abilities. Remember: intelligence is what we use when *we don't already know* what to do.

We wish that 25 years ago the Albert Einstein College of Medicine thought of doing side-by-side comparisons of different kinds of dancing, to find out which was better. But we can figure it out by looking at *who* they studied: senior citizens 75 and older, beginning in 1980. Those who danced in that particular population were former Roaring Twenties dancers (back in 1980) and then former Swing Era dancers (today), so the kind of dancing most of them continued to do in retirement was what they began when they were young: freestyle social dancing (basic foxtrot, swing, waltz and maybe some Latin).

Richard has been watching senior citizens dance all of his life, from his parents (who met at a Tommy Dorsey dance), to retirement communities, to the Roseland Ballroom in New York. He almost never sees memorized sequences or patterns on the dance floor. He sees easygoing, fairly simple social dancing, freestyle lead and follow. Of course, even simple freestyle social dancing isn't that simple. It requires a lot of split-second decision-making, in both the Lead and Follow roles.

At this point, we want to clarify that we're not demonizing memorized sequence dancing or style-focused pattern-based ballroom dancing. There are stress-reduction benefits of any kind of dancing, cardiovascular benefits of physical exercise, and the further benefits of feeling connected to a community of dancers. All kinds of dancing can have major benefits.

But when it comes to preserving (and improving) mental acuity, some forms are significantly better than others. While all dancing requires *some* intelligence, we encourage you to use your *full* intelligence when dancing, in both the Lead and Follow roles. The more decision-making we can bring into our dancing, the better.

## Who Benefits More, Follows or Leads?

In social dancing, the Follow role automatically gains this benefit, by making hundreds of split-second decisions as to what to do next, sometimes unconsciously so. As we've mentioned before, women don't "follow," they *interpret* the signals their partners are giving them, and this requires intelligence and decision-making, which is active, not passive.

This benefit is greatly enhanced by dancing with different partners, not always with the same fellow. With different dance partners, you have to adjust much more and be aware of more variables. This is great for staying smarter longer.

But men, you can also match her degree of decision-making, *if* you choose to do so.

Here's how:

1) Really pay attention to your partner and what works best for her. Notice what is comfortable for her, where she is already going, which signals are successful with her and which aren't, and constantly adapt your dancing to these observations. That's rapid-fire, split-second decision making.

2) Don't lead the same old patterns the same way each time. Challenge yourself to try new things. Make more decisions more often.

The huge side-benefit is that your partners will have much more *fun* dancing with you when you are attentive to their dancing and constantly adjusting for their comfort and continuity of motion. And as a result, you'll have more fun too.

## Full Engagement

Those who fully utilize their intelligence in dancing, at all levels, love the way it feels. Spontaneous leading and following both involve entering a flow state. Both leading and following benefit from a highly active attention to possibilities.

That's the most succinct definition we know for intelligent dancing: **a highly active attention to possibilities.** And we think it's wonderful that both the Lead and Follow role share that same ideal.

The best Leads appreciate the many options that the Follow must consider every second, and respect and appreciate the Follow's input into the collaboration of partner dancing. The Follow is finely attuned to the here-and-now in relaxed responsiveness, and so is the Lead.

Once this highly active attention to possibilities, flexibility, and alert tranquility are perfected in the art of dance partnering, dancers find it even more beneficial in their other relationships, and in everyday life.

## Dance Often

The study made another important suggestion: **do it often**. Seniors who solved crossword puzzles four days a week had a measurably lower risk of dementia than those who solved them once a week. If you can't take classes or go out dancing several days a week, then dance as much as you can. More is better.

And do it now, the sooner the better. It is essential to start building your cognitive reserve now. Some day, you'll need as many of those stepping stones across the creek as possible.

Don't wait—start building them now.

# THE SWING WALTZ

# Even More Ways to Waltz

While the waltzes we have described so far can provide more than enough enjoyment to last a lifetime, it's also fun to experiment with other things we can do in waltz time. Here are a few ways to add even more variety to your waltzing by adapting other dance forms to 3/4 time, and adapting waltz steps to 4/4 time.

*Note:* In some cases, we will describe how to dance the basic step in waltz time. In other cases, for dances in which doing this would be more difficult, we will simply describe how to adapt the traditional step to waltz time, assuming that you have learned or will learn the traditional step elsewhere.

## Country Walking Waltz
### (One-Step in Waltz Time)

*A leisurely traveling waltz for any tempo (usually slower, but most tempos work).*

Nothing could be simpler than this. Simply walk with your partner while a waltz is playing, and do walking variations that you know from other dances (like one-step, Texas two-step, or any of the waltzes), in one of many different positions: closed position (Follow backing), closed position (promenade), half-closed position promenade, hand-in-hand promenade, shadow position, cradle position, skater's position, and any other positions you may know. In traditional Country Waltz, shadow (varsovienne, sweetheart) position is especially popular.

## Swing Waltz
### (a.k.a Waltz Swing)

*Easygoing swing figures done on the spot, for in-between waltz tempos.*

Swing waltz is the ideal choice for music that's in the awkward in-between tempos between slow (cross-step, box step) and fast (rotary, Viennese) waltz, i.e., in the 124-132 bpm range.

There are two basic forms of swing waltz, which you can smoothly alternate between.

### 1. Nightclub Two-Step in Waltz Time

The Lead and Follow face each other squarely in waltz position.

1: The Lead steps side left with his left foot while the Follow mirrors him, stepping side right with her right foot.

2: The Lead places his right foot behind his left and takes weight on his right foot while the Follow mirrors him, taking weight on her left foot behind her right.

3: The Lead replaces weight onto his left foot while the Follow mirrors him, replacing weight onto her right foot.

4-5-6: The Lead does exactly what the Follow did, and vice-versa.

Easily verbalized and remembered as "side-rock-step." In traditional 4/4 time nightclub two-step, many dancers start rock-step first. While also possible in Swing Waltz, we find that sidestep first is almost always more musical in 3/4.

*Optional Styling:* Rise up on counts 2 and 5.

*Variations:* Everything from nightclub two-step works.

*In 4/4 Time:* To dance traditional nightclub two-step in 4/4 time, simply perform the steps described above in slow-quick-quick (1—3-4, 5—7-8) timing to music in 4/4 time around 152 to 176 bpm (164 bpm is optimal).

## 2. East Coast Swing Figures in Waltz Time

Simply get yourself into swing out position, and then walk through the swing figures you know, using counts 1-2-3-4 to walk through the figure. Start facing your partner, and end facing your partner, walking forward and backward as necessary to make this happen, exactly as you would in swing. Then rock step, back-forward, on 5-6.

As an interesting aside, this way of walking through the figures splits the difference between single-step and triple-step east coast swing: in single-step, you have four steps for each figure, and in triple-step, you have eight steps for each. In the case of swing waltz, you have six for each figure.

*In 4/4 Time:* You can also do this in nightclub two-step by walking through swing figures in slow-quick-quick (1—3-4, 5—7-8) timing (walk 1—3-4-5—, rock-step 7-8). Or you can do them traditionally, in east coast swing (walk-walk-rock-step in slow-slow-quick-quick timing).

# Waltz-Time Hustle
## (a.k.a Three-Count Hustle a.k.a. Hustle)

*An energetic form of swing that's already in waltz time.*

Of course, you can also do the same swing figures twice as fast in waltz time by doing them in three-count hustle. Three-count hustle is usually danced against four-count music, but it works just as well to energetic waltz music around 120 bpm. You'll now be hitting every count 1, instead of shifting across the music as you would in 4/4 time.

If you happen to know the 1970s disco six-count American hustle (touch-close-touch-walk-walk-walk), or Latin hustle (touch-close-tri-ple-step-walk-walk), you can dance these six counts of steps to the six counts of waltz music.

## West Coast Waltz
### (West Coast Swing in Waltz Time)

*Another kind of swing waltz, slinky and smooth.*

Similarly, six-count west coast swing figures can be danced to slow waltz music (around 110 bpm), simply by dancing the six counts of the figure to the six counts of the music. As in waltz-time hustle, you'll now be hitting every count 1, instead of shifting across the music as you would in 4/4 time.

Eight-count west coast swing figures are trickier in waltz time, because simply dancing them in waltz time shifts across the music in a messy way. However, eight-count figures can sometimes be adapted to waltz time by either removing two counts and weight changes (usually counts 5 and 6), in which case it is a new kind of six count figure, or by adding a ninth count without changing weight, in which case it is a new nine-count figure that shifts you to the other downbeat (count 4) in the waltz music.

## Fox Waltz
### (Foxtrot in Waltz Time)

*A leisurely traveling waltz for very slow waltz tempos (around 80 bpm).*

Occasionally, you'll hear a waltz that is too slow for dancing anything else. In that case you might try waltz-time foxtrot: simply dance any slow-slow-quick-quick (Magic Step) figures you may know, with one slow step on 1, one slow step on 2, and two quick steps on 3-and.

*Music:* "Strong Enough" by Sheryl Crow is great for waltz-time foxtrot, as is the latter half of "Fake Empire" by The National.

## Latin Waltz
### (Salsa in Waltz Time)

*Another waltz in place for in-between tempos (around 141 bpm).*

The Lead and Follow face each other squarely in waltz position.

1: The Lead steps forward into his partner with his left foot, while the Follow steps back on her right foot.

2: The Lead replaces weight back onto his right foot while the Follow replaces weight forward onto her left foot.

3: The Lead steps back with his left foot while the Follow steps forward with her right foot.

4-5-6: The Lead does exactly what the Follow did, and vice-versa.

Easily verbalized and remembered as "break-step-walk." (Some teachers teach salsa as "break-step-close," which also works as a basic step, but "break-step-walk" facilitates variations.)

*Optional Styling:* Latin hips, more air under the armpits than regular waltz position.

*Variations:* Everything from salsa works.

*In 4/4 Time:* To dance traditional salsa in 4/4 time, simply perform the steps described above in quick-quick-slow (1-2-3—, 5-6-7—) timing to music in 4/4 time around 172 to 200 bpm (188 bpm is optimal).

## Three-Slide Galop
### (Galop or Polka in Waltz Time)

*A waltz for high energy music at cross-step waltz tempo, this one travels at great speed.*

This simply splits the difference between a polka and a Four-Slide Galop. Slide three times, turning on the third, with a hop to prepare for the next slide: "slide-and-slide-and-turn-hop."

*In 4/4 Time:* For full descriptions of the polka and Four-Slide Galop, see p. 104-105.

## Vals Cruzado
### (Tango in Waltz Time)

*A meandering waltz for very fast waltz music (around 200 bpm).*

Simply do any tango figures you may know by taking one slow step for each measure of waltz (1-2-3), and do quick-quick steps in canter timing (weight changes on 1 and 3).

For example, the timing of the basic tango fan is:     S      S      Q   Q   S
                                                   (1-2-3) (4-5-6) (1) - (3) (4-5-6)

*Note:* You can also use this trick to dance slow waltzes to fast waltz music. The first step gets three counts, the second step gets two counts, and the third gets one count, i.e., 1——4—6.

## Bluesy Waltz

While all of these dance forms are worth dancing for whole songs, another fun way to dance these figures is to mix them all together, as inspired by the music, to create a hybrid dance form called bluesy waltz (thanks to Campbell Miller and Chris Mayer of Austin, Texas). With your entire focus on your partner and the music, dance whatever feels right in the moment, stealing figures from all the dances that you know, and interspersing them with simple waltz steps, either the ones we've described, or ones even simpler: balancing (step-close-close) forward and back or side to side, or even simply swaying to the music (on count 1 and 4). Here are a few waltzes recommended for bluesy waltz:

- "Why Don't You Try" by Kelly Clarkson (117 bpm)
- "Not the Same" by Mingo Fishtrap (117 bpm)
- "The Air That I Breathe" by Maroon 5 (120 bpm)
- "Candycoatedwaterdrops" by Plumb (120 bpm)
- "Can't Let You Go" by Matchbox Twenty (126 bpm)

**Waltzing in 4/4 Time**

In addition to adapting 4/4 figures to 3/4 music, we can also adapt 3/4 figures to 4/4 music.

There are two basic ways to do this:

## 1) Dance against the music (as in hustle).

For example, dance cross-step waltz to one-step music (or other walking tempo tunes in 4/4), exactly as you would to cross-step waltz music (one step per beat), ignoring the counts, hearing each beat as a generic beat. For the musically and mathematically inclined, you'll shift across the music, hitting the the downbeat with every other primary cross-step (or if you're counting by eights, it will take twice as long).

| Music | 1 2 3 4 / 1 2 3 4 / 1 2 3 4 // repeat |
|-------|----------------------------------------|
| Steps | 1 2 3 / 4 5 6 / 1 2 3 / 4 5 6 // repeat |

This can also be done with other waltzes and music of appropriate tempos in 4/4, but it's not all that common. The other way of dancing these steps in 4/4 is seen much more frequently.

## 2) Modify the dance to fit the music, using slow and quick steps (as in foxtrot).

For example, dance cross-step waltz (or box step waltz) in slow-quick-quick rhythm to foxtrot music, to get cross-step foxtrot (or box step foxtrot).

| Music | 1 2 3 4 / 1 2 3 4 // repeat |
|-------|------------------------------|
| Steps | 1 2 3 / 4 5 6 // repeat |

Or, as you saw in the descriptions of some of the advanced waltz and polka variations on p. 147, dance a faster waltz (rotary waltz, reverse waltz, or advanced variations thereof) in quick-quick-slow rhythm to polka music.

| Music | 1 2 3 4 / 1 2 3 4 // repeat |
|-------|------------------------------|
| Steps | 1 2 3 / 4 5 6 // repeat |

Finally, some steps that work in waltz time can be danced to 4/4 music by adding or subtracting steps, as in the Three-Slide Galop (p. 192) and the Waltz Galop (p. 148).

Another example of this, developed earlier this year by Nick Enge and Danielle Baiata, is **triple-step waltz**, which is cross-step waltz with a triple-step along LOD on counts 3-and-4 (and 7-and-8) in place of a single step along LOD on counts 3 and 6. The triple-step not only fills in the extra beat of music in 4/4 time, but allows extra movement to happen at the end of each half waltz (you get half a second more at 120 bpm, and two extra quick steps), enabling more complex cross-step waltz style variations. The triple-step can be a smooth triple, as in cha cha and west coast swing, or a swung triple as in triple-step swing and lindy hop. Triple-Step waltz can be danced by itself, or as a variation of those dances.

Here's a list of common waltz adaptations in 4/4 time, and music that works well for each:

| | |
|---|---|
| cross-step one-step (QQQ) | one-step, polka, hustle |
| cross-step foxtrot (SQQ) | foxtrot, club two-step, schottische, tango |
| triple-step waltz (SSQQS) | cha cha, west coast swing, lindy hop |
| box step foxtrot (SQQ) | slow foxtrot, tango |
| rotary foxtrot (SQQ) | fast foxtrot, fast club two-step |
| rotary/reverse waltz in polka time (QQS) | polka, one-step, hustle |
| redowa, mazurka, etc in polka time (QQS) | polka, one-step, hustle |

# Improvisation

One of the defining features of social dance is that it is spontaneously creative—improvised.

Of course, this is not to devalue choreography, which has its own benefits. It is simply to say that most of what happens on the social dance floor is completely unscripted. The same is also true of life: we're constantly improvising our way through our days.

Fortunately, in the Department of Theater and Performance Studies at Stanford, we are blessed with two gurus of improvisation: Dan Klein and Patricia Ryan Madson, who teach the art of making stuff up. We also have an improv troupe, the Stanford Improvisors, which Nick performed in a few years back.

To help you improvise your dancing and your life, we want to pass on a few improv maxims, which are laid out in detail in Madson's book, *Improv Wisdom: Don't Prepare, Just Show Up.* The maxims (headings) are hers, the applications are ours.

## Don't Prepare, Just Show Up

The overwhelming tendency for beginning improvisors—onstage, on the dance floor, and in life—is to try to plan everything out in advance.

For Leads, this means choreographing every move ahead of time: "two more turning basics, then a grapevine turn, then two more basics, and he-goes-she-goes." The Follow's equivalent is trying to guess what's next: "oh, a grapevine, I'll take three steps and then turn myself."

The problem with this approach is that things don't always go as planned. There isn't always floor space for he-goes-she-goes, and grapevines can be longer, not always three steps.

How would an experienced improvisor approach this?

He'd follow this maxim: "Don't prepare, just show up." Rather than choreographing his moves in advance, he'd simply show up and dance with his partner, choosing each step based on what's happening in the moment (or in the Follow's case, interpreting them in the moment).

Before we go any further, however, it is essential to differentiate between two kinds of preparation, only one of which is avoided by an experienced improvisor. The first kind of preparation is **learning**. The second is **getting ahead of oneself**.

The first kind of preparation—learning—is essential. **The best improvisors, whether onstage or on the dance floor, have taken many classes and practiced for many hours outside of the classroom in order to be able to improvise as successfully as they do**.

So by all means, take as many classes as you can, learn as many figures as you can, and practice as much as you can with as many different partners as you can. All of this will make you a better dancer, and a better improvisor.

As the saying goes, "chance favors the prepared mind."

The second kind of preparation—getting ahead of oneself—is the kind which improvisors try to avoid. **Rather than focusing on planning (or guessing) the next three moves, focus on dancing the move that you're currently dancing, and then see what flows smoothly from there, in the moment.**

## Say Yes

Without having a plan in advance, improvisors need some way of inventing a plan as they go. To do this, they simply use the magic word: **YES.**

"This is going to sound crazy," writes Madson. **"Say yes to everything. Accept all offers. Go along with the plan. Support someone else's dream."** This is the key to improvisation.

Improvisors begin by taking a first step. *Any* first step. Then they simply take turns saying "Yes" to each others' offers, building a story, or a dance, step by step.

Actually, what improvisors really say is *Yes, And...* They not only **affirm**, but also **build on** each offer: the Lead turns the Follow, *so she turns herself more*, then *her momentum suggests his next move*. If the Follow's interpretation takes them somewhere unexpected, then the Lead stays right there with her the whole time, leading into something unexpected.

*Yes, And...* is the basis of all successful improvisation, and as a result, all successful social dancing. The Lead makes a suggestion and the Follow says *Yes, And...*, then the Lead says *Yes, And...* to the Follow's *And...*, and the Follow says *Yes, And...* to the Lead's *And...* They pass ideas back and forth, always building on what came before. In this way, they create a whole journey from that first step, one *Yes, And...* at a time.

Of course, there are always exceptions to the rule, and sometimes we need to say "No," as in the case of harm or injustice. On stage, "No" is usually a "Yes, And..." in disguise, where the word "No" is what is needed to move the scene forward. In social dancing, we can take a similar approach, what we might call **"a No with a Yes in your heart."** In both roles, if your partner is going to crash, you can say "a No with a Yes in your heart" by pulling them away from it, perhaps dampening their fun, but saving them from danger. This "No" is really a "Yes, And..." in disguise, as it is exactly what is needed to move the dance forward. The same applies in cases of harm and injustice, where taking a stand with the word "No" is exactly what is needed to move ourselves and society forward.

"Don't Prepare, Just Show Up" and then just "Say Yes." This is the essence of improvisation, and everything else follows naturally from that.

There are several other tips that Madson offers, however, which we can use to further improve our improv, both on the dance floor and throughout our lives.

## Make Mistakes, Please

**Be willing to make mistakes.** As Madson puts it, "When I say, 'Make mistakes, please,' what I really want is for you to do something risky or challenging, something out of your comfort zone, where mistakes are possible (and likely), and to proceed boldly."

Ask someone new to dance, maybe even someone "risky": your role model, the teacher, or that cute guy or girl. Leads, try leading that new variation you just learned… or the one you just saw… or the one you just invented… or the one you haven't invented yet.

Then, when something unexpected happens, treat it as if were the best thing that could've happened, immediately adapting to it and flowing with it. **Welcome chance intrusions**. Give the impression, if you can, that there was no mistake, simply a new and exciting invention. Learn the arts of **resilience** and **mid-course correction,** turning **mistakes into opportunities**.

## Be Average

We hear it all the time: "Be original."

There is a common misconception that improvisation necessarily involves extraordinary feats of originality, that in order to improvise, we must do something that no one has ever done before. Madson has different advice: "Be average."

Remember the words of William B. DeGarmo:

> No two persons write alike. A man cannot write his own name twice the same. There is no duplicate in nature. No two persons dance alike.

The essential wisdom of DeGarmo, and in Madson's advice to be average, is this:

> **There is no need to *be* original. We already *are* original.**

As Martha Graham put it:

> There is a vitality, a life force, an energy, a quickening that is translated through you into action, and because there is only one of you in all of time, this expression is unique. And if you block it, it will never exist through any other medium and it will be lost. The world will not have it. It is not your business to determine how good it is nor how valuable nor how it compares with other expressions. It is your business to keep it yours clearly and directly, to keep the channel open.

When you're dancing improvisationally, don't stress yourself by trying to be extraordinary. Be average. Or better yet: **just be yourself**. Trust in the fact that even your most ordinary dancing is already unique.

## Wake Up to the Gifts

Inspiration abounds on the dance floor, and we can improve our improv by **paying attention to this inspiration**, and saying "Yes, And…," further enriching our dance experience.

We can take inspiration from different qualities in the music. We can creatively use the space on the dance floor, taking advantage of free space with larger variations, and using more compact ones to get through a tight squeeze. Leads, you can take inspiration from other variations that you glimpse across the dance floor. (Follows, if he's looking around, he's not checking out the other girls, he's trying to get ideas for what to lead next.)

With these forms of inspiration, and the continual flow of offers from our partner, we have more than enough to build an entire dance, without having anything planned in advance.

## Take Care of Each Other

Dance for your partner.

We've said it many times, but it's worth saying again, this time for slightly different reasons. Now, it's not just that dancing for your partner is the *kind* thing to do (which it is), or that dancing for your partner will be the most *fulfilling* course of action (which it will be). **Dancing for your partner also helps you improvise.**

*Leads:* As you're dancing, ask yourself: **"What will my partner most enjoy now?"** Answering this question will lead you to your next step, in a much more concrete way than simply pondering the hundreds of things you *could* lead next. It's a more focused question, which is easier to answer. Don't worry about answering "incorrectly." It is not a multiple choice test where you must discern and lead her favorite variation every time. The idea is simply that by asking this question: (1) you'll have a clear path forward, and (2) that path forward will almost certainly be more satisfying for her (and for you) than a randomly chosen path.

*Follows:* As you're dancing, ask yourself the same question: "What will my partner most enjoy now?" In your case, this might be translated as: "What is my partner asking me to do now?" By answering this question, you too will find a clearer and more mutually satisfying path.

Dancing for our partner, and knowing that our partner is dancing for us also increases **our confidence to improvise**. We're not coming up with the whole dance on our own—only our half of it, and we have our partner's help. Our partner is taking care of us. We're embarking on an exciting adventure, *together.*

## Enjoy the Ride

Finally, whatever you choose to do, **have fun!**

The point of social dancing is having fun. The point of *improvised* social dancing is having *even more* fun. For some dancers, this is automatically true. Other dancers *learn* to enjoy improvisation. And some dancers want to stay far away from it.

If you're one of those dancers who prefers knowing exactly what is going on, having fun repeating the step you know, or practicing a choreographed sequence, we wholeheartedly encourage you to enjoy doing that. We're certainly not saying that you must improvise your waltzing—we're simply giving you tips on how to do it better. And even if you're not the improvising type, many of these tips can still help you improve your dancing.

> "There are people who prefer to say 'Yes,' and there are people who prefer to say 'No.' Those who say 'Yes' are rewarded by the adventures they have, and those who say 'No' are rewarded by the safety they attain. There are far more 'No' sayers around than 'Yes' sayers, but you can train one type to behave like the other."
> — Keith Johnstone, improv pioneer

# PerForMance vs. Just For Fun

## by Nicholas Chin
an essay from Social Dance 2

I grew up in a musical family, and everyone knew how to play at least one instrument. For me it was the violin and piano. Although I had some aptitude for music and enjoyed performing, it was not something that I yearned to spend the bulk of my time doing. Practicing endlessly for my violin examinations was extremely frustrating.

In contrast, I love social dancing because it's like playing with friends. Instead of being responsible for the music, I can enjoy the music and share this joy with my partner. I no longer have to worry about how I look in front of my audience; my focus is on my partner. As long as she is having fun, then I'm having fun.

I view social dancing as two people having a **conversation set to the music.** The Lead brings up a point and the Follow interprets and responds. **If it's a choreographed dance, it would be like having a pre-scripted conversation.** It could still be beautiful, but less exciting for those who are performing it.

I love the sense of the unknown, wondering whether a move will work perfectly or fail gloriously. The times that it does work are truly magical moments, and I look into my partner's eyes and see them giving me the same look back saying, "Wow, that really worked!"

# Bouncing Back

## by John Sanderson
an essay from Social Dance 2

The following observation came while I was sick and sitting in the balcony. By now I have come to know who some of the most experienced dancers are. I had a good vantage point from the balcony to notice which Leads seemed to have the most headroom; these were the Leads for whom the dances were easy enough that they had some capacity to be playful with variations.

In observing these Leads, I was struck by the fact that **they made mistakes just as frequently as everyone else. They just bounced back from them more easily.** Whereas less confident dancers would be thrown off for several measures by such a mistake, those I was observing were promptly right back in the swing of things, laughing it off with their partners. They seemed to have better internalized the idea we all strive for, to dance for the sheer enjoyment of it, with less concern for doing perfect footwork.

Recently, I've been reading about the habits that top students (straight A students, or otherwise high achieving students who run balanced, relaxed lives) have in common. A common misconception is that they are just a very organized, driven breed, who put in place solid time management systems, and show indefatigable discipline in adhering to them throughout college. Interviews with them, however, have shown that they are just as prone to "get off track" or to fall behind in classes. They are distinct though, in their ability to bounce back, to get back on track, and to contain the damage of momentarily falling behind.

**Apparently excellence in dancing, as in academics, is more about resilience than about immaculate consistency.**

> "Intelligence is not the absence of mistakes, but the ability to quickly find a way to make them good."
> — Bertolt Brecht, playwright

> "Things work out best for those who make the best of how things work out."
> — John Wooden, basketball coach

# Oops, Sorry

If you could eavesdrop at a social dance, the two words most commonly uttered are probably "Oops!" and "Sorry."

Dr. Frank Clayton, an orthopedic surgeon, related a funny story about "Oops."

Dr. Clayton said that when he was in medical school, they told him that if he slipped up and made a mistake during surgery, never *ever* say "Oops." The patient might be conscious, and upon hearing that word, will become very worried.

The instruction was to retrain your automatic response: if you make a mistake, instead of saying "Oops," say, *"There!"*

So if you ever mess up while dancing, just smile at your partner confidently and say, "There!"

# What Is A Mistake?

## by Gregory Manker
### an essay from Social Dance 1

I signed up for Social Dance this quarter because I thought it would be cool to know some dances, but I didn't expect that it would cause me to think about the nature of making mistakes, and more importantly, cause me to change the way I deal with "messing up."

When I started dancing, I was ashamed of missteps and botched moves. I interpreted errors as a sign of my stupidity, and I'd apologize to my partner whenever I did something wrong. Doing so, I felt, was the right thing to do. Doesn't it always make things better to admit one's mistake and move forward?

In certain situations, admission of one's error is critical. Companies facing product problems often do it and emerge stronger than before because people like honesty. Apple admitted the iPhone 4 had cell reception issues, and in doing so, quelled a potential media and consumer backlash.

Social dance, however, isn't a competitive marketplace. People dance for many reasons, chief amongst them to have fun. My job, as a Lead, is to ensure that my partner is enjoying herself as much as possible, and I found that one way to have more fun is to stop admitting mistakes.

What is a "mistake"? A mistake is defined by perception. People are usually so focused on their own dancing that they won't notice a problem unless it's pointed out to them. **A mistake only exists if it gets labeled as such. After a certain point, I stopped apologizing for missteps and ambiguous leads and learned to smile and keep going, and my dance experience improved dramatically.** Even if a partner notices that I "messed up", what good does it do to point it out? One of the best dances I had, in fact, was a Tango in which I had forgotten all of the moves and my partner led me through it. I think we were laughing so hard, she forgot some steps.

So what did this quarter of social dance teach me? It taught me how to do swing, waltz, tango and a variety of other dances. And I learned much more. I might forget the dance moves with time, but the lessons I learned about failure will stick with me as I weave them into my approach to interacting with people. I am often very hard on myself, and there are moments when I get myself into a prolonged funk over my mistakes, when in fact, I need to smile and keep dancing.

> "Creativity is allowing yourself to make mistakes.
> Art is knowing which ones to keep."
> — Scott Adams, cartoonist

# Smile

What do you do if your partner "messes up" and does something unexpected?

If you've taken our classes, you know the answer: *smile* and keep on dancing.

But *why* is smiling so important that we mention it as often as we do in our classes?

Let's begin with the most obvious reason: it reassures your partner that the mess-up wasn't a problem. They're probably wondering, so a reassuring smile is much appreciated.

But this isn't the only reason to smile. Smiling has many additional benefits. For example, smiling simply feels good, for the person who smiles, and for those who see it.

Positive feelings evoke a smile, but it can also work the other way: a smile itself can evoke positive feelings. **Even choosing to smile for no reason can significantly boost our mood**, in a powerful effect known as *facial feedback*.

Interestingly, the smile doesn't need to be our own to do this. In addition to neurons which create a two-way link between the expression and experience of an emotion, we have other neurons, called *mirror neurons*, which create a two-way link between our emotional experience and the emotional experience of others. **Seeing someone smile engages many of the same neurons as smiling ourselves, and carries with it similar mood benefits.**

But while the mood benefits of smiling are worth smiling about, the main adaptive purpose of smiling is social—creating, sustaining, and building relationships—and at this task, it performs exceedingly well.

In a recent experiment involving a game of trust, participants were shown six-second videos of several different people they could play with, including one who was smiling genuinely, and one who was not smiling. In a survey before the game, participants rated smiling people as significantly more **likable**, more **attractive**, and more **trustworthy** than people who were not smiling, and they expected the smiling people to be significantly more likely to cooperate with them in the game.

When asked to choose someone to play with, participants were **ten times as likely to choose a smiling partner**. Later, while playing the game, those who were playing with a smiling partner were nearly **three times as likely to choose to cooperate with their partner**, compared to those who were playing with a partner who wasn't smiling.

After the game was over, players with smiling players were more willing to play with their partner again, and more interested in meeting their partner outside the lab.

All of this from one simple smile.

*How* shall we smile? With our eyes, and often. All of these benefits of smiling are multiplied when we "smile with our eyes," as compared to just raising the corners of our mouths. And of course, the more we choose to smile, the more we, and those around us, will benefit.

# Laugh

While we encourage dancers to smile when they "mess up," we often find that laughter also ensues. And we're happy to hear this, because laughter is also beneficial.

Although physiologically distinct from smiling, **laughter also serves to boost our mood**, even more so than smiling. But laughter not only raises our spirits: it also physically eases our pains, as **laughter triggers the release of endorphins**, the brain's own brand of morphine. And laughter, like smiling, is highly contagious, meaning that its benefits quickly spread.

**Laughter also serves to soothe our partners.** Evolutionary researchers note that while laughter was eventually co-opted for less noble purposes, i.e., to manipulate, deride, and subvert, laughter's primary purpose was, and still is, to signal positive social intention and strengthen social bonds to enhance cooperation.

Even laughter at humor is a co-option of laughter's original function. According to a study of laughter in daily conversation, only 10 to 20% of laughs were preceded by anything remotely funny. The other 80 to 90% of laughs served **laughters' primary purpose: casting an otherwise ambiguous social situation in a more obviously positive light**.

Perhaps the most unique and essential benefit of laughter, however, is its remarkable ability to defuse our fears. As Stephen Colbert put it, "you can't laugh and be afraid at the same time." And "that's not a philosophical statement," he clarified, "it's a physiological statement. When you laugh, you're not afraid."

The evidence seems to bear out Colbert's instinct. When young children are exposed to something unexpected, they generally have one of two divergent reactions. If they are surprised and feel threatened, they will start to cry. But if they are surprised and feel safe, they will laugh instead.

Depending on the context and our emotional state, laughter and fear are two alternative reactions that we can have in situations where we face something unexpected. And to the degree that we can consciously influence these reactions, laughter and fear are alternative choices in a world filled with shocking twists and turns.

As neuroscientist Gregory Berns explains, when our brains sense pain, or anticipate loss, we tend to hold onto what we have. When the fear system of the brain is active, exploratory activity and risk-taking are turned off, depriving us of exactly the creative ability we need to get ourselves out of a fearful situation.

Laughter, on the other hand, is, as psychologist Dacher Keltner puts it, "a lightning bolt of wisdom, a moment in which the individual steps back and gains a broader perspective upon their lives and the human condition."

**Where fear closes doors, laughter opens them.**

In an era in which our fears are increasing, along with the importance of trying new things to build a saner, more sustainable world, this laughing lesson rings especially true.

# Musicality

Music has often been described as the spirit or soul of dance. It drives our dancing, both physically and emotionally.

Thus, ideal dance partnering is often described as a three-way collaboration between the Lead, the Follow, and the music, with each contributing equally to the dance.

Whenever we ask what qualities dancers most admire in their partners, someone mentions that they love partners who dance musically. Others in the group always agree.

Fortunately, musicality isn't some mysterious gift which some people are born with, but rather a few easy awarenesses that can help enhance our dancing.

For both Leads and Follows, **musicality primarily arises from truly listening to the music.**

Music has many layers, dynamics and textures. It isn't just a metronome. Rather than counting the beats, or analytically thinking about the elements of music, *feel* its emotional content. Lose yourself in the music. Let it carry you along its journey. Embody it with your dancing. As the saying goes, "dancing is music made visible."

## Musicality for Leads

Here are three specific suggestions for musical dancing for Leads. If these suggestions are too much to think about simultaneously, then **focus on truly listening to and feeling the music**. That's the most important part, and if you do that, the rest will follow automatically.

### 1) Match the Beats

Step exactly to the beat of the music, not ahead or behind the beat or faster or slower than the tempo. There are both positive and negative motivations for doing this. In the positive, it's a wonderful sensation to feel exactly in sync with a dance partner as you move together to music. In the negative, Follows hate being led to dance off the beat.

*Note:* By "off the beat," we mean disconnected from the beat. Steps that are connected to the beats in more complex ways, such as triple-steps ("1-and-2"), canter steps ("1, 3"), and hemiolas (two against three), aren't "off the beat." In fact, these steps can be quite satisfying, especially when they match the quality of the music.

In order to step with more precise timing, imagine that your stepping is the drummer for the music that's being played. Step more lightly than a drummer would hit his drums, but just as precisely. Of course, while the drummer in the music may be doing something more complex, you'll want to drum simply, tapping out precisely the rhythm of the dance you're dancing.

In addition, make sure you're dancing on the downbeat of the music, beginning the dance on count 1 of the measure. And in waltz, polka, schottische, and other dances with two halves, make sure the halves of the dance are aligned to the phrases of the music, with the first half of the dance step on the first half of the musical phrase. If you find that you're off the music, simply pause for a moment and get a more musical start. Your partner will appreciate it.

*Note:* This advice is the best starting point. In the future you may encounter exceptions, like some blues and tango dancing that encourages dancers to play around with the timing, as a jazz singer would.

## 2) Match the Punctuation and Phrasing

While aligning your footwork to the music is a good start, it is even better when you can align your figures to it. Music has punctuation marks, so to speak: commas, semicolons, periods, exclamation marks, etc. Dance has similar punctuation marks. Punctuate the music with your dancing.

This often requires a few seconds of delayed gratification. Your inclination might be to lead a variation the moment it pops into your head. To you, that would be spontaneous, intuitive dancing. But she isn't actually reading your mind (even if it seems like it). She is dancing to the music. So when the idea of a variation occurs to you, hold that thought for a few seconds and lead it when you feel the music best expresses the pulse of that variation. While she'll probably enjoy the variation in any case, this way will leave her thinking, "Wow, everything's so musical with *him!*" You want to be that *him.*

When transitioning from one waltz form to another, time the transition to occur when the music changes, often at the end of an eight bar phrase, where the Follow will most likely expect a change. She will appreciate it happening where she expected it, as if you were reading her mind.

## 3) Match the Energy and Quality

Finally, you can add even more to your musicality by matching your choice of variations not only to the changes in the music, but to the energy and quality of the music.

Matching the energy is easy. Use large movements for high-energy music, gentle and understated movements for quiet music, and explore all of the subtler degrees in between.

Qualities to match might include undulation, edginess, sweetness, mysteriousness, delight, silliness, and so on, infinitely. If the music is repetitiously trance-like, you might want to settle into a trance-like repeating basic step. Latin-sounding music can be matched by dancing with salsa, tango, or flamenco styling. Our friend Lucas turned the "Imperial March" from Star Wars into a waltz and sure enough, everyone was soon dancing a bombastic "cross-step march."

## 4) Adopt Your Partner's Musicality

The Follow can add just as much musical styling as the Lead, perhaps even more so, since the Follow role often hears the music more directly. Notice the way your partner is moving to the quality of the music (undulating, edgy, mysterious, silly, etc.) and match her style. In other words, it's possible to have a kind of partnering teamwork where he is leading the figures, choosing the right musical moments for each one, while she leads the quality of musical styling. She follows his figures while he follows her styling.

# Musicality for Follows

While the Follow doesn't need to think about leading variations at musical moments, she contributes just as much to the musicality of the partnership. Here are some specific tips for Follows:

## 1) Match the Energy and Quality

Read #3 on the previous page. All of that also applies to the Follow role, who can lead the musical movement style of the dancing, while he is leading the figures. In this case, he follows the quality of her movement as she follows his figures.

## 2) Amplify the Music

As we noted in "Role Reversal," because the Follow role has "all of her antennae open" to pick up and act on any incoming signal, she often hears the music more clearly than he does, distracted as he may be by planning or navigating. Thus, as a Follow, you can greatly help him by carefully keeping the beat, giving him an amplified, physical signal of the music.

*Note:* If he's still off the beat, you can either kindly let him know, or you can test your own following skills by matching his timing, which can actually be quite a fun challenge!

In addition to keeping and amplifying the beat, you can also match the qualities of your movements to the music, which not only makes your dancing more enjoyable but helps him sense those qualities too.

## 3) Be Ready for Anything at Musical Moments

While you will likely want to have "all of your antennae open" all the time, be particularly attentive at musical moments, ready for any change that may come (or not).

Just as Follows find it particularly satisfying when Leads lead changes at musical moments, Leads find it particularly satisfying when Follows are ready for anything at those moments, allowing the changes to happen so naturally that it feels like the decision to change was mutual.

A potential danger of this pointer is that expecting something to happen at musical moments can become one more way for us to unnecessarily disapprove of our partners, not to mention another way to disappoint ourselves. Thus, be *ready* for anything, while *expecting* nothing. Another potential danger is that you might interpret this advice to mean that you can pay less attention in the middle of a musical phrase, but of course that is not what we're suggesting. Be ready for anything all the time, just *particularly* ready in those musical moments.

## 4) Be Patient and Encouraging

If he leads something that isn't particularly musical, or misses an opportunity to be especially musical, be patient with him. He has a lot on his mind. Musicality takes time to develop, and is often forgotten in the heat of the moment. Be understanding and encouraging of his musical development.

If you want to help him become even more musical, be particularly encouraging of his musical successes, either verbally ("that was so musical!") or simply by giving him an even bigger smile. He'll see how much you enjoy those moments, and seeking to please you, become even more musical in the future.

## Developing Musicality

As with all of the other aspects of dance, developing musicality takes time, and follows the trajectory described in "Conscious Competence" (p. 75).

First, you won't even be aware of musicality (*Unconscious Incompetence*). Then you'll be aware of it, but know you're not very good at it (*Conscious Incompetence*). However, as you progress through your dancing education, you'll slowly begin to dance more musically by devoting more conscious attention to the music, perhaps even counting the beats and phrases in your head (*Conscious Competence*). Eventually, when you spend enough time with dancing and dance music, musicality will simply become a part of your dancing without having to count it out or think about it, and you will naturally adjust your dancing to the music, even when the song is one that you haven't heard (*Unconscious Competence*).

*Note:* If you think "but I'm just not a musical person" refer to "Mindsets" on p. 73. Everyone can develop their musicality.

Developing musicality is an ongoing journey, and the ideas about musicality we've presented in this chapter are just the beginning. There are many other ways to interpret music, and we encourage you to explore them all.

We can always get better at dancing musically, just as we can always get better at dancing for our partners. Put these two pursuits together, and you will gain the enhanced pleasure of a truly musical conversation between yourself, your partner, and the music, moving together in perfect three-part harmony.

# Dancing in 5/4 Time

Occasionally, you'll find a song written in 5/4 time, like Dave Brubeck's "Take Five," or the Naruto ending theme "Wind" by Akeboshi. What, you may wonder, can I dance to this?

Here are a few ideas. Some are vintage 19th century variations. Others are brand new.

## Five-Step Waltz

**Five-Step Waltz (Easy Version):** Simply waltz six steps of rotary waltz in five counts: three in three counts and three in two counts (smooth polka timing, 1-and-2, quick-quick-slow).
    "1-2-3, 4-and-5," turning 180° on each part, 360° total
    "1-and-2, 3-4-5 is also possible if it fits better with the music

*Note:* All of the variations described here can be modified to better fit the phrasing of the music: does it sound more like 3+2 or 2+3? The former pattern, 3+2, is more prevalent, but there are always exceptions.

**Five-Step Waltz (Original Pivot Version from 1847):** Half of a rotary waltz, then one 180° pivot step on count 4 to finish the turn on counts 4-5, ready to waltz again on count 1.
    "waltz-2-3, pivot," turning 180° on each part, 360° total
    If you prefer, you can do a hopped pivot (step-hop) as in schottische, on counts 4-5
    Or you can do two pivot steps on counts 4-5, turning 540° total to repeat opposite

**Five-Step Viennese Step:** The Viennese Step (p. 152), with even timing throughout.
    "waltz-2-3, leap-click," turning 180° on each part, 360° total

All of the above can be done with Leap Waltz or Redowa (p. 147) in place of rotary waltz.

**Five-Step Mazurka:** Mazurka Step (p. 150), then a 180° leap and a hop. Repeat opposite.
    "ma-zur-ka, leap-hop," turning 180° total, repeat opposite

**Five-Step Carlowitzka/Gitana:** Three gliding, turning hops then two gliding, turning hops, turning 180° during each section (p. 151), then Five-Step Mazurka, turning another 180°.
    "glide-hop-hop, glide-hop, ma-zur-ka, leap-hop," turning 540° total, repeat opposite

**Five-Step Newport:** Half Newport, half Waltz Galop (p. 148).
    "leap side-close side-close, leap side-close," turning 360° total

**Five-Slide Galop:** Combinations of Three-Slide Galop (p. 192), polka, and Pivots.
    "three-slide + polka," repeat, or "polka + polka + pivot," repeat opposite
    There are other possibilities, but you get the idea.

All of the above can also be reversed, with counterclockwise rotation.

# Ten Count Swing

In addition to waltzing in 5/4 time, you can dance swing in 5/4 time (or rather, 10/8 time).

Many songs identified as being in 5/4, such as the "Mission Impossible Theme" or "Living in the Past" by Jethro Tull, are actually written 10/8. And 10/8 is often sub-divided 1-2-3, 1-2-3, 1-2, 1-2, or slow-slow-quick-quick.

**Ten-Count Swing:** Thus, six-count east coast swing (slow-slow-quick-quick) can be danced in 10/8 time simply by dancing the slow and quick steps of the dance in concert with the slow and quick impulses in the music. (For the mathematically inclined, step 1, 4, 7, and 9.)

**Ten-Count Foxtrot:** The same logic works for slow-slow-quick-quick (Magic Step) foxtrot. In fact, the Mission Impossible Theme is one of our favorite songs for foxtrotting.

# Music in 5/4 Time

## Songs in 5/4 Time

- "Take Five" by Dave Brubeck

- "Wind" by Akeboshi

- "Oh God" by Jamie Cullum

## Songs in 10/8 Time

- "Mission Impossible Theme" by Danny Elfman

- "Living in the Past" by Jethro Tull

- "Don't Be Afraid" (from Final Fantasy VIII) by Nobuo Uematsu

## Songs in Mixed Meters including 5/4 Time

- "5/6" by Jason Mraz (5/4 and 3/4)

- "In My Blood" by Starsailor (5/4 and 3/4)

- "Harbor" by Vienna Teng (5/4 and 7/4)

*Note:* While the songs in the "Discography of Waltz Music" (p. 223) are all readily available and ready to play, these songs are not all available for digital purchase, and they are not necessarily ready to play without editing (for tempo, extra beats, and non-5/4 or 10/8 bars.)

# Dancing in 7/4 Time

While even more rare than songs in 5/4 time, songs in 7/4 time do exist. For example, Yanni's "Waltz in 7/8," and "The Majestic Tale (of a Madman in a Box)" from Doctor Who (Series 6). How might we imagine dancing in 7/4 time?

Here are a few of the ideas we've come up with.

## Seven-Step Waltz

**Seven-Step Waltz (Hop Version):** Rotary waltz with a hop to fill the extra count. This turns like regular rotary waltz, slowing the rotation a bit on the half with the hop.
    "waltz-2-3, waltz-5-6-hop," turning 180° on each part, 360° total
    "waltz-2-3-hop, waltz-6-7" is also possible if it fits better with the music

*Note:* All of the variations described here can be modified to better fit the phrasing of the music: does it sound more like 4+3 or 3+4?

**Seven-Step Waltz (Pivot Version):** Rotary waltz with a single pivot step to fill the extra count. This turns an additional 180°, meaning that it repeats on the other foot.
    "waltz-2-3, waltz-5-6, pivot," turning 540° total, repeat opposite

**Seven-Step Waltz (Slow and Quick Version):** Nine steps of rotary waltz in seven counts, three in three counts and six in four (smooth polka timing, 1-and-2, quick-quick-slow). Nine steps gets you on the other foot, so the steps that are quick and slow will switch every time.
    waltz: "1-2-3, 4-and-5, 6-and-7," turning 540° total, repeat opposite

All of the above can be done with Leap Waltz or Redowa (p. 147) in place of rotary waltz.

**Seven-Step Polka Mazurka:** Polka Mazurka (p. 150) with a hop on the end.
    "glide-cut-lift, glide-cut-leap-hop," turning 180° total, repeat opposite

**Seven-Step Carlowitzka/Gitana:** La Carlowitzka (La Gitana) (p. 151) with a fourth turning hop on the first foot in the first half, and a hop on the end of the second half.
    "glide-hop-hop-hop, glide-hop-hop, glide-cut-lift, glide-cut-leap-hop,"
turning 540° total, repeat opposite. *Note:* As described, this mixes 4+3 and 3+4.

**Seven-Step Newport:** Full Waltz Galop, half Newport (p. 148) and repeat opposite.
    "leap side-close, leap side-close, leap side-close side-close,"
turning 540° total, repeat opposite

**Seven-Slide Galop:** Combinations of Four-Slide Galop, Three-Slide Galop, polka, and Pivots.
    "four-slide + three-slide" and repeat
    "three-slide + polka + polka" and repeat opposite (or other combos of three and two)
    "polka + polka + polka + pivot" and repeat
    There are other possibilities, but you get the idea.

All of the above can also be reversed, with counterclockwise rotation.

# Music in 7/4 Time

## Songs in 7/4 (or 7/8) Time

* "Rusty Lance" by Akeboshi

* "Waltz in 7/8" by Yanni

* "The Majestic Tale (of a Madman in a Box)" by Murray Gold

## Songs in Mixed Meters including 7/4 Time

* "Harbor" by Vienna Teng (7/4 and 5/4)


*Note:* While the songs in the "Discography of Waltz Music" (p. 223) are all readily available and ready to play, these songs are not all available for digital purchase, and they are not necessarily ready to play without editing (for tempo, extra beats, and non-7/4 bars.)

# Zwiefacher

Zwiefacher (**zwee**-fah-ker, **zvee**-fah-ker) is a Bavarian folk dance, characterized by its irregular rhythms, combining several different steps in hundreds of different patterns in order to match the music, which alternates between 3/4 and 2/4 time.

Depending on the pattern, zwiefacher calls for stringing together different kinds of footwork: mostly waltz steps and pivots (German: *dreher*), but occasionally polka and schottische steps.

In some traditions, zwiefacher travels LOD, with waltzes and pivots exactly as we have described them in this book: a bar of waltz turns 180°, as does one pivot step. In other, older traditions, zwiefacher stays mostly in place, with waltz and pivot steps that rotate on the spot. Both ways of dancing zwiefacher can be satisfying. In either case, be especially careful not to run into other couples, or to get in the way of other couples. Safety is more important than a perfectly danced pattern.

Because it rotates rapidly and changes often, requiring a strong connection, zwiefacher tends to be danced in barrel hold: both partners holding both shoulders, his arms under hers.

## Zwiefacher Patterns

The easiest pattern, known as "Alte Kath," is $W_2P_2$ meaning two bars of waltz, then two pivot steps. It sounds like "**oom**-pah-pah, **oom**-pah-pah / **oom**-pah, **oom**-pah."

The waltzes happen on the "oom-pah-pah"s and the footfall of the pivots happens on the following "oom" and "oom," i.e.,waltz-2-3, waltz-2-3, pivot, pivot.

As noted above, there are literally hundreds of other patterns. Here are a few popular ones:

| | |
|---|---|
| Alte Kath | $W_2P_2$ |
| Wintergrün | $W_4(P_2W_2)_2$ |
| Eisenkeilnest | $(P_2W_2)_2(PW)_2P_2W_2$ |
| Zipfi-Michi (or Sommermichl) | $(P_4W_2)_4W_4(P_4W_2)_2((WP_2)_3W_2)_2$ |
| Suserl | some combination of $P_2(WP_2)_2W_2$ and $(P_2WP_2)_2P_2(WP_2)W_2$ |
| S'Luada | $(P_2W_2)_4P_{32}$    Yes, you read that right: 32 pivots! |

*Naming Note:* The same names are often used to refer to multiple patterns, and one pattern often has multiple names. These are some of the most popular and unambiguously named patterns, but there are always exceptions.

*Dancing Note:* Four pivots can be replaced by a slow full polka turn, if that's easier or more fun. Likewise, one pivot can be replaced by a QQS waltz (as in 5/4 and 7/4 waltzing). In any case, make sure that you and your partner have the same expectations going in. The default assumption is regular waltzes and pivots, but it's always a good idea to check.

When you actually dance zwiefacher at a social dance event, it could be any one of hundreds of different patterns.

Sometimes the band or DJ will be clear in announcing the pattern, but other times they won't. In any case, zwiefacher remains an exciting challenge for even the most experienced waltzers.

## Tips for Surviving Zwiefacher

- Dance zwiefacher in whichever way you know that you and your partner will be able to do it comfortably. If that means traveling around the perimeter of room, wonderful. If that means rotating in place on one spot in the middle of the floor, great. Even stepping in place without rotating works, as does simply walking out the rhythm in promenade position. Do whatever is most comfortable and fun.

- Dance for your partner's footwork, rather than your own. Focus on helping them get the timing, and helping them rotate, if you happen to be traveling.

- *Relax.* This is the perfect time to practice "Dynamic Equanimity" (p. 55).

- When you or your partner makes an alternate interpretation of the song, don't worry. Just stay relaxed and keep on dancing. Or, if you prefer, pause for a moment, getting out of the way of other couples, or walking to keep up with the flow of traffic. Restart yourselves when you pick up the pattern again. In either case, remember the advice of "Bouncing Back" (p. 199): resilience is more important than perfection.

## Zwiefacher Music

If you want to try dancing zwiefacher, here are some sample tunes, available on iTunes, representative of the patterns listed on the previous page:

| Pattern | Song Title | Artist |
|---|---|---|
| Alte Kath | "Da Hemauer" | Tanngrindler Musikanten |
| Wintergrün | "S'Deandl vom Wintergrea" | Karl Edelmann |
| Eisenkeilnest | "Eisenkeilnest" | Störnsteiner Blasmusik |
| Zipfi-Michi | "Da Zipfe Michi" | Karl Edelmann |
| Suserl | "S'Suserl" | Karl Edelmann |
| S'Luada | "S'Luada" | Karl Edelmann |

# Going Out Dancing

*How to have more fun,*
*and how to let your dance partners have more fun*

## A Few Ground Rules (Musts)

- Floorcraft. Please take extra care not to bump other couples, i.e., don't step on anyone (!), don't throw your partner into someone else (!!), and don't ram into another couple (!!!). Always be aware of the others around you. If you do bump into someone, apologize.

- Leads, look where you are going to lead her *before* you send her there. Don't begin a move unless there is room. Protect her from collisions.

- For dances that travel line of direction: The fast lane is on the outside. Please don't block or slow down traffic. Dance in the fast lane only if you can keep up. Choose variations which keep up with that flow—don't be a rock in the rapids. The slow lane, and the place for stationary steps, is in the center, the eye of the hurricane.

- If you're not dancing for the moment, clear completely off the floor. The dancers will appreciate it.

- Don't wear perfumes or colognes to a social dance. Most people don't consider it very sociable, and some have allergies. And similarly:

- Dance hygiene! We often can't smell our own odors so it is important that you brush your teeth, shower, use deodorant, and put on clean clothes before going out dancing, including to dance classes.

## Further Suggestions
(Optional, but Highly Recommended)

- Don't be sketchy (p. 137).

- Don't exhibit a pedantic attitude on the dance floor, attempting to correct your partners to conform to your preferred style. True social dancing is about having fun and letting your partners enjoy themselves. Criticizing your partner is antisocial and simply isn't fun.

- If your partner's style of dancing is different from your own, we encourage you to be flexible and go more than halfway toward adapting to your partner's style. You'll impress your partner with your generosity (i.e., that you're nice), open-mindedness (i.e., that you're intelligent), and as a side bonus, you may learn something new that you'll like.

- If you are far more experienced than your partner, simplify your dancing somewhat for your partner's comfort. Yes, some challenges and surprises are fun, but being pushed around uncomfortably isn't.

- We encourage you to dance with people you don't already know. Most dancers will be happy to dance with someone new.

- If you think you might get sweaty while dancing, bring a spare dry shirt or two. Most dancers hate to hold on to a clammy wet shirt.

- If there is live music, don't treat the musicians like canned music. Let them know that you appreciate their presence and their talent.

- Relax. During the inevitable mess-ups, smile and keep on dancing. Truly exceptional dancers will almost always make a mistake look like something they planned, whenever possible. There are no mistakes in dancing, only new moves.

- Dance for your partner. But also dance *with* your partner—have fun yourself, and let your partner know that you're having fun with them.

*Illustration by Richard Powers*

# Where Can I Go Dancing?

This question used to be easy to answer, for a century and a half.

In the 19th century, the average American and European citizen knew how to waltz, polka, schottische, galop, and dance quadrilles. There were opportunities to go to balls and private soirées every week.

Similarly, most people knew how to social dance during the Ragtime Era and Roaring Twenties, now dancing the tango, foxtrot, one-step, maxixe, hesitation waltz, and Charleston. Dance halls sprung up like mushrooms, and hotels turned any available space into a dance floor, even their rooftops.

The next era saw a proliferation of *dine and dance* clubs, for swing, shag, the Big Apple, rumba, and samba, while foxtrot and tango continued.

So 1) most people knew how to do a wide variety of dances, and 2) there were many places to go out dancing.

**Today is different.** Most towns and cities have *specialized* dance groups, like a salsa club, west coast swing night, hustle club, Argentine tango milonga, or a Lindy hop group. They do their one specialty all night long, so their technique and vocabulary of moves goes deep and complex, often overwhelming beginners trying to join the group. The only place to find a wide variety of partnered dances may be at a competition-based ballroom dance studio, but their dance technique is also specialized and challenging.

Where can you find non-competitive social dancing? We have three answers.

## Mostly-Waltz Groups

There are more than thirty groups in the U.S. that hold weekly or monthly evenings of waltz-based classes and dance parties. The fact that rotary and cross-step waltz feel like two different dances could already keep an evening interesting, but most groups also play music for swing, tango, cha cha, polka, salsa, and many other social dances at their parties.

An updated list of mostly-waltz groups, with a map and links to their Web pages, can be found at: waltzingbook.com/waltzgroups

## Workshops

These are a wonderful way to escape into another world for a weekend or week, while learning new dances and meeting new people. Some are held in especially beautiful locations, set up as a dance vacation.

We don't know of a comprehensive list of all dance workshops, but an updated list of our waltz weekends and workshops is here: waltzingbook.com/workshops

# Do It Yourself!

This isn't as difficult as it might seem. All of those dance groups were started by someone. Here are some suggestions for starting a local waltz or social dance scene.

## Venues

You'll probably begin by looking for a place to hold your dances. You'll want a space that is conveniently located and has a friendly, welcoming atmosphere. Avoid a room with support posts that dancers can run into.

You'll also want an affordable space because you'll probably start small, before word-of-mouth grows, and you don't want to lose money on high rent right at the beginning.

1) Churches are often a good choice. Some churches rent out a large room, but better yet, many churches sponsor groups that they feel are a benefit to the community. Show them this book, to help explain the many ways that a social dance group will be good for the community, and also for the personal growth of the participants. Show them chapters like "Love Thy Neighbor," "Giving," and "The Third Place."

2) Lodges like the Odd Fellows, Elks, Eagles, Shriners, and Masons tend to have great spaces for dancing, often on the top floor of a downtown building (top floors usually don't have posts). As above, they often rent their space, or may sponsor a group that they feel is compatible with their mission or will benefit the community.

3) Dance studios are sometimes affordable, and if so, may be a good place to start because they tend to be small.

## Starting Small

Avoid starting out in a large hall. A dozen dancers in a large room will feel unsuccessful, as if no one came. The same dozen in a smaller room will feel full and successful, in a nicely intimate way, like a small party. Then you can move to a larger space when the group grows.

If you're wondering how many dancers fit into a room, we've found that 0.025 dancers per square foot works best for a class. More can fit into a room for a dance party or ball

# More

This chapter could go on for pages. Since this topic is a specialized interest, we have put the rest of our suggestions on our website. You will find further information on rentable halls, event insurance, music and sound systems, ASCAP fees, publicity, mailing lists, arranging an evening of classes and dances, and the best nights of the week for a successful dance event. Go to: waltzingbook.com/diy

"Dance, even if you have nowhere to do it but your living room."
— Mary Schmich, author

# Connections

One of greatest benefits of social dance is simply that it's *social*, and by dancing socially, we are building connections. This is important because of all the positive aspects of life that we've studied, the benefits of connection are some of the most dramatic.

As Robert Putnam writes in *Bowling Alone,* connection is *essential* to our happiness and health. According to dozens of scientific studies, **people who are socially disconnected are between two and five times more likely to die from all causes, compared to similar individuals who have close ties with family, friends, and the community.**

"As a rough rule of thumb," Putnam advises, "if you belong to no groups but decide to join one, you cut your risk of dying over the next year in half."

Putnam also notes that the single most common finding from a half century's research on the correlates of life satisfaction, not only in the United States but around the world, is that **happiness is best predicted by the breadth and depth of one's social connections.**

Joining an organization like a social waltz group "is the happiness equivalent of getting a college degree or more than doubling your income."

Of course, it makes a difference whom we connect with.

As Nicholas Christakis and James Fowler demonstrate in *Connected,* when we join a social network, we subject ourselves to all kinds of unexpected social contagion. By analyzing decades of data from thousands of socially-connected people, Christakis and Fowler have discovered that the relationship between people's happiness extends to three degrees of separation, meaning that your happiness depends on and influences the happiness of your *friends' friends' friends.*

**As a result, people who surround themselves with happy people—social dancers, for example—are significantly more likely to become and stay happy than those who are surrounded by unhappy people.**

They have also discovered that many other conditions and behaviors are socially contagious over three degrees of separation, including obesity, sleeping habits, drinking habits, drug use, feelings of loneliness, and charitable giving. It seems your mother was right: choose your friends carefully.

But while this is true to some degree, Christakis and Fowler clarify that "although bad things can spread through networks, the overall effect of a close personal connection is usually positive: **on average, every friend makes us happier and healthier.**"

Finally, it's not just *that* we're connected to other people. It's ***how*** we're connected to them, ***how*** we interact with them—the different kinds of relationships we form.

Interacting with our partners in a loving way, as we propose in this book, affects us, and affects our partners, in a different (and much more beneficial) way than interacting with them in a controlling, pedantic way. As a result, we end up being better people, living together in a better world.

# Recommended Reading on Connections

- *Connected: How Your Friends' Friends' Friends Affect Everything You Feel, Think, and Do* (2009) by Nicholas Christakis and James Fowler

- *Bowling Alone: The Collapse and Revival of American Community* (2000) by Robert Putnam

- *Consequential Strangers: The Power of People Who Don't Seem to Matter . . . But Really Do* (2009) by Melinda Blau and Karen L. Fingerman

- *Creating Community Anywhere: Finding Support and Connection in a Fragmented World* (2005) by Carolyn R. Shaffer and Kristin Anundsen

# The Third Place

People come for the dancing, but it's not the only reason they stay and come back to the dance hall week after week.

The dance hall itself provides many benefits, complementary to but independent from the dancing. It's a beautiful example of a place so rare today, a place which Ray Oldenburg calls *the third place*.

If *the first place* is home, and the *second place* is work, the *third place* is an essential space away from both, a public social space that forms the heart of a community.

In his book, *The Great Good Place: Cafés, Coffee Shops, Bookstores, Bars, Hair Salons and Other Hangouts at the Heart of a Community*, Oldenburg describes the qualities and benefits of the third place.

## Qualities of the Third Place

- The third place is an accommodating space conveniently located to serve our needs for relaxation and sociability, providing escape from work and home.

- Conversation is the main activity of the third place, whether it's in the form of talking or waltzing. In fact, "conversation" comes from the Latin *com-* "with" *vertere* "to turn."

- The third place is neutral ground, where we may come and go as we please. No one is required to play host, so everyone can feel at home and comfortable.

- By being open to all and emphasizing qualities that are not confined to the usual status distinctions, the third place acts as a social leveler.

- The third place has a playful mood, as well as regulars who help set this mood and welcome new faces to the community.

All together, the third place is a home away from home, where regulars can feel free to be themselves, while simultaneously contributing to something greater.

## Benefits of the Third Place

- The third place provides friends by the set. Through these affiliations and friendships, we feel that we belong to a larger group, which is different from and just as important as having pairwise relationships.

- The diverse population of the third place fosters a unique richness of human contact. By bringing together people of diverse backgrounds, professions, interests, and ideas, the third place allows unrelated people to relate, providing much needed perspective.

- The third place raises our spirits, as we enjoy our experience there. We leave feeling better about ourselves, for having received and bestowed such warm acceptance.

- The third place also provides social benefits, like encouraging community affiliation and countering the negative effects of mass media. People who isolate themselves at home and watch the news often get the feeling that "people out there" have become untrustworthy and dangerous. Social exchanges at the third place are an important reminder that real people are as wonderful as ever, in so many ways.

Perhaps the most essential benefit of the third place is its potential to inspire a positive culture shift.

"The third place is largely a world of its own making," Oldenburg writes, "quite independent of the institutional order of the larger society. If the world of the third place is far less consequential than the larger one, its regulars find abundant compensation in the fact that it is a more decent one, more in love with people for their own sake, and, hour for hour, a great deal more fun."

As a result, he says, "the third place is a force for good. It affords its habitués the opportunity for more decent human relations than prevail outside, and it is their habit to take advantage of that opportunity."

But something even more magical happens in the third place. As Oldenburg observes, this "promotion of decency in the third place is not limited to it."

**Those who come to the third place leave transformed.**

Once we have experienced the ways of being and relating that are possible in the third place —and on the dance floor—we simply cannot help but wonder **"what if the rest of the world was like this?" and act toward making this dream a reality.**

# Discography of Waltz Music

### Cross-Step Waltz
*3/4 time*
*Acceptable Tempo: 108 bpm to 120 bpm*
*(Sweet Spot: 114-116 bpm)*

- "Love Is the End" by Keane (110 bpm)
- "Enchantment" by Chris Spheeris (115 bpm)
- "Run" by Ludovico Einaudi (117 bpm)
- "I Miss You" by Incubus (117 bpm)
- "Winter Waltz" by Kitaro (117 bpm)
- "Lucky" by Bif Naked (118 bpm)
- "Another Trip to Skye" by Materdea (119 bpm)
- "Nickindia" by Nerina Pallot (120 bpm)
- "Lore of the Loom" by Secret Garden (120 bpm)
- "Scarborough Fair" by Sarah Brightman (120 bpm)

### Box Step Waltz
*3/4 time*
*Acceptable Tempo: 86 bpm to 110 bpm*
*(Sweet Spot: 100 bpm)*

- "At This Moment" by Michael Bublé (86 bpm)
- "Could I Have This Dance" by Anne Murray (88 bpm)
- "See the Day" by Girls Aloud (93 bpm)
- "Moon River" by Henry Mancini & His Orchestra (93 bpm) [one of many versions]
- "Through the Dark" by KT Tunstall (93 bpm)
- "Edelweiss" by New 101 Strings Orchestra (96 bpm) [one of many versions]
- "Open Arms" by Journey (101 bpm)

### Rotary Waltz (Moderate)
*3/4 time*
*Acceptable Tempo: 138 bpm to 160 bpm*
*(Sweet Spot: 144 bpm)*

- "Primavera" by Ludovico Einaudi (138 bpm)
- "You and Me" by Lifehouse (140 bpm)
- "Flora's Secret" by Enya (142 bpm)
- "After the Fall" by Two Steps from Hell (144 bpm)
- "Helplessly, Hopelessly" by Jessica Andrews (145 bpm)
- "Echo" by Jason Walker (149 bpm)
- "The Last Crossing" by Celtic Spirit (150 bpm)
- "Amas Veritas" by Alan Silvestri (153 bpm)
- "Together" by Michelle Branch (156 bpm)
- "Breakaway" by Kelly Clarkson (160 bpm)

## Rotary Waltz (Fast)

*3/4 time*
*Acceptable Tempo: 160 bpm to 190 bpm*
*(Sweet Spot: 168 bpm)*

- "Erin Shore (Instrumental)" by The Corrs (160 bpm)
- "Love Will Come Through" by Travis (160 bpm)
- "Waltz of Destiny" from Capital Scandal Soundtrack (162 bpm)
- "With You, Tonight" by Matt Wertz (162 bpm)
- "Sho's Song" from The Secret World of Arrietty Soundtrack (165 bpm)
- "I'm in Love" by Geoff Byrd (166 bpm)
- "Time" by Chantal Kreviazuk (167 bpm)
- "Utopia" by Within Temptation (171 bpm)
- "More Than a Memory" by Hoobastank (176 bpm)
- "Andalucia" by Pink Martini (186 bpm)

## Polka

*4/4 time*
*Acceptable Tempo: 104 to 124 bpm*
*(Sweet Spot: 114 bpm)*

- "Save a Horse, Ride a Cowboy" by Big & Rich (102 bpm)
- "Black Horse & The Cherry Tree" (106 bpm)
- "A Little Less Conversation [JXL Radio Edit Remix]" by Elvis Presley (116 bpm)
- "Ghostbusters" by Ray Parker, Jr. (116 bpm)
- "Zydeko" by Cirque du Soleil (117 bpm)
- "Love Today" by MIKA (124 bpm)
- "Per Colpa Di Chi" by Zucchero (126 bpm)

## Schottische

*4/4 time*
*Acceptable Tempo: 74 to 82 bpm*
*(Sweet Spot: 78 bpm)*

- "Elusive Butterfly" by Geoff Byrd (75 bpm)
- "Wavin' Flag (Coca-Cola Celebration Mix)" by K'Naan (76 bpm)
- "Misery" by Green Day (81 bpm)
- "The Way You Do the Things You Do" by UB40 (81 bpm)
- "You Make My Dreams Come True" by Hall & Oates (82 bpm)
- "I'll Do Anything" by Jason Mraz (82 bpm)
- "Don't Care What Time It Is" by Rachel Platten (83 bpm)

## Make Your Own Waltzes

Stanford student Lucas Garron created a Web site that converts your favorite songs into waltzes. Most music is written in duple (4/4) time. Lucas' script converts it to waltz (3/4) time. You simply drag and drop an audio file of a song onto the page and it "waltzifies" it for you. For a link to that page, visit: waltzingbook.com/music

# The Power of Music

While many of the benefits of social dancing are the result of moving in concert with a partner, others are the result of the concert of music that fills the air in social dance halls everywhere.

To begin with the obvious, we feel good when listening to music. In one study, students were randomly asked throughout the day whether they were listening to music, and if so, how it made them feel. **Time with music was more frequently associated with feelings of happiness-elation and nostalgia-longing, while time without music was more frequently associated with anger-irritation, boredom-indifference, and anxiety-fear.** And even nostalgia-longing can be beneficial. David Huron proposes that sad music can actually be quite comforting, because it tricks the brain into producing prolactin, a tranquilizing hormone associated with orgasm, birth, and breast-feeding.

In general, neuroscientist David Levitin reports that "music activates the same parts of the brain and causes the same neurochemical cocktail as a lot of other pleasurable activities like orgasms or eating chocolate."

But the effects of music are not purely emotional: music can also benefit us physically, influencing our heart rate, blood pressure, and breathing, among other essential bodily functions, which are each affected by the tempo and quality of the music, an effect which scientists call *entrainment*.

This capacity of music to "play the body" gives it the ability to affect our physical health. **Calming music, for example, can ameliorate the effects of stress**, stopping the rise of cortisol after a stressful experience, and significantly accelerating its decline thereafter.

**Music can also soothe our pains.** Surgical patients who listen to comforting music recover more quickly, report fewer complications, feel less pain, and require less anesthetics, analgesics, and sedatives than those who suffer in silence.

Music therapy has even been shown, almost miraculously, to help Parkinson's patients walk, to help stroke victims speak, to help the autistic connect with other people, and to help Alzheimer's patients remember. In addition, *social dance therapy* has been shown particularly effective in the treatment of Parkinson's. And as we've noted before (p. 183), social dancing is an effective preventive measure against dementia.

According to Levitin, music is able to have such wide-ranging positive effects because music engages nearly every region of the brain, involving almost every neural system, as if it were conducting a grand "brain orchestra." By creating cross-talk between these areas, music is activating and building neural networks, synchronizing our bodies and minds.

In addition, by synchronizing *many different bodies and minds* at the same time on the dance floor, music has the power to build social networks too. While it's fun to hear our favorite music together, a large part of what make concerts and social dances so special is that they are shared experiences in which we are all physically entraining to the same beat.

As WWII veteran William McNeill writes in his book *Keeping Together in Time*, the effects of these experiences can be quite profound, especially when they involve shared movement. Here he reports on his experience in basic military training.

> Words are inadequate to describe the emotion aroused by the prolonged movement in unison that drilling involved. A sense of pervasive well-being is what I recall; more specifically, a strange sense of personal engagement; a sort of swelling out, becoming bigger than life, thanks to participation in collective ritual.

Social dancers will recognize this feeling, the soaring transcendence of moving together as one. A recent study discovered a possible source of this feeling: **moving in synchrony releases a flood of endorphins, beyond those already released by solo movement.**

Reviewing the impact of this transcendent feeling as experienced in synchronized dance and drill throughout history, McNeill concludes that

> human beings desperately need to belong to communities that give guidance and meaning to their lives; and ... euphoric response to keeping together in time ... is the surest, most speedy, and efficacious way of creating and sustaining such communities that our species has ever hit upon. ... It is something to mull over, wonder about, and —for bolder spirits—to experiment with.

## Recommended Reading on the Power of Music

- *This Is Your Brain on Music: The Science of a Human Obsession* (2006) by Daniel J. Levitin

- *Keeping Together in Time: Dance and Drill in Human History* (1995) by William H. McNeill

- *Dancing in the Streets: A History of Collective Joy* (2006) by Barbara Ehrenreich

- *The World in Six Songs: How the Musical Brain Created Human Nature* (2008) by Daniel J. Levitin

- *The Power of Music: Pioneering Discoveries in the New Science of Song* (2011) by Elena Mannes

- *The Music Instinct: Science and Song* (2009) directed by Elena Mannes (PBS Special)

# Gratitude

To have three minutes of heavenly dancing with another human being in your arms, again and again for hours on end. It's hard to imagine anything better.

It's enough to fill one's heart with gratitude.

Which, as it turns out, is a wonderful thing, as gratitude is a powerful force for good in the world. Albert Schweitzer maintained that "the greatest thing is to give thanks for everything. He who has learned this has penetrated the whole mystery of life."

The new psychology of gratitude is beginning to show that there is truth to this claim.

In pioneering studies, psychologists Robert Emmons and Michael McCullough have shown that *cultivating gratitude* can have dramatic and lasting impacts on our health and well-being.

In their experiments, participants were randomly assigned to cultivate gratitude by writing down five things they were thankful for each day, as opposed to writing down five hassles, or five neutral things that happened to them. **Those who kept a gratitude journal reported feeling more positive emotions, fewer negative emotions, greater satisfaction with their life, and more optimism about their future.** These beneficial changes were observed not only by the gratitude journalers themselves, but also by their significant others.

Participants who counted their blessings also began to adopt other beneficial habits: exercising more, sleeping more and better, and experiencing fewer symptoms of illness.

Finally, gratitude journalers reported **feeling more connected with others**, and were more likely to offer their help and support to people around them.

That waltzing inspires a sense of gratitude, and likely brings with it some of the aforementioned benefits, is more than enough reason for us to be thankful.

But the connection between waltzing and gratitude runs deeper, as social dance etiquette requires us to *express* our gratitude, thanking every partner we dance with. This simple practice has many benefits: for ourselves, for our partners, and for the rest of the world.

First, and perhaps most obviously, it simply feels good to express and receive gratitude. In fact, in a recent review of positive psychology interventions, **sincerely expressing thanks face-to-face was the single most powerful mood booster studied.**

The other immediate impact of thanking is that gratitude builds and sustains relationships. In new relationships, like those created on the dance floor, gratitude acts as a relationship jump starter. When either partner feels gratitude, both partners perceive the relationship more positively. The same is true as the relationship develops, except that later on, gratitude acts as a booster shot, reminding both partners why they value the relationship.

Then, the essential benefits of thanking our partners extend beyond ourselves and our partners, to improve the lives of everyone around us. Studies of gratitude have shown that when James sincerely says "thank you" to Emily, James and Emily both become more likely to act generously toward each other—**and also toward unrelated others**—in the future.

Emily, having been thanked for her kindness, feels good about her good deeds and is motivated to repeat them, not only with James, but with the rest of the world. James, having received the benefits of Emily's kindness, is motivated pay it back to Emily, and also to pay the kindness forward to the world.

It is with this understanding that sociologist Georg Simmel called gratitude "the moral memory of mankind," writing, "if every grateful action, which lingers on from good turns received in the past, were suddenly eliminated, society (at least as we know it) would break apart." His use of the phrase "good turns" is remarkable. While it is unlikely that Simmel meant waltzing literally here, as we do, we know from his other writing that he was acquainted with the waltz.

In closing, it is worth noting once again, explicitly, that **gratitude is not just a feeling that comes over us, but rather, a state of mind that we can consciously cultivate.**

Frank Andrews expresses this beautifully in *The Art and Practice of Loving*, suggesting that we can simply exclaim "Thank you!" throughout the day, noting that as a declaration, it inspires us look around to see what we might experience in a thankful way. It frees us from taking everything for granted, from acknowledging only the most unusual blessings."

Then, when we have found something that we want to be thankful for, we can practice what Andrews calls "All-Out Appreciation," or "the practice of intentional loving."

> You devote a period of time solely to appreciating whatever is before you. You value it, enjoy it, esteem it. You approach it from a powerful yes, determined to use all the sensitivity you are capable of to experience it through that interpretation. You practice mindfulness, keeping in mind that your purpose here is to appreciate, and sensitivity, as you learn to appreciate nuances that you might never have even noticed before. … Slow down your senses, as you would to look at a famous painting, and revel in what is before you.

Try this with your partner the next time you're waltzing.

By repeatedly putting us in situations where it is all but impossible not to feel grateful, and further, by cultivating a tradition of thanks, waltzing inspires us to more deeply appreciate our lives.

## Recommended Reading on Gratitude

- *Gratitude Works!: A 21-Day Program for Creating Emotional Prosperity* (2013) by Robert Emmons

- *Thanks!: How the New Science of Gratitude Can Make You Happier* (2007) by Robert Emmons

- *The Gift of Thanks: The Roots and Rituals of Gratitude* (2008) by Margaret Visser

# Integration

Many of us aspire to live a holistic life, integrating **mind**, **body**, and **spirit**. The goal is complete, holistic wellness: not just avoiding disease, but maximizing our potential for a rich, fulfilling life.

This book has many chapters on the *mind* and *body*. But what do we mean by *spirit*?

Everyone seems to have their own definition of spirit, some equating it with *soul*, some viewing it differently. Here's one way that we like to think about it.

## Spirit

Imagine a sphere the size of a basketball.

Visualize an array of arrows pointing inward to the center of the sphere; then a second array of arrows emanating from the surface of the sphere, radiating outward.

In this model, the arrows pointing inward are analogous to **soul**, pointing to **who we really are at our core**, beneath the facade of our persona. The arrows pointing outward are analogous to **spirit—our connections with others**. Spirit, in this view, refers to our connectedness.

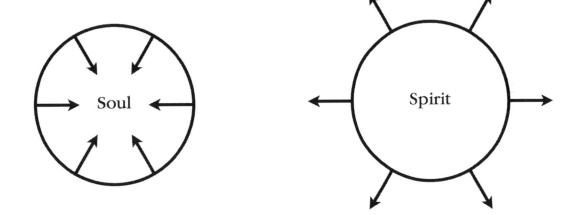

"A human being is a part of the whole, called by us "Universe," a part limited in time and space. He experiences himself, his thoughts and feelings as something separate from the rest—a kind of optical delusion of his consciousness. The striving to free oneself from this delusion is the one issue of true religion. Not to nourish it but to try to overcome it is the way to reach the attainable measure of peace of mind."
—Albert Einstein

"As I quiet down and I feel my connection to the universe more, I realize that I'm part of a family, I'm part of a community, I'm part of a nation state, I'm part of an ecosystem, I'm part of a species. And I recognize that a part of my path is to honor my involvement with each of these."
—Ram Dass

As dancers, we know how important connections are in our life. Hopefully you've already read our chapters on "Connections" (p. 219) and "The Third Place" (p. 221).

But simply mingling in a crowd does not automatically equate to feeling connected. We're all familiar with the stories about feeling completely isolated while living in New York City. **Going out dancing, being on a dance floor, will not dispel feelings of loneliness until you genuinely make an effort to connect with people**, in the myriad ways we have described in this book.

In doing so, you'll enhance not only your own, but also others' sense of connectedness, of *spirit*.

## Integration

**Integration means together now.**

Integration is different from balance, which is compensatory. Balance isn't bad—it's better than imbalance—but it isn't as complete as integration.

If your goal is simply to pursue a balanced life, you can do some mind work on Friday, some body work on Saturday, and some spiritual work on Sunday morning, hoping that everything will balance out over the course of the week.

Integration, on the other hand, means that in any one moment you are balanced and whole.

Developing our minds is good. Developing our bodies is good. But developing our minds and bodies at the same time, while simultaneously feeling our connectedness, is even better.

This is the opportunity that social dancing offers us. **If we choose, we can use our dancing as a perfect practice for the simultaneous development of mind, body, and spirit.**

And perhaps this interplay of positive factors is the most important consideration of all. It is not just physical activity to be healthier, not just the healing power of touch, not just the stress-reducing benefits of accepting and being accepted, not just the health benefits of feeling connected, but the holistic integration of all of these factors.

Dancing is integration in action!

# About the Authors

**Richard Powers** is a social dance instructor and historian at Stanford University's Dance Division. Richard's focus since 1975 has been the research and reconstruction of American and European social dance forms, working from a personal collection of over a thousand historic dance manuals.

Richard's grandfather taught social dance at Virginia Polytechnic Institute and his parents met at a swing dance. At Stanford, he was a student in the early years of the Product Design program. He also was one of the first students to pursue an individually designed major. He graduated from Stanford with a masters degree in design and the creative process.

He moved to Cincinnati, Ohio, where he was Vice President of Genesis Design Group and did freelance design work for other companies. He holds eight U.S. and international patents, and was recipient of 25 Art Directors awards for graphic and multimedia design. While in Cincinnati, he founded an artist's collective and received the Post-Corbett Award for Artist of the Year, Cincinnati's foremost arts recognition. He exhibited his multimedia constructions at The Contemporary Arts Center and at the Cincinnati Arts Consortium. He also founded the Clifton Court Dancers (Renaissance and Baroque dance), the Flying Cloud Academy of Vintage Dance (19th and 20th century dance), and the Fleeting Moments Waltz & Quickstep Orchestra.

Richard became a full-time instructor at Stanford University's Dance Division, joining the faculty in 1992. He was selected by the Centennial Issue of Stanford Magazine as one of Stanford University's most notable graduates of its first century, and was awarded the Lloyd W. Dinkelspiel Award for distinctive and exceptional contributions to education at Stanford University.

Richard has choreographed for dozens of stage productions, including Broadway and off-Broadway, and for films and television. He has taught over five hundred dance workshops across the U.S. and abroad.

You can find further information, including Richard's workshop schedule, photos, and examples of his design and illustration, at: http://richardpowers.com

**Nick Enge** recently graduated from Stanford University with a bachelors in Atmosphere/Energy Engineering and a masters in Earth Systems. At Stanford, in addition to his ecological interests, he developed a passion for social dancing, psychology, and writing.

Over the past five years, Nick has served as a course developer and teaching assistant for more than twenty-five iterations of ten different courses at Stanford, including Valuescience, Public Speaking, Electric Automobiles and Aircraft, and Energy Efficient Buildings.

Although he only began taking Richard's social dance classes in 2011, he is now a frequent instructor at Friday Night Waltz, and a substitute teacher for Richard when he travels.

Nick served as a chair of Stanford's 36th Annual Viennese Ball in 2013, and is currently a choreographer for the Opening waltz and polka for the 37th Annual Viennese Ball.

You can find further information on Nick's other projects at: http://nickenge.com

# Acknowledgements

**From Richard:**

This book is built upon a foundation of many talented and inspiring people. What appears to be the work of two authors is actually a life-long collaboration of friends and colleagues from many disciplines.

Nick Enge has been a joy to work with. This book has been simmering on my to-do list for years, and probably would have remained there for a few more years without Nick's multifaceted help in co-writing, editing, and organizing this large and complex project. I have also enjoyed the high energy of our daily exchanges of ideas and feedback, which is far more engaging than sitting in a room writing alone.

Angela Amarillas has been more than my teaching partner for the past twenty years. She has been a continual part of the process of developing both the ideas and dances described in this book. I also appreciate the valuable feedback and suggestions that Angela provided in editing this book.

I am grateful for the continual support and assistance of my wife Tracey. Many people agree that she is the best teammate ever, in so many ways, including help with information technology (she's a software engineer at Google). I'm very blessed to have Tracey as my life teammate. I'm also happy that Tracey and Angela are close friends. Some ideas in this book are the result of this three-way friendship.

Every time that someone comments on my positive outlook on life, I immediately give credit to my mom, Janet ("Tommy") Powers, who has always been my inspiration and prototype for actively appreciating what is good in life, in art, and in people. I'm grateful to both of my parents, for being the best possible teachers and exemplars for leading a fulfilling life.

I am indebted to Jackie Ling Wong for first introducing me to movement, through t'ai chi. I could have never guessed where that path would eventually lead. I am also grateful to my dance partners in those first years, Nancy Baugh, Melanie Cougarstar, and Cheryl Stafford.

I feel particularly lucky to have studied with inspiring teachers, most notably Ingrid Brainard, Elizabeth Aldrich, Catherine Turocy, Julie Sutton, and Angene Feves. I am thankful for the wonderful collaborations that I had with my first colleagues in historical social dance—Desmond Strobel, Carol Téten, Patri Pugliese, and František Bonuš, and also for my ongoing exchanges with Patrick Nollio, Marie Dauvois, Susan de Guardiola, Marc Casslar, and Dmitry Filimonov. I am also indebted to a few dancers in particular who set a prototype for creative approaches to dance and "coloring outside the lines." These include Steve Kreimer, Frank Clayton, Deb Henigson, Walter Dill, and Andy Jewell.

Joan Walton has been a long-time collaborator in the art of teaching dance. I've enjoyed working with Joan for the past thirty years, exchanging ideas on ways to present such ephemeral material as clearly as possible.

I'm also appreciative of the flow of ideas and feedback from Mirage Marrou, my teaching partner for the past six years. Mirage partnered the Waltz Lab, as well, and co-created many of its variations.

I am deeply grateful to Susan Cashion, with the help of Jerry Helt, for inviting me to teach at Stanford. Stanford University continues to provide the perfect intersection of talent, motivation, and resources for developing the ongoing evolution of social dance forms.

I would like to thank Sid Hetzler for providing the inspiration and "home away from home" for the first decade of waltz weekends. Sid also let me use his writer's cabin in Georgia, where I wrote the first draft of several chapters in this book. Thank you!

A vast coalition of dancers contributed to the creation and development of waltz forms and variations described in this book. The list could go on forever but must include James Mendoza, Ryan and Monica Shen Knotts, Campbell Miller, Zachariah Cassady, Lilli Ann Carey, Nick Enge and Danielle Baiata, Bill Boling and Beata Csanadi, Tim Lamm and Paula Harrison, Woodley Packard, Timmie Wong, Sven Jensen, Acata Felton, Lucas Garron, Donald Harvey, George Yang, and Ari Levitt, plus over a hundred more innovators in the Waltz Lab. I also thank Google for providing their Danceplex studio as the first home for the Waltz Lab.

We all appreciate Scott Gamble and Tom Hill for creating Friday Night Waltz, a home for waltzing in the Bay Area since 2001. And Scott provided many of the Do-It-Yourself suggestions for starting one's own dance group.

Nick and I thank Tam King, Manuel Avendano, and David Siegel for contributing their beautiful artwork to this book. We would also like to thank Dr. Ellen Langer, Dean Paton, Vienna Teng, and many other authors for letting us quote their writing in this book. And thanks to Jeff Kellem for his proofreading.

Finally, I wish to thank all of my students that I've had the honor of teaching for the past few decades. Each class has been a two-way exchange and I have learned much from each session. Thank you for your feedback and inspiration.


**From Nick:**

Even after a year of working on this book, I still can't believe that I have the honor of collaborating with my dance hero, Richard Powers. I have learned so much from Richard over the past few years, about dancing, teaching, DJing, writing, and living, and it's been truly amazing to have this opportunity to work together. I am deeply grateful for his support and encouragement, and for his research, his writing, and his insightful feedback.

In a blast from the past, I want to thank Holly Cornelison for introducing me to the joy of waltzing many years ago, and my first waltz partners at California Theater Center. To this day, I take inspiration from the exuberance of Elena Kuhn, the girl who always wanted to waltz. For all of the good times I had in the theatre, I want to thank all of my directors and teachers, particularly Bear Capron, Ron Huizing, Holly Cornelison, Charlie Shoemaker, Kay Kostopoulos, and Dan Klein, and all of the actors I had the privilege of playing with.

I loved waltzing then as I love it now, but for one reason or another, it faded out of my life. Years later, I am indebted to Elizabeth Lowell, Elise Fabbro, Vivian Chau, Jasmeen Miah, and Kevin Hsu, my friends who relentlessly encouraged me to dance again. None of this would have happened without their persistent nagging, nagging for which I will always be grateful.

I want to thank Scott Gamble and Tom Hill of Friday Night Waltz, for providing me a weekly place to dance outside of class, and later, for providing me with the opportunity to begin teaching and DJing there. My dancing, teaching, and DJing skills would not be the same without the fruitful opportunities they have provided and continue to provide.

It's true what they say about the romance of the waltz. Dancing at Friday Night Waltz, I fell deeply in love with Danielle Baiata, my incomparable partner in dancing, teaching, and life. I am continually grateful for her love and support. Reading an early version of this book aloud to me, Danielle helped me find many ways to improve it. She impresses and amazes me even more each day, and I can't wait to see what wonderful surprises the future will hold for us.

I am sincerely thankful for the opportunities that Joan Walton has provided to Danielle and to me, in allowing us to use College of San Mateo as our dancing "home away from home," giving us the opportunity to perform our first choreographies there, supporting all of our dancing endeavors, and teaching us about the arts of dancing and teaching. I am also grateful to Campbell Miller, who has provided long-distance support and encouragement.

My research skills were honed through years of participation in the Friends of Millard Fillmore (FOMF) trivia hunt. I want to thank the late Robert Hunter for founding the Hunt, and Dave Lowell for advising the Castilleja team and taking on the role of Hunt Director to continue this great tradition of research education. I also want to thank everyone who has FOMFed with me at Castilleja over the years. For my writing skills, I have many people to thank, but in particular, I want to thank Paige Price, Nancy Buffington, and Wendy Goldberg for introducing me to long-form writing, and Marcia Stefanick and Wes Alles for giving me the opportunity to develop my writing in preparation for my annual guest lectures in their class.

Many of the ideas in this book have been shaped through years of conversation with my fellow instructors and students in the Valuescience class at Stanford. My worldview, and my life, would not be the same without the lessons I have learned from David Schrom, Robin Bayer, Hilary Hug, Chris Tyler, Andrew Nepomuceno, and all of the students who have been our partners in inquiry over the years, teaching us as much as we have taught them. For their help in living better, I will always be grateful.

Likewise, I am deeply grateful for all of the fruitful discussions that I have had with my friends over the years, including late-night-driving buddy Urvi Nagrani (who also provided my About the Author picture), roommate of two years, Kevin Hsu, as well as Jasmeen Miah, Leila Beach, Ferris Jabr, Jeff and Laura Hamilton, Elise Fabbro, Josie Menkin, and Juliann Ma.

I also want to thank Jen Ying Zhen Ang, my dear friend and co-chair of the 36th Annual Viennese Ball, for joining me on that crazy adventure, and keeping me sane and smiling the throughout it. I also want to thank her for providing me the opportunity to teach her about dancing, DJing, and teaching. Through those teaching experiences, she has taught me as much—if not more than—I was supposed to be teaching her.

I am excited to be embarking on a similar journey with Melissa Carvell, my co-choreographer for the Opening waltz and polka at the 37th Annual Viennese Ball. Melissa has been a joy to work with thus far, and I look forward to continuing and developing our partnership.

I also want to thank all of the members of the Viennese Ball Steering and Opening committees, past, present, and future, for their efforts in keeping the tradition alive.

I'm deeply grateful to my dancing grandparents, Mildred Plank and Harald and Grete Enge, from whom I am sure I inherited my love of dancing, and to the many generations of teachers in my family, from whom I am sure I inherited my love of teaching.

Per and Elaine Enge are the best parents I could possibly imagine. They have given me all I could hope for in my life and more, and have supported me every step of the way, enabling me to achieve my wildest dreams. And as they could tell you, I've had some wild dreams.

Finally, I wish to reiterate my thanks to everyone I have danced with over the years. Thank you for sharing those marvelous moments with me, and making the world a better place, little by little, one dance at a time. If I haven't yet danced with you, I hope to dance with you soon.

# References

For further dance references, see Richard's collection of dance manuals:
   http://socialdance.stanford.edu/powers/WebBiblio.htm

## What Is Waltz?

*Etymologically speaking, the word "waltz":* Harper, Douglas. (2012). "Waltz." *Online Etymology Dictionary.* http://www.etymonline.com/index.php?term=waltz

*variously defined by Merriam-Webster:* Merriam-Webster. (2012). "Waltz." *Merriam-Webster Dictionary.* http://www.merriam-webster.com/dictionary/waltz

## Waltzing Essentials

*keep the frame somewhat open and expansive:*
   Maintaining an open and expansive frame may also have unexpected physiological and psychological benefits. In a recent study, simply maintaining an open, expansive posture for one minute significantly decreased participants' levels of the stress hormone cortisol compared to baseline, while maintaining a hunched, contractive posture for one minute significantly increased them. In an earlier study, researchers found that maintaining an expansive, upright posture for three minutes subsequently led to increased persistence on a frustrating task, as compared to spending three minutes in a hunched posture.

   Carney, Dana R.; Cuddy, Amy J.C.; Yap, Andy J. (2010). "Power Posing: Brief Nonverbal Displays Affect Neuroendocrine Levels and Risk Tolerance." *Psychological Science 21*: 1363. See also: Cuddy, Amy. (2012). "Your Body Language Shapes Who You Are." TED Global 2012. http://www.ted.com/talks/amy_cuddy_your_body_language_shapes_who_you_are.html

   Riskind, John H.; Gotay, Carolyn C. (1982). "Physical Posture: Could It Have Regulatory or Feedback Effects on Motivation and Emotion?" *Motivation and Emotion 6(3)*: 273.

## Cross-Step Waltz

*"Cross Walk Boston":* Norman, Frank H. (1914). *Complete Dance Instructor.* Montreal. 63-64.

*"may be introduced into the Waltz":* D'Egville, Geoffrey. (1919). *How and What to Dance.* London: C. Arthur Pearson, Ltd. 62.

*beginning with the Lead's right foot:* Collier, Adèle. (1919). *Feldman's How to Dance the Fox-Trot.* London: B. Feldman & Co.

*"the crossing of the feet is popular and effective":* "To-Day in the Ballroom." *Dancing Times Magazine,* March 1920. 439.

*Parisian dance and music magazines:*
   "Numéro Spécial: Dansomanie." *La Baïonnette Magazine, May 1919.*
   "Les danses a la Mode." *Musica-Album Magazine, 1919.*

*dance manuals:*
   "Pas croisés." Boucher, Paul. (1922). *Toutes Les Danses Pour Tous.* Paris.
   "Pas titubé." (c. 1923). Levitte, L. *Les 15 Danses Modernes.* Paris.

*Groovie Movie:* Jason, Will (dir). (1944). *Groovie Movie*. United States: Loew's.

*widespread in outdoor parks in Beijing:* "Chinese Waltzing." (September 29, 2007). *YouTube*. http://www.youtube.com/watch?v=wSatuU0eJaM

# Play

*waltzing … is a quintessential form of play:*
In *Man, Play, and Games,* Roger Caillois describes four different *forms* of play: 1) *agon,* or competition, as in chess, 2) *alea,* or chance, as in roulette, 3) *mimicry,* or role playing, as in cops and robbers, and 4) *ilinx,* or vertigo, as in children spinning until they fall down. In addition, Caillois notes that play exists on a continuum of *structure* from *ludus,* structured play with explicit rules, to *paidia,* unstructured and spontaneous play. Social waltzing is a beautiful example of three of Caillois' different forms of play at once: chance (as we ask "what will the next song be?" and "who will ask me to dance?"), mimicry (as we do dramatic dances like tango), and vertigo (as we get deliciously dizzy). In addition, waltzing represents a fifth form of play that we see as just as essential a form of play as competition, a form we might call *syn,* or cooperation. Likewise, social waltzing spans the entire continuum of structure in play, from spontaneous bluesy waltz to structured choreographies. More recently, The Institute for Play has described seven different patterns of play: 1) *attunement (connection),* 2) *body (moving self),* 3) *object (moving things),* 4) *social (interacting),* 5) *imaginative (role playing),* 6) *narrative (story-telling),* 7) *transformative (transcendent).* Once again, *social waltzing is a beautiful example of most, if not all, of these seven different forms of play at once.*
    Caillois, Roger. (1961). *Man, Games, and Play.* Champaign: University of Illinois Press. 12-13.
    Institute for Play. (2009). "The Patterns of Play." http://www.nifplay.org/states_play.html

*"to dance, leap for joy":* OED. (2012). "Play." *Oxford English Dictionary.* http://oed.com/view/Entry/145475

*many animals play by dancing:* Kay Redfield Jamison recounts many endearing examples, in Jamison, Kay Redfield. (2004). "Playing Fields of the Mind." *Exuberance: The Passion for Life.* New York: Vintage Books. 40-65.

*harbor … seals play by waltzing underwater:* Seal Conservation Society (2012). "Harbour Seal." http://www.pinnipeds.org/seal-information/species-information-pages/the-phocid-seals/harbour-seal
    For a (very cute) picture of this behavior (known as "rolling"), see: http://www.flickr.com/photos/ucumari/2840783232/in/set-72057594087623331

*apparently purposeless, or at least done for its own sake:* Brown, Stuart; Vaughn, Christopher. (2009). *Play: How It Shapes the Brain, Opens the Imagination, and Invigorates the Soul.* New York: Avery. 17.

*it's simply fun:* Neuroscientist Jaak Panksepp describes play as the "brain source of joy," and studies of play in rats have linked social play to the opioid systems of the mammalian brain. Panksepp, Jaak. (1998). *Affective Neuroscience.* New York: Oxford University Press. 248.
        For example, see: Vanderschuren, L.J., et. al. (1995). "Social Play Alters Regional Brain Opioid Receptor Binding in Juvenile Rats." *Brain Research 680*: 148-156.
        Interestingly, the positive emotions evoked by play may themselves contribute to play's ability to facilitate learning. For more on this idea, see the "broaden-and-build" theory of Barbara Fredrickson: Fredrickson, Barbara L. (2004). "The Broaden-and-Build Theory of Positive Emotions." *Philosophical Transactions of the Royal Society London B Biological Sciences 359(1449)*: 1367-1378.

*other key characteristics of play:* Brown, Stuart; Vaughn, Christopher. (2009). *Play: How It Shapes the Brain, Opens the Imagination, and Invigorates the Soul.* New York: Avery. 17.

See also Huizinga, Johan. (1955). *Homo Ludens: A Study of the Play-Element in Culture*. Boston: Beacon. 7-8.

*overworked and starved for play*: See Keil, Steve. (2011). "A Manifesto for Play, for Bulgaria and Beyond." *TEDxBG*. http://www.ted.com/talks/
steve_keil_a_manifesto_for_play_for_bulgaria_and_beyond.html

*throughout the human lifespan:*
As Stuart Brown notes, humans are the "most neotenous" of species. Neoteny is the retention of youthful traits into adulthood, which makes us "the most youthful, the most flexible, the most plastic of all creatures." Add to that the observation by Karl Groos that "perhaps *the very existence of youth is due in part to the necessity for play*; the animal does not play because he is young, he has a period of youth because he must play," along with the benefits of play we discuss in this chapter, and the importance of play throughout our lives is clear.
    Brown, Stuart. (2008). "Play is More than Fun." *Serious Play 2008*.
    http://www.ted.com/talks/stuart_brown_says_play_is_more_than_fun_it_s_vital.html
    Groos, Karl; Baldwin, E.L. (tr.). *The Play of Animals*. New York: D. Appleton and Company. xx.

*play is a vital facilitator, shaper, and motivator*: Jamison, Kay Redfield. (2004). *Exuberance: The Passion for Life*. New York: Vintage Books. 41.

*in play we can imagine and experience*: Brown, Stuart; Vaughn, Christopher. (2009). *Play: How It Shapes the Brain, Opens the Imagination, and Invigorates the Soul*. New York: Avery. 34.

*"play is an acting out of options"*: Heinrich, Bernd. (1999). *Mind of the Raven*. New York: Cliff Street Books. 294.

*increasingly intelligent and creative ways* and *physically promotes neuron growth and plasticity:* See research reviewed in Jamison, Kay Redfield. (2004). "Playing Fields of the Mind." *Exuberance: The Passion for Life*. New York: Vintage Books. 40-65, particularly 58-62.

*building rapport and partnership:* For a review of animal studies of this, see: Jamison, Kay Redfield. (2004). *Exuberance: The Passion for Life*. New York: Vintage Books. 53-58.

*"animals that play together tend to stay together"*: Marc Bekoff, quoted in Jamison, Kay Redfield. (2004). *Exuberance: The Passion for Life*. New York: Vintage Books. 54.

*couples who play together often:* Aron, Arthur, et. al. (2000). "Couples' Shared Participation in Novel and Arousing Activities and Experienced Relationship Quality." *Journal of Personality and Social Psychology 78(2)*: 273-284.

*"deep play"*: Diane Ackerman as quoted in Globerman, Missy. (1997). "'Deep play' isn't child's play, says Diane Ackerman." *Cornell Chronicle*. http://www.news.cornell.edu/chronicle/97/7.24.97/Ackerman.html

## Touch

*Throughout the history of social dancing:* For an introduction to the history of anti-dance sentiment, see: Knowles, Mark. (2009). *The Wicked Waltz and Other Scandalous Dances: Outrage at Couple Dancing in the 19th and Early 20th Centuries*. Jefferson: McFarland & Company.
    If you want to delve deeper into this historical topic, see Richard's collection of anti-dance treatises: http://socialdance.stanford.edu/powers/antidance.htm

*As Tiffany Field reports:* Field, Tiffany. (2001). "Massage Therapy Facilitates Weight Gain in Preterm Infants." *Current Directions in Psychological Science 10(2)*: 51-54.

For ideas about why this might be, see: Goleman, Daniel. (1988). "The Experience of Touch: Research Points to a Critical Role." *The New York Times*. http://www.nytimes.com/ 1988/02/02/science/the-experience-of-touch-research-points-to-a-critical-role.html

*Mothers who participate:* See Field (2001), above.

*fathers who participate:*
Infants with father-infant touch therapy are observed to greet their fathers with more eye contact, smiling, vocalizing, reaching, and orienting responses while showing less avoidance behaviors. Fathers were more involved and expressive and showed greater warmth and enjoyment.
> Scholtz, K.; Samuels, C. A. (1992). "Neonatal bathing and massage intervention with fathers: Behavioral effects 12 weeks after birth of the first baby." *International Journal of Behavioral Development 15*: 67-81.
> Cullen, C.; Field, T.; Escalona, A.; Hartshorn, K. (2000). "Father-infant interactions are enhanced by massage therapy." *Early Child Development and Care 164*: 41-47.

*basic human need:* "Like diet and exercise, we need a daily dose of touch." Field, Tiffany. (2003). *Touch*. Cambridge: MIT Press. 115.

*wide range of positive outcomes:* For an even longer list of the benefits of touch, see hundreds of journal article summaries at: http://www6.miami.edu/touch-research/Massage.html

*holding someone's hand in a stressful situation:*
The reduction in stress is strongly correlated with the quality of relationship we have with the person. A stranger's hand attenuates stress to a degree, but a spouse's hand does so to a greater degree. Among spouses, increased marital quality is correlated with increased stress attenuation.
> Coan, James A., et. al. (2006). "Lending a Hand: Social Regulation of the Neural Response to Threat." *Psychological Science 17(12):* 1032-1039.

*hug as many people as possible:* Clipman, J.M. (1999, March). "A Hug a Day Keeps the Blues Away: The Effect of Daily Hugs on Subjective Well-Being in College Students." Paper presented at the 70th Annual Meeting of the Eastern Psychological Association, Boston. Quoted in Lyubomirsky, Sonja. (2007). *The How of Happiness: A New Approach to Getting the Life You Want*. New York: Penguin Books. 148-149.

For more on the positive emotional impacts of touching, see:
> Fisher, Jeffrey D., et. al. (1976). "Hands Touching Hands: Affective and Evaluative Effects of an Interpersonal Touch." *Sociometry 39(4)*. 416-421. (Touch led to a more positive evaluation of a librarian.)
> Aguilera, D.C. (1967). "Relationship Between Physical Contact and Verbal Interaction Between Nurses and Patients." *Journal of Psychiatric Nursing and Mental Health Services 5*: 5-21. (Touch led to a more positive evaluation of medical staff.)

*recognize ... by touch alone:*
> Kaitz, M., et. al. (1992). "Parturient Women Can Recognize Their Infants by Touch." *Developmental Psychology 28*: 35-39.
> Kaitz, M., et. al. (1994). "Fathers Can Also Recognize Their Newborns by Touch." *Infant Behavior and Development 17*: 205-207.
> Kaitz, M. (1992). "Recognition of Familiar Individuals by Touch." *Physiology and Behavior 52*: 565-567.

*eight distinct emotions:* Hertenstein, Matthew J., et. al. (2009). "The Communication of Emotion via Touch." Emotion 9(4): 566–573. See also:
> Hertenstein, Matthew J., et. al. (2006). "Touch Communicates Distinct Emotions." *Emotion 6(3)*: 528-533.

*can actually be communicated more accurately:*

Compared to facial expressions: Haidt, Jonathan; Keltner, Dacher. (1999). "Culture and Facial Expression: Open-Ended Methods Find More Expressions and a Gradient of Recognition." *Cognition and Emotion 13(3)*: 225-266.

Compared to non-verbal vocal expression, like "aww": Simon-Thomas, Emiliana R., et. al. (2009). "The Voice Conveys Specific Emotions: Evidence From Vocal Burst Displays." *Emotion 9(6)*: 838–846.

For a direct comparison between body language, facial expressions, and touch in communicating status emotions, survival emotions, and prosocial emotions, see: App, B.; McIntosh, D.N.; Reed, C.L. Hertenstein, M.J. (2011). "Nonverbal Channel Use in Communication of Emotion: How May Depend on Why." *Emotion 11(3)*: 603-617.

*touch facilitates bonding and cooperation:* Kraus, M. W.; Huang, C.; Keltner, D. (2010). "Tactile communication, cooperation, and performance: An ethological study of the NBA." *Emotion 10*: 745-749.

For more on touch facilitating cooperation, see:
Kurzban, Robert. (2001). "The Social Psychophysics of Cooperation: Nonverbal Communication in a Public Goods Game." *Journal of Nonverbal Behavior 25(4)*. 241-259.

Morhenn, Vera B., et. al. (2008). "Monetary sacrifice among strangers is mediated by endogenous oxytocin release after physical contact." *Evolution and Human Behavior 29*: 375–383.

For more on touch and pro-social behavior, see:
Willis, F.N.; Hamm, H.K. (1980). "The Use of Interpersonal Touch in Securing Compliance." *Journal of Nonverbal Behavior 5(1)*: 49-55. (Touch led to increased support for a science museum petition.)

Kleinke, Chris L. (1977). "Compliance to Requests Made by Gazing and Touching Experimenters in Field Settings." *Journal of Experimental Social Psychology 13*: 218-223. (Touch led to increased helping behavior.)

Crusco, April H.; Wetzel, Christopher G. (1984). "The Midas Touch: The Effects of Interpersonal Touch on Restaurant Tipping." *Personality and Social Psychology Bulletin 10(4)*: 512-517. (Touch led to increased tips for a waitress.)

*In Grooming, Gossip, and the Evolution of Language:* Dunbar, Robin. (1996). *Grooming, Gossip, and the Evolution of Language.* Cambridge: Harvard University Press. 146-148.

*As psychologist Dacher Keltner summarizes:* Keltner, Dacher. (2010). "Hands On Research: The Science of Touch." *Greater Good: The Science of a Meaningful Life.* http://greatergood.berkeley.edu/article/item/hands_on_research/

For even more on touch, see the following reviews:
Gallace, Alberto; Spence, Charles. (2010). "The Science of Interpersonal Touch: An Overview." *Neuroscience and Biobehavioral Reviews 34(2)*: 246-259.

Hertenstein, Matthew J. (2006). "The Communicative Functions of Touch in Humans, Nonhuman Primates, and Rats: A Review and Synthesis of the Empirical Research." *Genetic, Social, and General Psychology Monographs 132(1)*: 5-94.

## The Three Worlds of Ballroom Dance

*"safeguarding of our mutual interests":* Charter of the Imperial Society of Teachers of Dancing, 1904.

*"all movement is easy, unaffected":* An Expert. (1923). *The Modern Ballroom Dance Instructor.* London: Geographia Ltd.

# Conditional Learning

For a general introduction to conditional learning, see: Langer, Ellen J. (1997). *The Power of Mindful Learning*. Cambridge: Da Capo Press.

*novice piano players:* Langer (1997), 26-27.

*consider tennis:* Langer (1997), 14.

*Smack-It Ball:* Langer (1997), 21.

*"I've learned, the hard way":* Radner, Gilda. (2009). *It's Always Something (20th Anniversary Edition)*. New York: Simon and Schuster. 254.

# "Lead" and "Follow"

*"Recollect that the desire of imparting pleasure":* Carpenter, D.L. (1854). *The Amateur's Preceptor on Dancing and Etiquette*. Philadelphia: M'Laughlin.

*"True, genuine politeness":* Fererro, Edward. (1859). *The Art of Dancing*. New York: Dick & Fitzgerald.

*the man was still the "boss":* Castle, Courtenay. (1958). *Learn to Dance*. London: Nicholas Kaye. 22-23.

*"weaker sex":* Murray, Arthur. (1953). *Ballroom Dancing*. New York. 39.

*had to "submit entirely":* Silvester, Victor. (1927). *Modern Ballroom Dancing*. London: Herbert Jenkins Ltd. 27.

*"she must not have a mind of her own":* Moore, Alex. (1943). *Ballroom Dancing*. London: Sir Isaac Pitman & Sons Ltd. 21.

*"you don't have much to say in the matter at all":* Castle, Courtenay. (1958). *Learn to Dance*. London: Nicholas Kaye. 22-23.

*"he should hold her firmer and give a stronger lead":* Heaton, Israel; Heaton, Alma (1954). *Ballroom Dance Rhythms*. Provo: Brigham Young University. 43.

# Il Tempo Giusto

*"There is more to life than increasing its speed.":* Honoré, Carl. (2004). In Praise of Slowness: Challenging the Cult of Speed. San Francisco: HarperSanFrancisco. Epigraph.

*Slow Food stands for:* Honoré (2004), 59.

*Slow Parenting encourages:* Honoré (2004), 271.

*"the slow philosophy can be summed up ...":* Honoré (2004), 15.

# Dynamic Equanimity

*"Real calmness should be found in activity itself":* Suzuki, Shunryu. (2010). *Zen Mind, Beginner's Mind (40th Anniversary Edition).* Boston: Shambhala. 31.

# Mindsets

*Growth vs. Fixed Mindsets:* Dweck, Carol. (2008). *Mindset: The New Psychology of Success.* New York: Ballantine Books.

*Performance vs. Mastery Goals:* Donald, Brooke. (2012, May 10). "Stanford psychologist: Achievement goals can be shaped by environment." *Stanford Report.* http://news.stanford.edu/pr/2012/pr-shape-achievement-goals-051012.html

*leads to a desire:* Diagram by Nigel Holmes in Krakovsky, Marina. (2007, March/April). "The Effort Effect." *Stanford Magazine.* http://www.stanfordalumni.org/news/magazine/2007/marapr/features/dweck.html

*these shifts in mindset tend to persist:* Donald, Brooke. (2012, May 10). "Stanford psychologist: Achievement goals can be shaped by environment." *Stanford Report.* http://news.stanford.edu/pr/2012/pr-shape-achievement-goals-051012.html

*the only problem is that they forget the yet:* Dweck, Carol. (2008). *Mindset: The New Psychology of Success.* New York: Ballantine Books. 25.

# Flow

*"when work on a painting was going well ...":* Nakamura, Jeanne; Csikszentmihalyi, Mihaly. (2002). "The Concept of Flow." *Handbook of Positive Psychology.* Edited by C.R. Snyder and Shane J. Lopez. Oxford: Oxford University Press. 89.

*qualities and conditions of flow (lists):* Nakamura, Jeanne; Csikszentmihalyi, Mihaly. (2002). "The Concept of Flow." *Handbook of Positive Psychology.* Edited by C.R. Snyder and Shane J. Lopez. Oxford: Oxford University Press.

*Quality of Experience as a Function of Skills and Challenges (Figure):* Adapted from Csikszentmihalyi, Mihaly. (1997). *Finding Flow: The Psychology of Engagement in Everyday Life.* New York: Basic Books. 31.

*"rhythmic or harmonious movements to generate flow."* Csikszentmihalyi, Mihaly. (1990). *Flow: The Psychology of Optimal Experience.* New York: Harper & Row. 99.

*suppose ... that a person is in the area:* Csikszentmihalyi, Mihaly. (1997). *Finding Flow: The Psychology of Engagement in Everyday Life.* New York: Basic Books. 32-33.

# Trust

*"Dance is the most reliable and quickest route:"* Keltner, Dacher. (2009). *Born to Be Good.* New York: W.W. Norton. 220.

*zero close friends that they trust enough to confide in:* McPherson, Miller; Smith-Lovin, Lynn; Brashears, Matthew E. (2006). "Social Isolation in America: Changes in Core Discussion Networks over Two Decades." *American Sociological Review 71.* 358.

*think people can generally be trusted:* General Social Survey. (1976 to 2006). "Can People Be Trusted." http://www3.norc.org/GSS+Website/Browse+GSS+Variables/Subject+Index/

*trust in social institutions:* General Social Survey, cited in Smith, Jeremy Adam; Paxton, Pamela. (2010). "America's Trust Fall." *The Compassionate Instinct.* New York: W. W. Norton & Company. 204.

*treat each other like old friends:* Kollock, Peter. (1994). "The Emergence of Exchange Structures." *The American Journal of Sociology 100(2):* 337-338.

*feeling trusted increases levels of oxytocin:* Zak, Paul J., et. al. (2005). "Oxytocin is Associated with Human Trustworthiness." *Hormones and Behavior 48:* 522-527.

*increased oxytocin leads to feeling trusting:* Kosfeld, Michael, et. al. (2005). "Oxytocin Increases Trust in Humans." *Nature 435:* 673-676.

*and being generous:* Zak, Paul J., et. al. (2007). "Oxytocin Increases Generosity in Humans." *PLoS One 11:* e1128.

*Increased oxytocin also leads to bravery:* Knobloch, H. Sophie, et. al. (2011). "Evoked Axonal Oxytocin Release in the Central Amygdala Attenuates Fear Response." *Neuron 73(3):* 553-566.

*aren't as prevalent as they used to be:* Putnam, Robert. (2000). *Bowling Alone: The Collapse and Revival of American Community.* New York: Simon & Schuster.

## Dancing as a Dream State

*dream research:* For the origin of this theory of dreaming, see: Hobson, J. Allan; McCarley, Robert W. (1977). "The Brain as a Dream State Generator: An Activation Synthesis Hypothesis of the Dream Process." *The American Journal of Psychiatry 134 (12):* 1335-1348. See also:
> Hobson, J. Allan. (1989). *The Dreaming Brain: How the Brain Creates Both the Sense and the Nonsense of Dreams.* New York: Basic Books.
> Hobson, J. Allan. (2003). *Dreaming. An Introduction to the Science of Sleep.* Oxford: Oxford University Press.
> For more on sleep in general, see: Dement, William; Vaughn, Christopher. (2000). *The Promise of Sleep: A Pioneer in Sleep Medicine Explors the Vital Connection Between Health, Happiness, and a Good Night's Sleep.* New York: Dell.

## Be Here Now

*moment-to-moment awareness:* Kabat-Zinn, Jon. (1990). *Full Catastrophe Living: Using the Wisdom of Your Body and Mind to Face Stress, Pain, and Illness.* New York: Dell. 2.

*"be here now":* Dass, Ram. (1971). *Be Here Now.* New York: Crown Publishing.

*focused attention* and *open monitoring:* Lutz, Antoine; Slagter, Heleen A.; Dunne, John D.; Davidson, Richard J. (2008). "Attention regulation and monitoring in meditation." *Trends in Cognitive Sciences 12(4):* 163-169.

*improving our ability to pay attention:* Brefczynski-Lewis, J.A.; Lutz, A.; Schaefer, H.S.; Levinson, D.B.; Davidson, R.J. (2007). "Neural correlates of attentional expertise in long-term meditation practitioners." *Proceedings of the National Academy of Sciences 104(27):* 11483–11488. See also:
  Slagter, Heleen A. (2007). "Mental Training Affects Distribution of Limited Brain Resources." *PLoS Biology 5(6):* 1-8.
  Davidson, Richard J. et. al. (2003). "Alterations in Brain and Immune Function Produced by Mindfulness Meditation." *Psychosomatic Medicine 65:* 564–570.

*reducing stress:* Dusek, J.A., et. al. (2008). "Genomic Counter-Stress Changes Induced by the Relaxation Response." *PLoS ONE 3(7):* e2576.

*soothing pain:* Kabat-Zinn, J. (1982). "An outpatient program in behavioral medicine for chronic pain based on the practice of mindfulness meditation." *General Hospital Psychiatry 4:* 33–47. See also:
  Kabat-Zinn, et. al. (1985). "The Clinical Use of Mindfulness Meditation for the Self-Regulation of Chronic Pain." *Journal of Behavioral Medicine 8(2):* 163-190.

*strengthening our immune system:* Davidson, Richard J. et. al. (2003). "Alterations in Brain and Immune Function Produced by Mindfulness Meditation." *Psychosomatic Medicine 65:* 564–570.

*heightening our senses:*
  Sight: Brown, Daniel, et. al. (1984). "Differences in Visual Sensitivity Among Mindfulness Meditators and Non-Meditators." *Perceptual Motor Skills 58:* 727-733.
  Touch: Kerr, Catherine E., et. al. (2008). "Tactile acuity in experienced Tai Chi practitioners: evidence for use dependent plasticity as an effect of sensory-attentional training." *Experimental Brain Research 188(2):* 317-322.

The benefits of mindfulness extend far beyond the ability of two pages to include them. If you are interested in learning more, we recommend that you begin by reading *Fully Present: The Science, Art, and Practice of Mindfulness* by Susan Smalley and Diana Winston, which covers the above and other benefits in greater depth.

*two hours of cumulative mindfulness practice:* Tang, Yi-Yuan, et. al. (2007). "Short-term meditation training improves attention and self-regulation." *Proceedings of the National Academy of Sciences 104(43):* 17152–17156.

*Matthew Killingsworth and Daniel Gilbert:* Killingsworth, Matthew A.; Gilbert, Daniel T. (2010). "A Wandering Mind is an Unhappy Mind." *Science 330:* 932. See also:
  Tierney, John. (2010, November 15). "When the Mind Wanders, Happiness Also Strays." *The New York Times.* http://www.nytimes.com/2010/11/16/science/16tier.html

## Some Days Just Suck

*mufarse:* Taylor, Julie M. (1976). *Tango: Theme of Class and Nation.* Champaign: University of Illinois.

## Stay Young, Go Dancing

*for every mile we walk:* Manning, Willard G. (1991). *The Costs of Poor Health Habits.* Cambridge: Harvard University Press. Quoted in Simon, Harvey B. (2006). *The No-Sweat Exercise Plan: Lose Weight, Get Healthy, and Live Longer.* New York: McGraw-Hill. xxi.

*burning 1,000 calories each week:* Lee, I-Min; Skerrett, Patrick J. (2001). "Physical activity and all-cause mortality: what is the dose-response relation?" *Medicine & Science in Sports & Exercise 33(6 Suppl):* S459-71.

*two to five hours of dancing:* Assuming cross-step waltz is like "strolling," it takes 5 hours to burn 1,000 calories, and assuming polka is like "jogging," it takes 2 hours to burn 1,000 calories. (For a dance comparison, ballet takes 2 hours and fifteen minutes to burn 1,000 calories.) Simon, Harvey B. (2006). *The No-Sweat Exercise Plan: Lose Weight, Get Healthy, and Live Longer.* New York: McGraw-Hill. 34.

*four of the ten:* ibid. xxi.

*Other studies have shown remarkably similar results:* Woodcock, James, et. al. (2010). "Non-vigorous physical activity and all-cause mortality: systematic review and meta-analysis of cohort studies." *International Journal of Epidemiology 40:* 121–138. Which cites:

> Nocon, M., et al. (2008). "Association of physical activity with all-cause and cardiovascular mortality: a systematic review and meta-analysis." *Eur. J. Cardiovasc. Prevent. Rehabil. 15:* 239–246.
> Physical Activity Guidelines Advisory Committee. (2008). *Physical Activity Guidelines Advisory Committee Report 2008.* Washington, DC: U.S. Department of Health and Human Services.
> Hamer, M., Chida, Y. (2008). "Walking and primary prevention: a meta-analysis of prospective cohort studies." *Br. J. Sports Med. 42:* 238-43.

*sitting is an independent risk factor:* Van Der Ploeg, H.P., et. al. (2012). "Sitting time and all-cause mortality risk in 222,497 Australian adults." *Archives of Internal Medicine 172(6):* 494-500. See also:

> Patel, Alpa V., et. al. (2010). "Leisure Time Spent Sitting in Relation to Total Mortality in a Prospective Cohort of US Adults." *American Journal of Epidemiology 172(4):* 419-429.
> Katzmarzyk, Peter T., et. al. (2009). "Sitting Time and Mortality from All Causes, Cardiovascular Disease, and Cancer." *Medicine & Science in Sports & Exercise 41(5):* 998-1005.
> Morris, J. N., et. al. (1953). "Coronary heart-disease and physical activity of work." *The Lancet 2:* 1111–1120.

*just as effective at reducing depression:* Blumenthal, James A., et. al. (1999). "Effects of Exercise Training on Older Patients with Major Depression." *Archive of Internal Medicine 159(25):* 2349-2356.

*it was later found to be even more effective:* Babyak, Michael, et. al. (2000). "Exercise Treatment for Major Depression: Maintenance of Therapeutic Benefit at 10 Months." *Psychosomatic Medicine 62:* 633–638.

*ten minutes of moderate physical activity:* The mood benefits described here sustained, but did not increase, as the students exercised for longer periods of time. Hansen, Cheryl, et. al. (2001). "Exercise Duration and Mood State: How Much Is Enough to Feel Better?" *Health Psychology 20(4):* 267-275.

*women taking an aerobics class:* Maroulakis, Emmanuel; Zervas, Yannis. (1993). "Effects of Aerobic Exercise on Mood of Adult Women." *Perceptual and Motor Skills 76:* 795-801.

*single most effective mood booster we know:* Thayer, Robert E.; Newman, J. Robert; McClain, Tracey M. (1994). "Self-Regulation of Mood: Strategies for Changing a Bad Mood, Raising Energy, and Reducing Tension." *Journal of Personality and Social Psychology 67(5):* 910-925.

*learned vocabulary words 20% faster:* Winter, Bernward. (2007). "High impact running improves learning." *Neurobiology of Learning and Memory 87:* 597–609.

*performance on a creative task also improved significantly:* Netz, Yael. (2007). "The Effect of a Single Aerobic Training Session on Cognitive Flexibility in Late Middle-Aged Adults." *Int. J. Sports Med. 28:* 82-87.

*76% reduction in dementia risk:* Verghese, Joe. (2003). "Leisure Activities and the Risk of Dementia in the Elderly." *New England Journal of Medicine 348:* 2508-2516.

# The Platinum Rule

*As Karl Popper wrote:* Popper, Karl. (2012). [1966]. *The Open Society and Its Enemies.* New York: Routledge. 501.

*as Walter Terence Stace points out:* Stace, Walter Terence. (1975). [1937]. *The Concept of Morals.* Gloucester: P. Smith. 136.

# Style in Social Dancing

Astaire, Fred. (1936). *The Fred Astaire Top Hat Dance Album: A Comprehensive Compendium on Ballroom Dancing.* London: Queensway Press.

De Garmo, William B. (1875). *The Dance of Society.* New York: W.A. Pond & Co.

Nachmanovitch, Stephen. (1990). *Free Play: Improvisation in Life and Art.* New York: Jeremy P. Tarcher 94-95.

# Dance for Your Partner

*"dance for your partner's benefit at the expense of your own":*
For example, Richard Dawkins writes that, "an entity, such as a baboon, is said to be altruistic if it behaves in such a way as to increase another entity's welfare at the expense of its own. Selfish behavior has exactly the opposite effect." Dawkins, Richard. (2006). *The Selfish Gene (30th Anniversary Edition).* Oxford: Oxford University Press. 4.

*set up so as to transcend the polarity:* Maslow, Abraham H. (1971). *The Farther Reaches of Human Nature.* New York: The Viking Press. 202.

*two people have arranged their relationship:* Maslow, Abraham H. (1971). *The Farther Reaches of Human Nature.* New York: The Viking Press. 209.

*"the lowest form of selfishness":* Ingersoll, Robert Green. (1929). "The Nobility of Selfishness." *The Works of Robert G. Ingersoll.* Volume XII. New York: The Ingersoll League. 355.

*"the way to be happy is to make others so":* ibid. epigraph.

*"being foolish selfish":* H. H. Dalai Lama. (2011). *Beyond Religion: Ethics for a Whole World.* Boston: Houghton Mifflin Harcourt. 48.

*"practice compassion":* Dalai Lama XIV; Cutler, Howard. (2010). *The Essence of Happiness: A Guidebook for Living.* New York: Riverhead Books.

# Giving

*"In general manners, both ladies and gentlemen":* The trick, as we will see, is that the other person's happiness actually is as important to our own happiness as our own happiness is, even if we don't yet realize it. By acting "as though the other person's happiness was of as much importance as their own," our beliefs and actions simply align with the reality of what naturally makes us happy. Maas. (1871). *The Nilsson Dance & Ball-Room Guide.* New York.

*a superior path to happiness:* Rudd, Melanie; Aacker, Jennifer. (2011). "Leave Them Smiling: How Small Acts Create More Happiness than Large Acts." Stanford Business School Working Paper. See also: For more support of this, see: Steger, Michael F., et. al. (2008). "Being good by doing good: Daily eudaimonic activity and well-being." *Journal of Research in Personality 42:* 22-42.

*spending money on others:* Dunn, Elizabeth W.; Aknin, Lara B.; Norton, Michael I. (2008). "Spending Money on Others Promotes Happiness." *Science 319:* 1687-1688. We're also happier recalling pro-social spending than personal spending—see Aknin, et. al. (2010) below.

*United States and Uganda:* Aknin, L.B., et. al. (2010). "Prosocial Spending and Well-Being: Cross-Cultural Evidence for a Psychological Universal." Harvard Business School Working Paper 11-038.

*even two-year olds:* Aknin, L.B.; Hamlin, J.K.; Dunn, E.W. (2012). "Giving Leads to Happiness in Young Children." *PLoS ONE 7(6):* e39211.

*acting kindly for the benefit of others:* See, for example:
> Lyubomirsky, Sonja, et. al. (2005). "Pursuing Happiness: The Architecture of Sustainable Change." *Review of General Psychology 9(2):* 111-131.
> Tkach, C. (2006). *Unlocking the Treasury of Human Kindness: Enduring Improvements in Mood, Happiness, and Self-Evaluations.* Doctoral Dissertation at the University of California, Riverside.
> Otake, Keiko. (2006). "Happy people become happier through kindness: A counting kindness intervention." *Journal of Happiness Studies 7:* 361–375.
> Alden, L. E.; Trew, J. L. (2012, May 28). "If It Makes You Happy: Engaging in Kind Acts Increases Positive Affect in Socially Anxious Individuals." *Emotion.* Advance online publication.
> Rudd, Melanie; Aacker, Jennifer. (2011, December 16). "Leave Them Smiling: How Small Acts Create More Happiness than Large Acts." Stanford Business School Working Paper.
> Mongrain, Myriam; Chin, Jacqueline M.; Shapira, Leah B. (2011). "Practicing Compassion Increases Happiness and Self-Esteem." *Journal of Happiness Studies 12:* 963–981.

There is also a positive feedback loop between prosocial action and happiness: when we act prosocially, we feel good, and we feel good, we're more likely to act prosocially.
> Aknin, L.B.; Dunn, E.W.; Norton, M.I. (2012). "Happiness Runs in a Circular Motion: Evidence for a Positive Feedback Loop between Prosocial Spending and Happiness." *Journal of Happiness Studies 13:* 347-355.

For more on positive mood as conducive to helping behavior, see:
> Isen, Alice M.; Levin, Paula F. (1972). "Effect of Feeling Good on Helping: Cookies and Kindness." *Journal of Personality and Social Psychology 21(3):* 384-388.
> Levin, Paula F.; Isen, Alice M. (1975). "Further Studies on the Effect of Feeling Good on Helping." *Sociometry 38(1):* 141-147.

*giving benefits to others activates the same reward circuits:*
> Rilling, J.K., et. al. (2002). "A Neural Basis for Social Cooperation." *Neuron 35:* 395-405.
> Moll, Jorge, et. al. (2006). "Human fronto–mesolimbic networks guide decisions about charitable donation." *Proceedings of the National Academy of Sciences 103(42):* 15623–15628.
> Harbaugh, W.T.; Mayr, U.; Burghart, D.R. (2007). "Neural Responses to Taxation and Voluntary Giving Reveal Motives for Charitable Donations." *Science 316(5831):* 1622-1625.

These principles were hinted at in the first sentence of the first book by Adam Smith, the father of modern economics: "How selfish soever man may be supposed, there are evidently some principles in his nature, which interest him in the fortune of others, and render their happiness necessary to him, though he derives nothing from it except the pleasure of seeing it." Smith, Adam. (1759). *The Theory of Moral Sentiments.* London: A. Millar.

*we feel bad about it and physically stress out:* Dunn, E.W.; Ashton-James, Claire E.; Hanson; Margaret D.; Aknin, Lara B. (2010). "On the Costs of Self-Interested Economic Behavior: How Does Stinginess Get Under the Skin?" *Journal of Health Psychology 15(4):* 627-633.

248

*teenagers who are more "generative" in high school:* "In particular, generative adolescents experienced fewer incapacitating chronic illnesses and limits placed on their activities by poor physical health in old age. They also reported higher life satisfaction; felt more peaceful, happy, and calm; and were less depressed." Wink, Paul; Dillon, Michele. (2007). "Do Generative Adolescents Become Healthy Older Adults?" in Post, Stephen G. (ed.). (2007). *Altruism and Health: Perspectives from Empirical Research*. Oxford: Oxford University Press.

There is also a strong correlation between generativity and happiness during adolescence: Magen, Zipora. (1996). "Commitment Beyond Self and Adolescence: The Issue of Happiness." *Social Indicators Research 37(3):* 235-267.

Giving teenagers also do better academically and personally in high school, and in college: Eccles, J. S., & Barber, B. L. (1999). Student council, volunteering, basketball, or marching band: What kind of extracurricular involvement matters? *Journal of Adolescent Research 14*: 10–43.

Barber, B. L., Eccles, J. S., & Stone, M. R. (2001). "Whatever happened to the jock, the brain, and the princess?" *Journal of Adolescent Research 16:* 429–455.

*older adults who are more giving:* For a recent review, see: Harris, Alex H. S.; Thoresen, Carl E. (2005). "Volunteering is Associated with Delayed Mortality in Older People: Analysis of the Longitudinal Study of Aging." *Journal of Health Psychology 10(6)*: 739-752.

For more specific results, see: Oman, Doug; Thoresen, Carl E.; McMahon, Kay. (1999). "Volunteerism and Mortality among the Community-dwelling Elderly." *Journal of Health Psychology 4(3)*: 301-316. In this particular study, there was a 44% reduction in mortality associated with high volunteerism after controlling for a wide array of potential confounds. This 44% reduction was "larger than the reductions associated with physical mobility (39 percent), exercising four times weekly (30 percent), and weekly attendance at religious services (29 percent), and was only slightly smaller than the reduction associated with not smoking (49 percent)."

For other studies, with similarly impressive results, see:

Musick, M. A.; Herzog, A. R.; House, J. S. (1999). "Volunteering and mortality among older adults: Findings from a national sample." *Journals of Gerontology: Series B: Psychological Sciences and Social Sciences 54(3)*: S173–S180.

Luoh, M.C.; Herzog, A. R. (2002). "Individual consequences of volunteer and paid work in old age: Health and mortality." *Journal of Health and Social Behavior 43(4)*: 490–509.

Shmotkin, D.; Blumstein, T.; Modan, B. (2003). "Beyond keeping active: Concomitants of being a volunteer in old-old age." *Psychology and Aging 18(3)*: 602–607.

Older adults also see psychological benefits: Musick, M.A.; Wilson, J. (2003). "Volunteering and Depression: The Role of Psychological and Social Resources in Different Age Groups." *Social Science & Medicine 56*: 259–269.

*"more blessed to give than to receive":* Brown, Stephanie L., et. al. (2003). "Providing Social Support May Be More Beneficial than Receiving It: Results From a Prospective Study of Mortality." *Psychological Science 14(4)*: 320-327. See also:

Brown, William M., et. al. (2005). "Altruism relates to health in an ethnically diverse sample of older adults." *Journals of Gerontology: Series B: Psychological Sciences and Social Sciences 60B*: 143-152.

Schwartz, C. E.; Sendor, R. M. (1999). "Helping others helps oneself: Response shift effects in peer support." *Social Science and Medicine 48*: 1563–1575.

Schwartz, C.E. (1999). "Teaching coping skills enhances quality of life more than peer support: Results of a randomized clinical trial with multiple sclerosis patients." *Health Psychology 18(3)*: 211-220.

The phrase "more blessed to give than to receive" is from Acts 20:35.

*an emotion called elevation:*

Schnall, S.; Roper, J.; Fessler, D.M. (2010). "Elevation leads to altruistic behavior." *Psychological Science 21(3)*: 315-320.

Haidt, Jonathan. (2000). "The Positive Emotion of Elevation." *Prevention & Treatment 3*: Article 3.

Haidt, J. (2003). "Elevation and the positive psychology of morality." In C. L. M. Keyes & J. Haidt (Eds.). *Flourishing: Positive Psychology and the Life Well-Lived*. Washington DC: American Psychological Association. (pp. 275-289).
Elevation can even temporarily boost our immune system: watching a film about Mother Teresa resulted in significant increases in salivary immunoglobulin A, and remained high for an hour in subjects who were asked to focus on times they had loved or been loved. McClelland, D., McClelland, D.C., & Kirchnit, C. (1988). "The effect of motivational arousal through films on salivary immunoglobulin A." *Psychology and Health 2*: 31-52.

*having experienced elevation, we feel inspired:* Algoe, S.B.; Haidt, Jonathan. (2009). "Witnessing excellence in action: the 'other-praising' emotions of elevation, gratitude, and admiration." *The Journal of Positive Psychology 4(2)*: 105–127.

*make us significantly more likely to give to others:*
Schnall, S.; Roper, J.; Fessler, D.M. (2010). "Elevation leads to altruistic behavior." *Psychological Science 21(3)*: 315-320.
Cox, Keith S. (2010). "Elevation predicts domain-specific volunteerism 3 months later." *The Journal of Positive Psychology 5(5)*: 333-341.
Freeman, Dan; Aquino, Karl; McFerran, Brent. (2009). "Overcoming Beneficiary Race as an Impediment to Charitable Donations: Social Dominance Orientation, the Experience of Moral Elevation, and Donation Behavior." *Personality and Social Psychology Bulletin 35(1)*: 72-84.
Something similar happens when we recall good deeds that we ourselves have done. Young, Liane; Chakroff, Alek; Tom, Jessica. (2012). "Doing Good Leads to More Good: The Reinforcing Power of a Moral Self-Concept." *Review of Philosophy and Psychology 3*: 325-334.

Note: There is one essential caveat in all this: it is unclear how thinking about the personal benefits of giving will effect giving and the benefits of giving. In one study about giving and happiness, people who read the results of the study linking spending on others to greater satisfaction gave more money to others (and subsequently experienced greater satisfaction as a result) compared to those who had not read the results of the study. In another study, however, about volunteering and mortality, people whose primary motivation for volunteering was to help others saw the usual reductions in mortality, *while people who volunteered for self-oriented reasons saw no reduction in mortality compared to non-volunteers.* In either case, it seems safe to say that the best way to think about the results presented in this chapter is that they are *beneficial side-effects that accompany the primary benefits of making others happy, i.e., making others happy.* See:
Anik, L.; Aknin, L.B.; Norton, M.I.; Dunn, E.W. (2009). "Feeling Good about Giving: The Benefits (and Costs) of Self-Interested Charitable Behavior." Harvard Business School Working Paper.
Konrath, Sara, et. al. (2012). "Motives for Volunteering Are Associated With Mortality Risk in Older Adults." *Health Psychology 31(1)*: 87–96.

## Dancing in the Rain

*"My formula for greatness …"*: Nietzsche, Friedrich Wilhelm; Kaufmann, Walter Arnold (tr.). (1968). "Ecce Homo." *Basics Writings of Nietzsche*. New York: Modern Library. 714.

*"Imagine living …"*: Andrews, Frank. (2010). *The Art and Practice of Loving: Living a Heartfelt Yes*. Palo Alto: Magic. 9.

## Creativity

*"effort-driven rewards circuit"*: Lambert, Kelly. (2010). *Lifting Depression: A Neuroscientist's Hands-On Approach to Activating Your Brain's Healing Power*. New York: Basic Books. For a summary of the

central idea, see: Kamps, Louisa. (2010). "DIY Therapy: How Handiwork Can Treat Depression." *Whole Living.* http://www.wholeliving.com/134137/diy-therapy-how-handiwork-can-treat-depression

*when ideas have sex:* Ridley, Matt. (2010). "When Ideas Have Sex." *TED Global 2010.* http://www.ted.com/talks/matt_ridley_when_ideas_have_sex.html

*thwarted by intense concentration:* See, as several different examples:
Wiley, Jennifer; Jarosz, Andrew F. (2012). "Working Memory Capacity, Attentional Focus, and Problem Solving." *Current Directions in Psychological Science 21*: 258-262.
White, Holly A.; Shah, Priti. (2011). "Creative Style and Achievement in Adults with Attention-Deficit/Hyperactivity Disorder." *Personality and Individual Differences 50(5)*: 673-677.
Carson, Shelley H.; Peterson, Jordan B.; Higgins, Daniel M. (2003). "Decreased Latent Inhibition Is Associated With Increased Creative Achievement in High-Functioning Individuals." *Journal of Personality and Social Psychology 85(3)*: 499–506.

*the Marshmallow Challenge:* Wujec, Tom. (2010). "Build a Tower, Build a Team." *TED 2010.* http://marshmallowchallenge.com/TED_Talk.html

*beginner's mind:* Wiley, Jennifer; Jarosz, Andrew F. (2012). "Working Memory Capacity, Attentional Focus, and Problem Solving." *Current Directions in Psychological Science 21*: 258-262.

*beginner's mind is a perspective we can cultivate:* Zabelina, Darya L.; Robinson, Michael D. (2010). "Child's Play: Facilitating the Originality of Creative Output by a Priming Manipulation." *Psychology of Aesthetics, Creativity, and the Arts 4(1)*: 57-65.

*students who have lived abroad:* Maddux, William W.; Galinsky, Adam D. (2009). "Cultural Borders and Mental Barriers: The Relationship Between Living Abroad and Creativity." *Journal of Personality and Social Psychology 96(5)*: 1047–1061.

*people who integrate multiple social identities:* Cheng, Chi-Ying; Sanchez-Burks, Jeffrey; Lee, Fiona. (2008). "Connecting the Dots Within: Creative Performance and Identity Integration." *Psychological Science 19(11)*: 1177-1183.

*have many acquaintances:* Ruef, Martin. (2002). "Strong Ties, Weak Ties and Islands: Structural and Cultural Predictors of Organizational Innovation." *Industrial and Corporate Change 11(3)*: 427-449.

*the benefits of working in a team:* Jones, Benjamin. (2010, May). "As Science Evolves, How Can Science Policy?" http://www.kellogg.northwestern.edu/faculty/jones-ben/htm/As_Science_Evolves.pdf

*intermediate intimacy:* Uzzi, Brian; Spiro, Jarrett. (2005). "Collaboration and Creativity: The Small World Problem." *American Journal of Sociology 111*: 447-504.

*constructive criticism is key:*
Donald, Taylor W.; Berry, Paul C.; Block, Clifford H. (1958). "Does Group Participation When Using Brainstorming Facilitate or Inhibit Creative Thinking?" *Administrative Science Quarterly 3(1)*: 23-47.
Nemeth, Charlan J.; Personnaz, Bernard; Personnaz, Marie; Goncalo, Jack A. (2004). "The Liberating Role of Conflict in Group Creativity: A Study in Two Countries." *European Journal of Social Psychology 34*: 365–374.

As a side note, being in the same room with your team is also key. In a study where different teams engaged in simulations involving nuclear disarmament and airline ticket pricing, teams working together face-to-face showed significantly higher levels of trust and cooperation, significantly lower levels of deception, and as a result, higher success, than teams communicating electronically. Teams communicating face-to-face fared significantly better than teams communicating via video chat, who in turn fared significantly better than teams communicating via email.

Rockmann, Kevin W.; Northcraft, Gregory B. (2008). "To be or not to be trusted: The influence of media richness on defection and deception." *Organizational Behavior and Human Decision Processes 107(2)*: 106-122

Note: In researching this chapter, Nick found many insights in Jonah Lehrer's *Imagine: How Creativity Works*. As you may know, Lehrer and his book has come under fire for the fabrication of Bob Dylan quotes, and *Imagine* has been pulled from the shelves. Nick has subsequently re-doubled his fact-checking efforts to make sure that everything in this chapter rests solidly upon evidence in primary sources, but would still like to acknowledge Lehrer for leading him to many of the primary sources cited in this chapter. For more on the Lehrer affair, see: Myers, Steve. (2012, July 30). "Jonah Lehrer resigns from New Yorker after fabricating Bob Dylan quotes in 'Imagine'." *Poynter.* http://www.poynter.org/latest-news/mediawire/183298/jonah-lehrer-accused-of-fabricating-bob-dylan-quotes-in-imagine/

## Welcome Chance Intrusions

*vertical thinking* versus *lateral thinking:* De Bono, Edward. (1973). *Lateral Thinking: Creativity Step by Step* New York: Harper & Row.

*The most fascinating part of swing dancing:* Blair, Skippy. (1978). Disco to Tango and Back. Downey: Blair.

## Dancing Makes You Smarter

*stress reduction:* Hanna, Judith Lynne. (2006). *Dancing for Health: Conquering and Preventing Stress.* Lanham: Altamira Press.

*increased serotonin level:* Jeong, Y.J., et. al. (2005). "Dance movement therapy improves emotional responses and modulates neurohormones in adolescents with mild depression." *International Journal of Neuroscience 115(12):* 1711-1720.

*dancing apparently makes us smarter:* Verghese, Joe, et. al. (2003). "Leisure Activities and the Risk of Dementia in the Elderly." *New England Journal of Medicine 348:* 2508-2516.

*Robert Sylwester:* Sylwester, Robert. (1995). *A Celebration of Neurons: An Educator's Guide to the Human Brain.* Alexandria: Association for Supervision and Curriculum Development.

*"intelligence is what you use":* This is actually a paraphrase of Piaget by William Calvin, but it's quite a nice way of packaging his ideas. Calvin, William H. (1996). *How Brains Think: Evolving Intelligence, Then and Now.* New York: Basic Books. 1.

## Improvisation

*Improv Wisdom:* Madson, Patricia Ryan. (2005). Improv Wisdom: Don't Prepare, Just Show Up. New York: Bell Tower.

For more on improvisation, see the work of Keith Johnstone:
Johnstone, Keith. (1981). *Impro: Improvisation and the Theatre.* New York: Routledge.
Johnstone, Keith. (1999). *Impro for Storytellers.* New York: Routledge.

*"chance favors the prepared mind":* Attributed to Pasteur, Louis. (1854). Lecture at University of Lille.

*"There is a vitality, a life force ..."*: Quoted in De Mille, Agnes. (1991). *The Life and Work of Martha Graham*. New York: Random House. 264.

# Smile

For an overview on smiling, see: Gutman, Ron. (2011). *Smile: The Astonishing Powers of a Simple Act*. TED Books.

*choosing to smile for no reason can significantly boost our mood*: Neuhoff, C.C.; Schaefer, C. (2002). "Effects of Laughing, Smiling, and Howling on Mood." *Psychological Reports 91(3 Pt 2):* 1079-1080.

*facial feedback:* "Even the simulation of an emotion tends to arouse it in our minds." Darwin, Charles. (1872). *The Expression of the Emotions in Man and Animals*. London: John Murray. 1st edition. 366.

*mirror neurons:* Botvinick M.; Jha A.P.; Bylsma L.M.; Fabian S.A.; Solomon P.E.; Prkachin K.M. (2005). "Viewing facial expressions of pain engages cortical areas involved in the direct experience of pain." *NeuroImage 25 (1):* 312–319. See also:
> Grahe, Jon E.; Williams, Kipling D.; Hinsz, Verlin B. (2000). "Teaching Experimental Methods While Bringing Smiles to Your Students' Faces." *Teaching Psychology 27(2):* 108-111.

*In a recent experiment involving a game of trust:* Krumhuber, Eva; Manstead, Anthony S.R.; Kappas, Arvid; Cosker, Darren; Marshall, Dave; Rosin, Paul L. (2007). "Facial Dynamics as Indicators of Trustworthiness and Cooperative Behavior." *Emotion 7(4).* 730-735. See also:
> Scharlemann, Jorn P.W.; Eckel, Catherine C.; Kacelnik, Alex; Wilson, Rick K. (2001). "The Value of a Smile: Game Theory with a Human Face." *Journal of Economic Psychology 22(5):* 617-640.
> Shore, Danielle M.; Heerey, Erin A. (2011). "The Value of Genuine and Polite Smiles." *Emotion 11(1):* 169-174.
> Rudd, Melanie; Aacker, Jennifer. (2011, December 16). "Leave Them Smiling: How Small Acts Create More Happiness than Large Acts." Stanford Business School Working Paper.

*smile with our eyes:* Ekman, Paul; Davidson, Richard J.; Friesen, Wallace V. (1990). "The Duchenne Smile: Emotional Expression and Brain Physiology II." *Journal of Personality and Social Psychology 58(2):* 342-353.

Another interesting finding: smiling in the face of adversity is especially important. Papa, Anthony; Bonanno, George A. (2008). "Smiling in the Face of Adversity: The Interpersonal and Intrapersonal Functions of Smiling." *Emotion 8(1):* 1-12.

# Laugh

*Although physiologically distinct from smiling:* Preuschoft, S.; Van Hooff, J.A.R.A.M. (1997). "The Social Functions of 'Smile' and 'Laughter': Variations across Primate Species and Societies." *Where Nature Meets Culture: Nonverbal Communication in Social Interaction*. Hillsdale: Erlbaum. 171-189.

*laughter also serves to boost our mood:* Foley, E.; Matheis, R. Schaefer, C. (2002). "Effect of Forced Laughter on Mood." *Psychological Reports 90(1):* 184. See also:
> Neuhoff, C.C.; Schaefer, C. (2002). "Effects of Laughing, Smiling, and Howling on Mood." *Psychological Reports 91(3 Pt 2):* 1079-1080.

*laughter triggers the release of endorphins:* Dunbar, Robin; et. al. (2012). "Social laughter is correlated with an elevated pain threshold." *Proceedings of the Royal Society B 279(1731):* 1161-1167.

Laughter is also effective against psychological pain: Keltner, Dacher; Bonanno, George A. (1997). "A Study of Laughter and Dissociation: Distinct Correlates of Laughter and Smiling During Bereavement." *Journal of Personal and Social Psychology 73(4)*: 687-702.

*laughter, like smiling, is highly contagious:* Provine, Robert. (1992). "Contagious Laughter: Laughter is a Sufficient Stimulus for Laughs and Smiles." *Bulletin of the Psychonomic Society 30(1):* 1-4.
> Of course, this is why many television shows employed, and in some cases still do employ, a "laugh track," which can and does increase viewers' inward evaluations of humor and overt expressions of laughter. See Smyth, M. M.; Fuller, R. G. (1972). "Effects of Group Laughter on Responses to Humorous Material. *Psychological Reports 30*: 132–134., among other studies.

*laughter's primary purpose was:* Gervais, Matthew; Wilson, David Sloan. (2005). "The Evolution and Functions of Laughter and Humor: A Synthetic Approach." *The Quarterly Review of Biology 80(4)*: 395-430.

*according to a study of laughter in daily conversation:* From Robert Provine's wonderful introduction to laughter science: Provine, Robert. (2000). *Laughter: A Scientific Investigation.* New York: Penguin Books. 40-41. The original article cited: Provine, Robert. (1993). "Laughter Punctuates Speech: Linguistic, Social and Gender Contexts of Laughter." *Ethology 95(4):* 291-298.
Other laughter insights from Robert Provine include:
> We are thirty times more likely to laugh in a social context than we are to laugh alone. Provine R.R.; Fischer K.R. (1989). "Laughing, Smiling, and Talking: Relation to Sleeping and Social Context in Humans." *Ethology 83(4)*: 295-305.
> In verbal contexts, 99% of laughter occurs at a point of punctuation. Provine, Robert. (1993). "Laughter Punctuates Speech: Linguistic, Social and Gender Contexts of Laughter." *Ethology 95(4):* 291-298.
> This punctuation effect is also seen in the laughter of deaf signers of American Sign Language. Provine, Robert; Emmorey, Karen. (2006). "Laughter Among Deaf Signers." *Journal of Deaf Studies and Deaf Education 11(4):* 403-409.
> Emoticons like :-) ;-) ^_^ :-P and lol, serve as a substitute for laughter in electronic communication, with 99% of emoticons serving to punctuate phrases with a clarifying display of emotion, usually positive. Provine, Robert R.; Spencer, Robert J.; Mandell, Darcy L. (2007). "Emotional Expression Online: Emoticons Punctuate Website Text Messages." *Journal of Language and Social Psychology 26(3)*: 299-307.

Another interesting finding: We are more likely to remember things that are followed by laughter. Nielson, K. A.; Powless, M. (2007). "Positive and negative sources of emotional arousal enhance long-term word-list retention when induced as long as 30 min after learning." *Neurobiology of Learning and Memory 88*: 40–47. See also:
> Nielson, K. A., Yee, D.; Erickson, K. I. (2005). "Memory enhancement by a semantically unrelated emotional arousal source induced after learning." *Neurobiology of Learning and Memory 84.* 49–56.
> Nielson, K.A.; Lorber, W. (2009). "Enhanced post-learning memory consolidation is influenced by arousal predisposition and emotion regulation but not by stimulus valence or arousal." *Neurobiology of Learning and Memory 92*: 70–79.
> Emotionally charged music facilitates learning in a similar fashion: Judde, Sarah; Richard, Nikki. (2010). "The effect of post-learning presentation of music on long-term word-list retention." *Neurobiology of Learning and Memory 94*: 13–20.

*As Stephen Colbert put it:* "Not living in fear is a great gift, because certainly these days we do it so much. And do you know what I like about comedy? You can't laugh and be afraid at the same time— of anything. If you're laughing, I defy you to be afraid." Kaplan, James. (2007, September 23). "After tragedy, TV funnyman Stephen Colbert says, "If you are laughing, you can't be afraid."" *Parade.* http://www.parade.com/articles/editions/2007/edition_09-23-2007/AStephen_Colbert
In a later interview, he clarified: "That's not a philosophical statement, I think it's a physiological statement. When you laugh, you're not afraid. And sometimes you laugh because you're afraid, but when you laugh, the [fear] goes away. And it's not just whistling past the graveyard. It actually just

254

goes away when you're laughing. And that's why I don't think I could ever stop doing what I'm doing, because I laugh all day long, and if I didn't, I would just cry all day long." Russert, Tim. (2007, October 21). "Interview with Stephen Colbert, Out of Character." *Meet the Press.*

*When young children are exposed:* Rothbart, Mary K. (1973). "Laughter in Young Children." *Psychological Bulletin 80(3):* 247-256. See also:

    Scarr, S.; Salapatek, P. (1970). "Patterns of fear development during infancy." *Merrill-Palmer Quarterly 16:* 53-87.

    This video is a wonderful example of the phenomenon: Mandkyeo. (2011, March 14). "Emerson - Mommy's Nose is Scary." http://www.youtube.com/watch?v=N9oxmRT2YWw

*"when our brains sense pain…":* Berns, Gregory. (2008, December 7). "In Hard Times, Fear Can Impair Decision-Making." *The New York Times.* http://www.nytimes.com/2008/12/07/jobs/07pre.html

For more on the science of the adaptive and maladaptive aspects of fear, and overcoming it, see:

    Gardner, Dan. (2008). *The Science of Fear: Why We Fear the Things We Shouldn't—and Put Ourselves in Greater Danger.* New York: Dutton.

    Glassner, Barry. (2010). *The Culture of Fear: Why Americans Are Afraid of the Wrong Things: Crime, Drugs, Minorities, Teen Moms, Killer Kids, Mutant Microbes, Plane Crashes, Road Rage, & So Much More.* New York: Basic Books.

    Wise, Jeff. (2009). *Extreme Fear: The Science of Your Mind in Danger.* New York: Palgrave Macmillan.

    Kushner, Harold S. (2009). *Conquering Fear: Living Boldly in an Uncertain World.* New York: Alfred A. Knopf.

    Jeffers, Susan. (1987). *Feel the Fear and Do It Anyway.* San Diego: Harcourt Brace Jovanovich.

    Yogis, Jaimal. (2013). *The Fear Project: What Our Most Primal Emotion Taught Me About Survival, Success, Surfing . . . And Love.* New York: Rodale.

*"a lightning bolt of wisdom":* Keltner, Dacher. (2009). *Born to Be Good.* New York: W.W. Norton. 143.

# Zwiefacher

*Zwiefacher patterns:* For a list of more than 200 recorded Zwiefacher patterns, see: http://www.folkdancing.com/Pages/seattle/Zwie-Pattern.html

# Connections

For an introduction to our need to connect, see: Baumeister, R.F.; Leary, M.R. (1995). "The Need to Belong: Desire for Interpersonal Attachments as a Fundamental Human Motivation." *Psychological Bulletin 117(3):* 497-529.

*people who are socially disconnected:* Putnam, Robert. (2000). *Bowling Alone: The Collapse and Revival of American Community.* New York: Simon & Schuster. 326.

*"if you belong to no groups but decide to join one":* Putnam, (2000), 331.

*happiness is best predicted by the breadth and depth of one's social connections:* Putnam, (2000), 332.

*"the happiness equivalent of getting a college degree":* Putnam, (2000), 332.

*your happiness depends on and influences the happiness of your friends' friends' friends:* Fowler, James H.; Christakis, Nicholas A. (2008). "Dynamic spread of happiness in a large social network: longitudinal analysis over 20 years in the Framingham Heart Study." *BMJ 337:* a2338.

*many other conditions and behaviors are socially contagious:*
Christakis, Nicholas A.; Fowler, James H. (2007). "The Spread of Obesity in a Large Social Network Over 32 Years." *New England Journal of Medicine 357(4)*: 370.

Rosenquist, J. Niels; Murabito, Joanne; Fowler, James H.; Christakis, Nicholas A. (2010). "The Spread of Alcohol Consumption Behavior in a Large Social Network." *Ann Intern Med. 152*: 426.

Mednick, Sara C.; Christakis, Nicholas A.; Fowler, James H. (2010). "The Spread of Sleep Loss Influences Drug Use in Adolescent Social Networks." *PLoS ONE 5(3)*: e9775.

Caioppo, John T.; Fowler, James H.; Christakis, Nicholas A. (2009). "Alone in the Crowd: The Structure and Spread of Loneliness in a Large Social Network." *Journal of Personality and Social Psychology 97(6)*: 977.

Fowler, James H.; Christakis, Nicholas A. (2010). "Cooperative Behavior Cascades in Human Social Networks." *Proceedings of the National Academy of Sciences 107(10)*: 1-5.

Carman, K.G. (2003, January). "Social Influences and the Private Provision of Public Goods: Evidence from Charitable Contributions in the Workplace." Stanford Institute for Economic Policy Research Discussion Paper 02-13.

Goeree, J.K., et. al. (2008, November 27). "The 1/d Law of Giving." http://www.hss.caltech.edu/~lyariv/Papers/Westridge.pdf

*choose your friends carefully:* Rook, Karen S. (1984). "The Negative Side of Social Interaction: Impact on Psychological Well-Being." *Journal of Personality and Social Psychology 46(5)*: 1097-1108.

*"on average, every friend makes us happier and healthier":* Christakis, Nicholas A.; Fowler, James H. (2009). *Connected: How Your Friends' Friends' Friends Affect Everything You Feel, Think, and Do.* New York: Back Bay Books. 29.

# The Third Place

*The Great Good Place:* Oldenburg, Ray. (1997). *The Great Good Place: Cafés, Coffee Shops, Bookstores, Bars, Hair Salons, and Other Hangouts at the Heart of a Community.* Philadelphia: Da Capo Press.

*"The third place is largely a world of its own making...":* Oldenburg (1997), 48.

*"the third place is a force for good...":* Oldenburg (1997), 78.

*"promotion of decency...":* Oldenburg (1997), 79.

# The Power of Music

*music was more frequently associated with feelings of happiness-elation:* Juslin, Patrik N., et. al. (2008). "An Experience Sampling Study of Emotional Reactions to Music: Listener, Music, and Situation." *Emotion 8(5)*: 668-683.

*sad music can actually be quite comforting:* Huron, David. (2011). "Why is sad music pleasurable? A possible role for prolactin." *Musicae Scientiae 15*: 146-158.

*"music activates the same parts of the brain and causes the same neurochemical cocktail":* Quoted in Dotinga, Randy. (2006, August 23). "Music Makes Your Brain Happy." *Wired.* http://www.wired.com/medtech/health/news/2006/08/71631

*gives it the ability to affect our physical health:* Mannes, Elena. (2011). *The Power of Music: Pioneering Discoveries in the New Science of Song.* New York: Walker & Company. 20-21. For examples of research supporting this idea, see:

Blood, Anne J.; Zatorre, Robert J. (2001). "Intensely pleasurable responses to music correlate with activity in brain regions implicated in reward and emotion." *Proceedings of the National Academy of Sciences 98(20)*: 11818–11823.

Bernardi, L. (2009). "Dynamic interactions between musical, cardiovascular, and cerebral rhythms in humans." *Circulation 119*: 3171-3180.

Bernardi, L., et. al. (2006). "Cardiovascular, cerebrovascular, and respiratory changes induced by different types of music in musicians and non-musicians: the importance of silence." *Heart 92:* 445-452.

*Calming music, for example, can ameliorate the effects of stress:*
Miluk-Kolasa, B., et. al. (1994). "Effects of Music Treatment on Salivary Cortisol in Patients Exposed to Pre-Surgical Stress." *Exp. Clin. Endocrinol. 102(2)*: 118-120.

Khalfa, S., et. al. (2003). "Effects of Relaxing Music on Salivary Cortisol Level after Psychological Stress." *Ann. N.Y. Acad. Sci. 999*: 374-376.

*Music can also soothe our pains*: See studies reviewed in Mannes, Elena. (2011). *The Power of Music: Pioneering Discoveries in the New Science of Song*. New York: Walker & Company. 168-169.

*Music therapy has even been shown*: See studies reviewed in Mannes, Elena. (2011). *The Power of Music: Pioneering Discoveries in the New Science of Song*. New York: Walker & Company. 167, 177-190. and Sacks, Oliver. (2008). *Musicophilia: Tales of Music and the Brain*. New York: Vintage Books. 270-283, 371-385.

*particularly effective in the treatment of Parkinson's*:
Hackney, M., et. al. (2007). "A study on the effects of Argentine tango as a form of partnered dance for those with Parkinson disease and the healthy elderly." *American Journal of Dance Therapy 29(2)*: 109-127.

Hackney, M. et. al. (2007). "Effects of Tango on Functional Mobility in Parkinson's Disease: A Preliminary Study." *Journal of Neurologic Physical Therapy 31*: 173-179.

*engages nearly every region of the brain*: Levitin, Daniel J. (2006). *This Is Your Brain on Music: The Science of a Human Obsession*. New York: Plume. 9.

*activating and building neural networks*: Mannes, Elena. (2011). *The Power of Music: Pioneering Discoveries in the New Science of Song*. New York: Walker & Company. 80. For an example of research supporting this idea, see:
Wan, Catherine Y.; Schlaug, Gottfried. (2010). "Music Making as a Tool for Promoting Brain Plasticity Across the Life Span." *Neuroscientist 16(5)*: 566-577.

*by synchronizing many different bodies and minds at the same time*: "Just as rapid neuronal oscillations bind together different functional parts within the brain and nervous system, so rhythm binds together the individual nervous systems of a human community." Sacks, Oliver. (2008). *Musicophilia: Tales of Music and the Brain*. New York: Vintage Books. 269.

*entraining to the same beat*: Mannes, Elena. (2011). *The Power of Music: Pioneering Discoveries in the New Science of Song*. New York: Walker & Company. 38.
Amazingly, even babies that are *two days* old share our ability to detect and anticipate the beat in music. Winkler, I., et. al. (2009, January 26). "Newborn Infants Detect the Beat in Music." *Proceedings of the National Academy of Sciences (Early Edition)*.

*words are inadequate to describe the emotion*: McNeill calls this phenomenon "muscular bonding." McNeill, W.H. (1995). *Keeping Together in Time: Dance and Drill in Human History*. Cambridge: Harvard University Press. 2.

For more on this feeling, see Émile Durkheim's concept of *collective effervescence* and Victor Turner's notion of *communitas*, as well as Ehrenreich, Barbara. (2006). *Dancing in the Streets: A History of Collective Joy*. New York: Holt.

*moving in synchrony releases a flood of endorphins*: Cohen, Emma E. A.; Ejsmond-Frey, Robin; Knight, Nicola; Dunbar, R.I.M. (2010). "Rowers' High: Behavioural Synchrony is Correlated with Elevated Pain Thresholds." *Biology Letters 6*: 106-108.

*human beings desperately need to belong to communities*: McNeill, William H. (1995). *Keeping Together in Time: Dance and Drill in Human History*. Cambridge: Harvard University Press. Main quote is from page 152, "euphoric response" section is from 150, and last sentence is from 157.
    Walter J. Freeman calls music and dance "the biotechnology of group formation." Freeman, Walter J. (1995). *Societies of Brains: A Study in the Neuroscience of Love and Hate*. Hillsdale: Lawrence Erlbaum Associates. 129.
    Joining the growing number of scholars who propose this, Daniel J. Levitin writes: "I believe the *synchronous, coordinated song and movement* were what created the strongest bonds between early humans, and these allowed for the formation of larger living groups, and eventually of society as we know it." Levitin, Daniel J. (2008). *The World in Six Songs: How the Musical Brain Created Human Nature*. New York: Plume. 50.
    For scientific studies of synchrony and cooperation which provide support for this idea, see:
        Valdesolo, P., & DeSteno, D. (2011). "Synchrony and the Social Tuning of Compassion." *Emotion 11*: 262-266.
        Valdesolo, Piercarlo, et. al. (2010). "The rhythm of joint action: Synchrony promotes cooperative ability." *Journal of Experimental Social Psychology 46(4)*: 693-695.
        Wiltermuth, S. S., & Heath, C. (2009). "Synchrony and cooperation." *Psychological Science 20(1)*: 1-5.

# Gratitude

*"the greatest thing is to give thanks for everything"*: Schweitzer, Albert. (1979). [1904]. "Gratitude—the Secret of Life." *Reverence for Life*. New York: Irvington. 41.

*In pioneering studies*: Emmons, R.A.; McCullough, M.E. (2003). "Counting Blessings Versus Burdens: An Experimental Investigation of Gratitude and Subjective Well-Being in Daily Life." *Journal of Personality and Social Psychology 84*: 377-389.
    Additional findings are reviewed in: Emmons, Robert. (2007). *Thanks!: How the New Science of Gratitude Can Make You Happier*. Boston: Houghton Mifflin. 186.

*feels good to express and receive gratitude*: Gordon, Cameron L., et. al. (2011). "Have You Thanked Your Spouse Today?: Felt and Expressed Gratitude Among Married Couples." *Personality and Individual Differences 50*: 339-343.

*single most powerful mood booster*: Seligman, M.E.P., et al. (2005). "Positive Psychology Progress: Empirical Validation of Interventions." *American Psychologist 60(5)*: 410-421.

*In new relationships*: Algoe, Sara B.; Haidt, Jonathan; Gable, Shelly L. (2008). "Beyond Reciprocity: Gratitude and Relationships in Everyday Life." *Emotion 8(3)*: 425-429.

*The same is true as the relationship develops*: Algoe, Sara B.; Gable, Shelly L.; Maisel, Natalya C. (2010). "It's the little things: Everyday gratitude as a booster shot for romantic relationships." *Personal Relationships 17*: 217-233. See also:
    Algoe, Sara B. (2012). "Find, Remind, and Bind: The Functions of Gratitude in Everyday Relationships." *Social and Personality Psychology Compass 6(6)*: 455-469.

Gordon, Cameron L., et. al. (2011). "Have You Thanked Your Spouse Today?: Felt and Expressed Gratitude Among Married Couples." *Personality and Individual Differences 50*: 339-343.

*Emily ... is motivated to repeat them:* Proposed and reviewed in McCullough, M.E., Kilpatrick, S.D., Emmons, R.A., & Larson, D.B. (2001). "Is gratitude a moral affect?" *Psychological Bulletin 127*: 249-266. Specific findings:

> Those who receive an expression of gratitude are more likely to help the expresser, and unrelated others, again. Grant, A.M.; Gino, F. (2010). "A Little Thanks Goes a Long Way: Explaining Why Gratitude Expressions Motivate Prosocial Behavior." *Journal of Personality and Social Psychology 98(6)*: 946-955. See also:

> Those who receive an expression of gratitude are more likely to rate the expresser positively and to help unrelated others. Deutsch, Francine M.; Lamberti, Donna M. (1986). "Does Social Approval Increase Helping?" *Personal and Social Psychology Bulletin 12*: 149-157.

> Thank you notes increase helping behavior. Clark, H. B., Northrop, J. T., & Barkshire, C. T. (1988). "The effects of contingent thank-you notes on case managers' visiting residential clients." *Education and Treatment of Children 11*: 45-51.

*James ... is motivated to pay it back:* Proposed in McCullough, M.E., Kilpatrick, S.D., Emmons, R.A., & Larson, D.B. (2001). "Is gratitude a moral affect?" *Psychological Bulletin 127*: 249-266. And reviewed in McCullough, Michael E.; Kimeldorf, Marcia B.; Cohen, Adam D. (2008). "An Adaptation for Altruism? The Social Causes, Social Effects, and Social Evolution of Gratitude." *Current Directions in Psychological Science 17(4)*: 281-285. Specific findings:

> Those who feel gratitude are more likely to help both their benefactors, and unrelated others. Bartlett, M.Y.; DeSteno, D. (2006). "Gratitude and prosocial behavior: Helping when it costs you." *Psychological Science 17(4)*: 319-325.

> Those who receive a good outcome through the intentional effort of another feel more gratitude, and subsequently help others (including the benefactor) more, than those who receive a good outcome by chance. Tsang, Jo-Ann. (2006). "Gratitude and Prosocial Behaviour: An Experimental Test of Gratitude." *Cognition and Emotion 20(1)*: 138-148. and Tsang, Jo-Ann. (2007). "Gratitude for Small and Large Favors: A Behavioral Test." *The Journal of Positive Psychology 2(3)*: 157-167.

> Those who keep a gratitude journal are more likely to provide support to others. Emmons, R.A.; McCullough, M.E. (2003). "Counting blessings versus burdens: An experimental investigation of gratitude and subjective well-being in daily life." *Journal of Personality and Social Psychology 84*: 377-389.

> Those who are are higher in dispositional gratitude (by self and peer report) engage in more prosocial behavior. McCullough, M.E.; Emmons, R.A.; & Tsang, J. (2002). "The grateful disposition: A conceptual and empirical topography." *Journal of Personality and Social Psychology 82*: 112-127.

*The Art and Practice of Loving:* Andrews, Frank. (2010). *The Art and Practice of Loving: Living a Heartfelt Yes*. Palo Alto: Magic. 105-106. Available for free download at heartfeltyes.com

# Integration

*"A human being is a part of the whole":* Calaprice, Alice. (2005). *The New Quotable Einstein*. Princeton: Princeton University Press. 206.

# Space for Your Thoughts

We have provided the following blank pages as a space to record your own thoughts on waltzing—notes, ideas, variations, or anything else you may want to set to paper.

If you want to share any of your thoughts on waltzing with us, feel free to send them to us at: authors@waltzingbook.com

**Space for Your Thoughts (Continued)**

# Space for Your Thoughts (Continued)

# Space for Your Thoughts (Continued)

This book is set primarily in ITC Garamond,
drawn in 1977 by Tony Stan for the International Typeface Corporation (ITC).
The cover and title page are set in Wisteria ITC and Cochin.
It is published by Redowa Press in Stanford, California,
and printed on-demand by CreateSpace.